SCOTTISH LITERATURE INTERNATIONAL

Writing Scottishness

Literature and the Shaping of Scottish National Identities

Edited by
IAN BROWN and
CLARISSE GODARD DESMAREST

Occasional Papers: Number 26
Association for Scottish Literature

Published by
Scottish Literature International
Scottish Literature
7 University Gardens
University of Glasgow
Glasgow G12 8QH

Scottish Literature International is an imprint of
the Association for Scottish Literature

www.asls.org.uk

ASL is a registered charity no. SC006535

First published 2023

© ASL and the individual contributors

All rights reserved. No part of this book may be
reproduced, stored in a retrieval system, or
transmitted in any form or means, electronic,
mechanical, photocopying, recording or otherwise,
without the prior permission of the
Association for Scottish Literature.

A CIP catalogue for this title
is available from the British Library

ISBN 978-1-908980-39-7

Contents

Introduction   v
     Clarisse Godard Desmarest

One   Inscribing Scottishness in Language, Space, and
     Performance since the Seventeenth Century   1
     Ian Brown

Two   Lethington, Marie Maitland, and the 'Maitland Quarto':
     Memorialisation and Performance in Times of 'Troubill'
     for Scotland   20
     Pamela King

Three   Translating Identities: Tracing the Transfer of a Scottish
     Origin Myth from Scotland to France *c*. 1519   44
     Bryony Coombs

Four   'Losing its religion'? Scottish Literature and
     Confessional Identity   65
     Gerard Carruthers

Five   Collective Identities and the *Other* in Scottish
     Jacobite Songs   84
     Kristel van Soeren

Six   Napoleon and Ossian: Celtomania and the Construction
     of French Nationhood   98
     Clarisse Godard Desmarest

Seven   Transatlantic 'Scott-land': Re-locating the Late
     Waverley Novels within a Transatlantic Discussion   121
     Pauline Pilote

| Eight | Questions of Identity on the Stevenson Trail in Scotland
Lesley Graham | 138 |

| Nine | The Safe Nationalisms of Hugh MacDiarmid and Compton Mackenzie
Béatrice Duchateau | 157 |

| Ten | Situating the Gael in Scottish Landscapes: Self-Identity and Change in Twentieth-Century Gaelic Poetry
Emma Dymock | 176 |

| Eleven | Critiquing Scotland's Clever Clocks and MacGrundies: Willa Muir's Nationalist Feminism
Emily L. Pickard | 197 |

| Twelve | 'This is Scotland, by Christ!': Cultural Nationalism and National (Re)Branding in the Cinematic Adaptations of Irvine Welsh
Anne-Lise Marin-Lamellet | 214 |

| Thirteen | George Davie's *Democratic Intellect* in Context
Robert Anderson | 232 |

| Fourteen | Writing Scottishness in Post-imperial, Post-devolution Theatre: a Conversation
Peter Arnott and Ian Brown | 249 |

Notes on contributors 263

Index 267

Introduction

CLARISSE GODARD DESMAREST

This book is published at a time of renewed interest, both in Scotland and further afield, in the relationship between culture, politics and nationalism. This renewed interest reflects growing shock at the progressive disintegration of what had, until recently, seemed to be a stable, international political and economic consensus – the consensus that Francis Fukuyama controversially proclaimed, exactly thirty years ago, as the 'end of history'. The fall of the Soviet Union and the end of the Cold War, Fukuyama argued, had confirmed the inevitable advent of a universal political and economic order of liberal democracy, globalised open markets, and transnational political and legal institutions. In this vision, the sovereign nation states which had dominated the political and cultural history of the eighteenth, nineteenth and twentieth centuries, with their potent alignment of political, cultural and economic identities, were destined to wither away in the face of the coming transition to the 'post-historical'.

Fukuyama has now himself conceded that history did not come to an end in 1990 and that 'liberalism is in peril'.[1] The democratic forms that came to Russia in the 1990s have been hollowed out from within as Vladimir Putin has tightened his control over the country's institutions of government and civil society, and through them over its economy, while the invasion of Ukraine has confirmed his disregard for international norms and expectations. China's economic liberalisation and integration into the global economy has vastly increased its wealth and military power, but without perceptibly weakening the Communist Party's authoritarian rule. In the USA, growing economic polarisation resulting, in considerable part, from China's growing dominance over the world's industrial production, has fuelled a corresponding political polarisation, symbolised by the 'America First' Presidency of Donald Trump. The fragile unity of the European Union – for Fukuyama as for his inspiration Alexandre Kojève, the archetype of the new transnational liberal order – has been threatened by Brexit and by the resurgence across Europe of the economic isolationism and cultural chauvinism of the extreme right.

Scotland, with its enduring commitment to a communitarian vision of civil society, has to a considerable extent avoided the rightward swerve of the contemporary west. But this has not precluded the reassertion of political nationalism. Indeed, far from shutting off the debate over independence 'for a generation', the 2014 referendum led to a dramatic growth in support for a definitive break from Westminster and the rest of the United Kingdom. Since then, partly as Brexit's direct consequence, there has been growing pressure for a second independence referendum – 'indyref2'. The maintenance of pro-independence majority in the Scottish parliamentary elections in May 2021 has only increased this pressure, leading the Scottish government to declare its intention to hold another referendum in October 2023. As such constitutional questions fall within the British government's reserved powers, this development promises to lead to even greater legal and political controversy over Scotland's place within the Union.

In this context, it seems particularly timely to think again about the long-held sense of Scottish cultural distinctiveness and its relationship to evolving political identities – not least the contemporary quest for Scottish independence. This is especially the case as Scotland's cultural and political identity has, both historically and in the present day, arguably displayed complexities that make it unusual in the context of historical and contemporary nationalisms. The recent development of the independence debate encapsulates this complexity. The Scottish National Party (SNP) has succeeded in maintaining a near monopoly on political expression of nationalist sentiment in spite of overtly rejecting traditional ethno-cultural nationalism. Instead, the party has adhered to a consciously progressive liberal democratic (and broadly pro-immigration) policy agenda. Progressive politics and overt political nationalism make unusual bedfellows and imply a particularly complex relationship between the cultural and political expressions of national identity. As Ian Brown's chapter in this book highlights, the inevitable political dimension to writing about Scottishness, and of expressing Scottish national identity in literature and performance, has made literature a particularly vivid expression of this complexity, and one which has far deeper roots than is sometimes realised.

In the medieval and Renaissance period, which marked a first stage in the articulation of a Scottish national identity, the country was part of an 'Auld Alliance' with France against England, while its internal ethno-linguistic identity was far from unified, with different groups and strata within society maintaining strong Gaelic, Scots, Latin and English cultures. Perhaps as a result of this, and in the face of the constant threat of English hegemony, Scottish identity then tended to coalesce around a strong martial culture celebrating the heroic oppressed. This transpired in both poetry and the visual arts and is exemplified by the cult of male heroes – best shown in the poetry of John Barbour (c. 1320–1395) and 'Blind' Hary (c. 1440–1492) – and the taste for castellated architecture.

Recognising that Early Scots writing underscores a *Braveheart* picture of a proud national culture that is designed for and defended by men (the film was inspired by Hary's *Wallace*), Pamela King's chapter focuses on the poetry in the so-called Maitland Quarto, a collection emanating from a literary family which provides auspicious grounds for seeking a female voice. Bryony Coombs's chapter offers an early and telling evidence for the transfer of ideas between Scotland and France, and for the role of the literary material in expressing Scottish national identity. By bringing together two heraldic manuscripts, one kept in Paris and one in Glasgow, Coombs analyses the extraordinary visual genealogy used by elite Scots to forge their identity and bolster political power at the turn of the sixteenth century. But the flowering of letters in the Renaissance, and the dialogue with the literatures of other countries like France, was stifled by the 1560s Reformation which not only challenged the 'Auld Alliance' whilst consolidating ties with Protestant England, but also imposed a puritanical approach to life and to the arts. This has meant that the theatrical tradition from the sixteenth to the eighteenth century was less dynamic than elsewhere, whether in England (where the Reformation was less radical than in Scotland and where also the established church maintained episcopal authority) or in France. The marginalisation of secular poetry has similarly been seen as a legacy of the Reformation. This view, however, has been challenged by some scholars who now consider that the intellectual achievements of the Enlightenment were inherited from the Reformation (which kept the vigour of religious poetry). Meanwhile, the Kirk opposed professional playhouse theatre which in the late seventeenth century it identified with anti-Presbyterian forces. This did not mean, however, that it sought to suppress all drama. Indeed, it required that schools use drama at least once a year to convey religious and political themes to which it was sympathetic. This not only allowed future professionals – including potential ministers – to develop skills in public speaking and role-playing but fostered interest in the polemical uses of theatrical performances. The enduring influence of Scotland's religious past on its literary culture is the focus of Gerard Carruthers's chapter. With references ranging from the Middle Ages to the twentieth century, it reveals the complexity of the religious allegiances that have characterised Scottish writing and especially the post-Reformation tensions between (and within) the Presbyterian majority and the Catholic and Episcopalian minorities.

Religious change also helped forge a growing rapprochement with England, as the two Protestant states developed the close dynastic links that led, in 1603, to the Union of the Crowns and culminated in 1707 with the Union of Parliaments. Increasing political integration initiated a process of increasing Anglicisation, mitigated only by a gradual reinforcement of the authority of the Kirk through successful resistance to attempts by the Anglo-Scottish monarchy to introduce to Scotland customs from the established church of their English domains. Linguistically, English gradually displaced Scots as Scotland's dominant written language, which meant that in the following century polite Scots sought to polish their language and 'drop their Scotticisms'. Focusing on this period of transition, Kristel van Soeren's chapter provides a case study of two Jacobite songs, explaining how their tunes and lyrics were quietly used to maintain a distinctive and unexpectedly multi-layered identity. This chapter confirms the complexity of the Jacobite movement, and shows that it needs to be read as being as much forward-looking (intellectually) as backward-looking (with its continuing adherence to the clans and the vertical loyalties they represented).

In spite of the increasing prominence of English, the Scots maintained vibrant traditions in both Scots and Gaelic-language literature. Scottish writer Allan Ramsay Senior developed a poetry using both English and Scots. Playing with the English classical styles and traditional metrical patterns, his poetry sat uneasily within the canon of classical taste. His editing of medieval Scottish authors also gave impetus to Scottish song and poetry, which not only laid the foundations for the work of Robert Fergusson but may also help account for the appeal of Robert Burns's poetry later in the century. Similar patterns of cross-fertilisation, and the challenges to which they could give rise, appear in the controversy over James Macpherson's 'Ossian' poetry (1760-62). Some, including such Enlightenment literati as David Hume and Hugh Blair, recognised the value of translating Gaelic poetry into contemporary English while others, including the notoriously Anglocentric English critic Samuel Johnson, denounced Macpherson's claim to be presenting a straightforward translation as a conscious fraud. The debates over the authenticity of the Ossianic corpus did not, however, seemingly diminish its wide appeal within and beyond the British Isles. Clarisse Godard Desmarest revisits Napoleon's fascination for Ossian through a reinterpretation of Girodet's painting *Ossian and his warriors welcoming in their aerial realm the shades of the French heroes*. Through considering how Napoleon negotiated Scotland's, France's and Europe's multiple pasts (Celtic, Roman, and Germanic), she shows how romantic taste for Gaelic poetry and the appeal of the remote Highland home of the Celtic 'noble' savage was able to provide a unifying identity for France's new culturally and ethnically diverse empire. It was the same unifying potential of the romantic Highlands that underlay Walter Scott's appeal in the nineteenth century. His ability to bring together a sense of Scottishness and greater Britishness was the foremost expression of the 'unionist nationalism' that characterised late Georgian and Victorian Scotland. The influence of Scott's vision spread widely, in part by means of the expanding periodical culture that characterised the period both in Britain and abroad. Pauline Pilote's chapter focuses on the cross-fertilisation between novels by Scott and by North American writer James Fenimore Cooper, and shows how some of Scott's novels integrate representations derived from American frontier stories. Pilote's contribution reflects a wider reappraisal of Scottish literature in the Victorian period, which has for too long been shaped by the pessimistic views of contemporaries like Thomas Carlyle, for whom the Enlightenment had stopped in the 1830s. Commentators like Alexander Broadie and Cairns Craig have now placed the Enlightenment within a continuum of intellectual achievement extending over a longer cultural durée. A similar concern for broadening, and contextualising, our understanding of the Scottish literary achievement in the eighteenth and nineteenth centuries is also evident in recent collected volumes, such as the *International Companion to Scottish Literature of the Long Eighteenth Century* and the *International Companion to Nineteenth-Century Scottish Literature*.[2] Urbanisation, industrialisation, imperial expansion and the broadening of voting rights have increasingly been highlighted as the context within which Robert Louis Stevenson's novels were written and published. Lesley Graham sets out to explore questions of identity in the travel accounts of writers who, since the late nineteenth century, have visited Scotland on the Stevenson trail, such writers including Clayton Hamilton, Nicholas Rankin, Gavin Bell, and Ian Nimmo.

The Scottish Literary Renaissance in the interwar years forms the focus of Béatrice Duchateau's chapter. Building on work by Scott Lyall, she offers fresh insights into establishment perceptions of Scottish identity through an exploration of the MI5 files kept on the towering but controversial figure of poet Hugh MacDiarmid and his foremost contemporary, the novelist Compton Mackenzie. Strikingly, Duchateau finds that, although militant Scottishness was expressed in their writings, MacDiarmid and Mackenzie fell outside the immediate priorities of the secret services who chose, rather, to counteract the threats of communism and fascism. Emma Dymock's chapter seeks to explore the way Gaelic poets have approached identity in the twentieth century and what it has meant to be Scottish and Gaelic, when the Gàidhealtachd has been subject to migration in and out while also forming part of a pan-Celtic and European context. Her work interrogates the relationship between language (writing in English, Scots or Gaelic), identity and worldview.

Seeking to address the question of gender in Scotland, and of a male-dominated society, Emily Pickard discusses the work of twentieth-century female novelist Willa Muir. Through an exploration of cinematic adaptations of Irvine Welsh's novels, Anne-Lise Marin-Lamellet's chapter shows how postindustrial despair coupled with anti-Thatcherite resentment led to the emergence of an alternative imagery of Scottishness represented by the urban underclass rather than the traditional romanticised imagery of the Highlands.

These developments reflected a wider breakdown of the post-war consensus, and as this happened the concern for self-assertion became political as well as cultural; the 1967 by-election victory of SNP parliamentary candidate Winnie Ewing in Hamilton, a Labour stronghold, marked a turning point in the direction taken by contemporary Scotland. The preconditions for this period of change are illuminated by Robert Anderson's chapter on George Davie, the author of the now classic and still controversial *The Democratic Intellect* (1961). Anderson revisits the context of publication of this seminal analysis of the transformation of post-Enlightenment university education in Scotland, which Davie considered to be the result of increasing Anglicisation and the erosion of the traditional Scottish curriculum's intellectual breadth and strongly philosophical foundation. Since the 1980s, Davie's pessimistic narrative has led a new generation of scholars to revisit the question of Scotland's supposed lack of confidence in its distinctive educational and cultural inheritance. Intellectuals like Craig Beveridge, Ronald Turnbull and Tom Nairn have sought to account for Scottish 'inferiorism' as a result of the damaging effects of Scotland's cultural and political incorporation within the Union. They sought to counter this by producing works in literature, history and the arts which emphasise the value of Scotland's autonomous political and cultural traditions, and its historical role as a nation in its own right.

The growing sense of democratic deficit felt by Scots since Margaret Thatcher's period in government has led to increasing intersections between Scottish literature and broader political questions. It has therefore been difficult to separate recent Scottish writing from the increasing polarised views on the constitutional future of the nation. It is now twenty years since devolution, and playwright and novelist Peter Arnott offers, in dialogue with Ian Brown, an insider's view of the way in which the world of letters has promoted and responded to this new constitutional order. Arnott offers an analysis of the perceived changes and continuities brought by devolution in contemporary literature.

Arnott's playwright's view adds to the rich diversity of voices and perspectives presented in this volume, which reflects the increasing maturity of Scottish Literature as a field of critical study. Until the twentieth century Scottish Literature was hardly taught at universities, except some key texts which had entered the English literary canon. Whereas English Literature became a university subject in the late eighteenth and early nineteenth centuries, Scottish Literature fought for its existence in the more recent 1970s and 1980s, later even than Irish Literature which had become independent from English in the earlier twentieth century.

Since then, the field of Scottish Studies has been enriched by the contribution of new scholars willing to bridge the disciplinary divides between history, geography, art and architecture, and literature, and has gained wider recognition both in Scotland and abroad. Scottish literary texts are now explored from new and more inclusive perspectives, ranging from postcolonialism to gender studies. International conferences on topics related to Scotland have been held elsewhere in the UK, in Ireland, France, Germany, Italy, Spain, Canada, the USA, China, India and New Zealand. The Eighteenth-Century Scottish Studies Society held, for example, its annual conference at the Sorbonne in 2013 on the topic 'Scotland, Europe and Empire in the Age of Adam Smith and Beyond'. This volume is itself testimony to the growing international interest in Scottish literary and cultural history. Its origins lie in the 20th Congress of the French Society for Scottish Studies held at the University of Picardie Jules Verne, Amiens, on 7–9 October 2021, which addressed the theme of 'Scotland and Nationalism: cultural and political aspects of Scottish identity from the medieval period to the present'. At the conference, contributors hailed from across Scotland, the wider UK, France and Italy, enabling them to consider the complex interrelationships between cultural, literary and political identity at a time when the resurgence of national feeling in Scotland has sparked international interest.

Combining papers from the conference on literary manifestations of Scottishness and a selection of specially commissioned chapters, this book also sheds new light on broader questions about nationalism and national identity as a cultural and political phenomenon. Scotland is an interesting case study in this respect because of its unique location and status. Throughout its history, this small nation has attempted to negotiate its identity within Britain, Europe and the wider world, from a position that is arguably at Europe's geographical and economic periphery. Yet, this has not stopped Scotland from contributing richly to the mainstream of European culture. Implicit within this, are perennial tensions between tradition and openness, particularity and universality, which gained especially forceful expression in the areas of Enlightenment and Romanticism, and which continue to shape our perceptions to this day. In Scotland, as in other examples of historical nations that feel themselves to be excluded from metropolitan cultural and political centres, such as Catalunya, or Bohemia and Hungary in the era of the Hapsburg monarchy, these tensions are especially keenly felt. The great paradox of Scotland is that while it could not express its national identity through the creation of a nation state it was able to do so through its cultural identity, including – perhaps most prominently – literature.

It is precisely the way that the chapters presented here provide direct insight into this complexity that makes this book of value not only for the specific field of Scottish Studies but for broader debates on nations and nationhood. The question of the nature and development of nationalism and national identity has, arguably, been studied from two dominant perspectives. The most pervasive we might call a modernist approach (associated primarily with Ernest Gellner and Benedict Anderson). For Gellner and Anderson, nations are 'invented' and nationalism is a by-product of modernity. Gellner considers that the nation-state works to homogenise its population through the mass dissemination of a national culture. For Anderson, too, the emergence of a common culture through the growing influence of the press, and through centralised education, are critical foundations for modern nationalism. The result is that the nation provides a new form of 'imagined community'. In contrast to this approach, Anthony D. Smith has developed an ethno-symbolic approach that holds that the nation was not *wholly* imagined as a result of modernity. According to

Smith, nationalism draws on ethnic and linguistic identities that long predate the modern nation state, in some cases by hundreds or even thousands of years. At the heart of this debate is the extent to which ethno-linguistic and cultural identity has historically aligned with political organisation, with Gellner and Anderson seeing the alignment between state and cultural nations as an essentially modern phenomenon and Smith arguing that it had much earlier roots. Scotland forms a particularly fascinating and challenging case study in this respect. The emergence in the high Middle Ages of 'national' narratives and identities in a culturally complex but politically coherent Scotland; the growth of a highly cohesive culture of 'Scottishness' in the eighteenth and nineteenth centuries without accompanying calls for political autonomy; and the contemporary articulation of political Scottishness with its conscious repudiation of traditional ethno-linguistic cultural nationalism – all these phenomena complicate and in certain respects counter the theoretical expectation of an inevitable convergence of political and cultural identity, whether perennially or at the specific moment when modernity was being made. Moreover, the question of how stable the current nationalist consensus is likely to be gives continuing relevance and interest to these themes in a specifically Scottish context. Whether Scotland can in fact realise an alternative form of nationalism that combines political autonomy with cultural inclusiveness remains to be seen, but the outcome, whatever it is, will have fundamental implications for the fate of nationalism and the nation state in the face of the pressures and opportunities of an ever more globalised – and in certain respects ever more fragmented – world.

INTRODUCTION

Endnotes

1. Francis Fukuyama, 'A Country of Their Own. Liberalism needs the nation', *Foreign Affairs* 101.3 (May/June 2022), www.foreignaffairs.com/articles/ukraine/2022-04-01/francis-fukuyama-liberalism-country.
2. Leith Davis and Janet Sorenson (eds), *The International Companion to Scottish Literature of the Long Eighteenth Century* (Glasgow: Scottish Literature International, 2021). Caroline McCracken-Flesher, Kenneth McNeil and Sheila Kidd (eds), *The International Companion to Nineteenth-Century Scottish Literature* (Glasgow: Scottish Literature International, 2022).

1. Inscribing Scottishness in Language, Space, and Performance since the Seventeenth Century

IAN BROWN

At the core of this chapter lies the conception that the ways in which 'Scottishness' is written into existence and performed are not simply matters of written words, however central the act of writing about – and so in a sense creating – Scottishness may be. The chapter will explore a variety of ways in which, over the centuries, conceptions of Scottishness (sometimes alongside Englishness and Britishness) have been performed and modified. In doing so, it recognises the insight of Thomas Owen Clancy and Barbara E. Crawford:

> In [language or landscape, politics, peoples or territory], Scotland during its earliest history is not a fixed and labelled destination, but a constantly shifting theatre of change. Even as late as the fourteenth century, Scotland as we know it was still evolving, first into a kingdom and then a nation, defining its borders and amalgamating its startling range of peoples and languages.[1]

The argument being developed here is that this evolution continued and continues in a variety of ways. It draws on the politics of the historical promotion and suppression of specific regional identities and different languages within Scotland. It considers Scottish scholars' development of the discipline of 'English Literature' as part of the Scottish Enlightenment and aspects of the impact of the post-Treaty of Union Hanoverian settlement. It outlines ways in which versions of Scottishness have been inscribed on townscapes and landscapes. It also addresses ways in which enactment through performance, including costume and political action, have embodied attitudes to different varieties of Scottish identities. It recognises that all these expressions may often be ambivalent, contributing, on the one hand, to what has been called the 'Scottish Cringe' especially with regard to languages and, on the other, to assertive Scottish identities both within a unionist context and, more recently, in the rise of the movement to re-establish Scottish independence.

The political manipulation of languages

One of the primary ways in which versions of Scottishness may be modified is by manipulation of the politics – one might even say power-politics – of language. The relationship between Gaelic-speaking and Scots-speaking magnates throughout the first half of the last millennium was, of course, highly politicised. Yet, despite James IV's suppression of the Lordship of the Isles in 1493, there was a general acceptance for many years of both languages in cultural discourse, often in unexpected interactions. James IV (r. 1488–1513) is, for example, considered to be the last king of Scots to understand Gaelic, having Gaelic-speaking bards, like Walter Kennedy from Carrick in Ayrshire – then an area with Gaelic speakers – as part of his court retinue. The early sixteenth-century Book of the Dean of Lismore, a key repository of medieval Gaelic poetry compiled in Highland Perthshire, uses Scots orthography and includes poems in both Gaelic and Scots. At the same time rivalry for political power was becoming more intense between those whose first language was one or the other. This rivalry was reflected also in approaches to history based on a fundamental paradox about the very historiography of Scotland and its inhabitants. As Ulrike Hogg and Martin MacGregor put it,

> The Gaels had become a stereotype inhabiting the margins of the history of the kingdom to which, so that history still asserted, they had given birth and autonomous existence; the very history which they themselves had once authored and nurtured.[2]

By the sixteenth century, Hogg and MacGregor suggest ownership 'of the Scottish past, however, was claimed for the Lowlands, while the original preservers of its records were side lined and rarely brought into the narrative unless as troublemakers'.³

It was out of such a mindset that the 1609 Statutes of Iona established a process under James VI and I of suppression of the Gaelic language, closely linked to attempts to suppress aspects of Scotland's culture associated with that language. After promulgation, they were followed by further legal enactments including regulations produced by the Scottish State Council in 1616. A key provision was that education of the children of any 'gentleman or yeoman' in possession of more than sixty cattle was to take place in Lowland schools where they 'may be found able sufficiently to speik, reid and wryte Englische'. Other provisions make clear this was not an isolated linguistic regulation. It was part of a larger attempt to reshape and redefine the nature of Highland society in terms more acceptable to the Lowland lawmakers, whose language at this point was Scots. Typical of accompanying requirements were provision and support of Protestant ministers to Highland parishes, banning of arms, and prohibition of general import and sale of wine and strong spirits, except to chiefs and other gentlemen who were permitted to purchase them from the Lowlands for household consumption. As if to emphasise the politico-cultural thrust of the Statutes, they included the outlawing of bards and other bearers of the traditional culture, all such persons to be apprehended, put in the stocks, and expelled from the Islands. I have argued elsewhere that long-standing and ingrained attitudes grew out of the Statutes' enactment, so that they underlie subsequent attempts to suppress Gaelic and the antipathy still shown by some non-Gaelic-speakers to the language's continued existence.⁴ As recently as March 2017, the north of Scotland newspaper the *Press and Journal* carried a front-page headline, 'Councillor blasts "Gaelic Gestapo" as region is forced to promote the language'.⁵ The inspiration for this sensational headline was identified as 'independent councillor George Alexander [who] fought the proposals and urged his fellow members to vote against progressing the scheme [to draw up a Gaelic language plan] – despite being warned that would bring the authority into "direct conflict" with SNP ministers'. Alexander's role was further highlighted when, on being told it would be against the law to defy an act of parliament, he was quoted as saying,

> I dread the idea of spending money because Bord Na Gaidhlig [sic] says we have to. They are behaving like a Gaelic Gestapo. The thought of road signs with Gaelic first and English second sends a shiver down my spine [...].[6]

It is, of course, offensive to our European neighbours and beyond rational comprehension that attempts to sustain the vitality of a much-reduced Scottish language should be compared to the operations of the Nazi state's secret police. Nonetheless, the fact that such remarks can be made in apparent seriousness in the last five years highlights the long-term impact of anti-Gaelic initiatives of the kind represented by the Statutes of Iona.

Parallel, if not quite so draconian, linguistic initiatives with regard to Scots-speaking developed after the 1706 Treaty of Union and the 1707 confirmatory Acts of Union, as political power began to be expressed in the language of Westminster. The Scottish bourgeoisie, especially in cities, sought lessons in English and English pronunciation. In 1725, for example, under the aegis of Allan Ramsay (1686–1758), the English actor Anthony Aston was welcomed by Edinburgh's council and social élite, as an actor bringing a theatrical company, but also as a tutor in newly post-Union 'polite' anglicised speech. As David Hume aspired to publication from the 1740s on, he sent his manuscripts away to have the 'Scotticisms' removed. In 1762, Edinburgh University created the Chair of Rhetoric and Belles Lettres, the first professorship in English Literature in the United Kingdom, but one the first word of whose title – 'Rhetoric' – implies concern with means of linguistic expression. The first holder of the chair, Hugh Blair had taught the subject at the university from 1759. While Blair was ostensibly an advocate of the worth of the Ossian texts, he contributed to the continuing dismissal of Gaelic language and culture. As Robert Crawford puts it, Ossian for Blair embodied 'Highland artworks [which] seemed "a fertile and cultivated country"; but his *Lectures* presented Gaelic as clearly both ancient and obsolete'.[7] Meantime, Hume, a native Scots-speaker, could write in a letter to a nephew:

> I believe all the officers of your Regiment consist of Englishmen or Scotchmen thouroughly [sic] naturalized; so that you have a good opportunity of learning the pronunciation exactly; and I beseech you not to neglect it. It is an agreeable Quality and easily carry'd about with you: I was too negligent in this particular when I was of your age.[8]

Clearly, despite the earlier eighteenth-century efforts of Ramsay in his own poetry and drama, the socially polite language of Enlightenment was English (though examinations at Edinburgh University were conducted in Latin as late as the mid-1820s).

That this had become so is evident in later developments in nineteenth-century and early twentieth-century educational language policies. The 1872 Education (Scotland) Act insisted on English, the *lingua franca* of British imperial rule, as the language of education, not Gaelic or Scots, presumably still the languages of the large majority of Scotland's indigenous population.[9] A dynamic in this promotion of improved teaching of English and other 'modern' subjects, supplanting time formerly given to Latin and Greek, was parental aspiration that their children should compete on an even playing field in joining the professions or such career gateways as the Indian Civil Service examinations. Although the 1918 Education Act required education authorities in Gaelic-speaking areas to make 'reasonable provision' for teaching Gaelic, it was not precise about what was reasonable. By the 1950s, when the present author attended primary school, it was still not uncommon to see a pupil humiliated in front of the class for using a perfectly proper Scots-language formulation like 'shouldnae'. Nonetheless, in the last Scottish census in 2011, more than one and a half million people said they could speak Scots, while another 267,000 said they could understand Scots but not read, write or speak the language.[10] The same census found that only 87,100 people aged three and over in Scotland (1.7 per cent of the population) had some Gaelic language skill. Of these, 32,400 (37 per cent) had full skills in Gaelic, that is could understand, speak, read and write Gaelic; 57,600 (66 per cent) could speak Gaelic; 6,100 (7 per cent) were able to read and/or write but not speak Gaelic; and 23,400 (27 per cent) were able to understand Gaelic but could not speak, read or write it.[11] The long-term impact of language policies is clear; the continuing relatively strong survival of Scots in this context is remarkable.

Robert Burns and monumentalising space

A factor contributing to this survival may be the continuing process of learning, speaking and listening to Scots in poetry and song. A key figure here is Robert Burns as poet and song-collector, whose impact in this regard is reinforced by the cult which developed very quickly after his death. A popular element in this is the annual celebration of his birth on 25 January 1759 by Burns Suppers, where some of his poems are recited and his songs sung. The first of these took place on 21 July 1801, actually marking the fifth anniversary of his death, when nine of his close friends gathered in his birthplace, by then serving as a tavern. Clark McGinn identifies the first Burns Supper outside Scotland happening in 1806 in Magdalen College, Oxford.[12] These events emphasised Burns's writing in Scots rather than English and quickly came internationally to mark identification of expatriates, whether temporary or permanent, as 'Scottish', a topic explored by Ronnie Young.[13] Noting one of the earliest Suppers in India, Nigel Leask observes:

> We are familiar with the manifold ways in which Burns's poetry buttressed Scottish identity in the British Empire (one of the earliest Burns Suppers was held in Calcutta [Kolkata] in 1812) but it is refreshing to think that his sturdy democratic sentiments and vernacular challenge to standard English played a part in resisting, as well as reinforcing, colonial ideologies.[14]

Other such events followed across the USA and Canada from the 1820s on.[15] The first Australian Supper was in 1841 (following an initial Burns Festival there in 1823).[16] As Christopher Whatley remarks,

> Burns was identified both with Scotland and with a wider set of causes (each, of course, with its Scots inflections) within the union and empire. Scottishness and broader British allegiances did not cancel one another out: nineteenth-century Scottish identity – unlike, perhaps, some of its later iterations – did not belong in a zero-sum game. Moreover, if anything, another lower layer of identity – that of localism and civic pride – was the prime focus of nineteenth-century Scottish commemorations of Burns.[17]

Clearly, here Whatley reinforces Graeme Morton's concept of unionist nationalism and concentric – local, Scottish national, British and imperial – loyalties.[18]

Whatley has, of course, written much on the public ceremonials attending the inauguration of Burns monuments.[19] Such monuments and statues of Burns exemplify further important inscriptions of Scottishness, as embodied in the poet, in townscapes and landscapes. An aspect of such monumentalising of Burns is that it offers means of enshrining his status as an internationally important poet. Again, this process began very soon after his death in 1796. In 1818 his remains were translated in St Michael's cemetery in Dumfries from the simple grave in which he was first interred to a large marble Mausoleum, which was modelled – significantly – on Dante's tomb in Ravenna, 'designed some thirty odd years earlier by Camillo Morigia'.[20] This dominant inscription in the townscape not only glorified Burns, but implicitly elevated him, as a national poet, to equivalence to the great national poet of Italy. Only two years later, the first fully public monument to him was completed in 1820 in Alloway, the village of his birth, overlooking the Brig o Doon which occupies such an important part in the narrative of 'Tam o' Shanter'. Johnnie Rodger, who builds upon Whatley and others to discuss such monuments from an architectural perspective,[21] observes this 'had no specific purpose apart from memorialising'.[22] As I have commented elsewhere,

> the memorial is based on the Choragic Monument of Lysicrates near the Acropolis in Athens, creating an associative link – in an age in

which people were well-versed in the classics – between the memory of Burns and classical Greece: a choragus was a citizen who paid for productions at the city Dionysia, the annual Athenian poetry-theatre-music festival for which the great tragedies of Aeschylus, Sophocles and Euripides were written. Both Dumfries mausoleum and Alloway monument enshrined statues of the 'Bard' in architectural contexts which related him to some of the greatest poets ever.[23]

The Alloway Burns Monument designed by Thomas Hamilton[24] provided the design for the 1831 Edinburgh Burns Monument, located as it is on the south side of Calton Hill near the Royal High School, whose design, also by Hamilton, as I have noted,

is based on the Temple of Hephaistos, and close to the New Town buildings of Regent and Royal Terrace. Burns is embodied in a neo-classical architectural composition, overlooking the royalty of Holyrood Palace and the commonality of the Canongate graveyard containing the headstone he arranged for his admired and poverty-stricken predecessor, Robert Fergusson. High above the valley and on the axis between the geological features of the Calton Hill and Arthur's Seat, he is not only Scotland's national poet configured within classical models and above all classes, but situated in the midst of the scenic effects of millennia of geological time as revealed by the Enlightenment pioneer of geology James Hutton. Nowhere is truly 'ageless', but such positioning is as close to marking Burns as physically and metaphorically ageless as may be.[25]

As Jen Harvie comments, 'memory is invested in and stimulated by sites. [...] site-specific performance can be especially effective at remembering and constituting identities that are significantly determined by their materiality and spatiality'.[26] Other nineteenth-century examples of such inscription of iconic figures embodying conceptions of Scottishness onto Scottish townscapes or landscapes include the Scott Monument (1844) in the centre of Edinburgh and the National Wallace Monument (1869) on

Abbey Craig, just north of Stirling and overlooking the site of Wallace's victory at the 1297 Battle of Stirling Bridge. The Scott Monument is situated on Princes Street, approximately half a mile to the west of the Burns Monument, embedding Scott in the city, while, as just outlined, Burns is placed with a view across the valley of Edinburgh in a wide and ancient landscape. These monuments include statues of the heroes they celebrate, that of Wallace being, of course, conjectural. The latter's monument also includes a 'Hall of Heroes' containing busts celebrating Scots who have achieved prominently in arts and sciences, including James Watt and Robert Burns. For well over a century the 'Scottishness' embodied in this hall of fame was exclusively male. It took until 2017 for females to be included: then, it was decided to include Mary Slessor and Maggie Keswick Jencks. Versions of Scottishness are often highly gendered, even though exceptions have existed: R. R. Anderson placed a large female statue of Caledonia outside the Scottish National Portrait Gallery, just above the entrance porch and placed Mary Queen of Scots in pride of place at the side of the gallery, thus celebrating Scotland as an ancient nation with its own ancient line of monarchs.[27]

The statues and busts included in the monuments remind us of another key means of inscribing embodiments of Scottishness into townscapes. Freestanding statues of Burns are found in over twenty public spaces throughout Scotland, while at the top of a high column in the centre of Glasgow's George Square stands one of Scott, close to a later Burns statue raised by public subscription. Such Burns statues are found, however, not only in Scotland. There are three in England but, more tellingly in view of the ways we have already seen Burns and his Suppers 'write' Scottishness into the cultural experience of overseas territories, fifteen are to be found in the United States, including a prominent one in New York's Central Park. There, he stands alongside such internationally renowned artists as Richard Wagner and William Shakespeare. Nine are found in Canada and seven in Australia. What is striking, moreover, about the prevalence of Burns statues is not only how widespread they are, but how much they outnumber those of another 'national bard', William Shakespeare. In England, there are only three public Shakespeare statues, the same number as of Burns, while in

Scotland, there are none in public spaces. The early nineteenth-century Edinburgh Theatre Royal, however, in now-vanished Shakespeare Square at the northeast end of the North Bridge, featured one on its façade as does Glasgow's current Citizen's Theatre in its foyer, transferred from its former façade. Here, though, the reference embodied is surely to drama rather than a national identity, a theory supported by the fact that two of the public English Shakespeare statues are in theatrical contexts: at the heart of London's West End theatre district in Leicester Square and in front of Stratford's Shakespeare Memorial Theatre. As John and Margaret Gold calculate, 'There are upwards of 180 monuments to Burns worldwide. This far outstrips Shakespeare or any other poet.'[28] It is clear, meanwhile, from the overseas examples cited that Burns provided a means of writing Scottishness into lands in which the Scottish diaspora settled and that the employment of Burns in this symbolism differed from the way in which the symbolism of Shakespeare as a 'national bard' was deployed.[29]

The process of marking national identity through statues and busts of those designated national icons is, of course, long established in many countries. In parallel, however, to the developing identity of Scottishness within the United Kingdom, an earlier example of establishing 'Englishness' as 'Britishness' which excluded Scottishness within that then-newly constituted British state can be found in 1734. Then, Richard Temple, Viscount Cobham had his gardener William Kent design and build the Temple of British Worthies at Stowe. This included busts of Alfred the Great, Francis Bacon, Sir Francis Drake, Edward the Black Prince, Elizabeth I, Thomas Gresham, John Hampden, Inigo Jones, John Locke, John Milton, Isaac Newton, Sir Walter Raleigh, William Shakespeare and William of Orange. Later, John Barnard MP and Alexander Pope were added. What is striking here is that all the so-called 'British' worthies, except William of Orange who became king by the 1688 invasion before the Union created a British state, were English. One is aware of the tendency in some English nationalist discourses to call Britain 'England', to the extent that in some countries, under such an influence, the local language's word for 'English' is used as a translation of 'British', as in Turkey where the British Council is translated as '*İngiliz Kültür Heyeti*'. Temple is simply part of that process of assimilating

Englishness to Britishness and vice versa. There is no sense in which discussing the way in which writing Scottishness into townscapes or landscapes is an example of Scottish exceptionalism. We are merely considering Scottish examples of a practice widespread internationally.

Historical memory and static performance

This practice often derives some of its impact from its selective use of versions of historical memory. Jen Harvie offers an insight into the workings of such processes when she observes with specific regard to theatre but also more generally,

> The act of remembering constitutes and produces identity, providing narratives or performances of events and times that are understood to define an individual or a community [...] Different versions of the 'same' memory serve different social functions and produce different effects of power. [...] Theatre and other forms of performance contribute importantly to the memory work of specific communities – especially [...] national communities. [...] Such performance engages audiences in negotiating, formulating, and changing their relationships to their pasts – and so also their presents and futures.[30]

In the context of this chapter, the presence of such statues and monuments can be seen as static 'performances' which, as Whatley has explored, were often inaugurated by elaborate inaugural public ceremonials.[31] Such monuments may even explicitly contain in their design text from historic documents of particular significance, in Harvie's words, in the 'narratives or performances of events and times that are understood to define an individual or a community'. One such Scottish example is the monument of the Royal Scots: the 1st or Royal Regiment of Foot in Edinburgh's West Princes Street Gardens. The regimental title and its relative antiquity and, so, status – founded in 1633 and existing until amalgamation in 2006 as the oldest and senior infantry regiment in the British Army – mark it as a particular embodiment of a Scottish military identity which has evolved and changed over the centuries.

The monument itself contains the regiment's battle honours and cameo profiles of every ruler of Scotland/Britain since 1633, including Oliver Cromwell, until the inauguration of the monument in 1952. It also includes a celebrated passage from the 1320 Declaration of Arbroath: 'It is not for glory, nor riches, neither is it for honours that we fight, but it is for the sake of liberty alone, which no true man loseth but at the cost of his life.' The Declaration marks a particular and historically crucial performative act of assertion of Scottishness against the imposition of another identity, in the specific case here, by England. In doing this, it draws, as Geoffrey Barrow has shown,[32] on a passage from Sallust's *War of Cataline*. In short, it writes into another version of Harvie's 'same' memory of Scottish history an element of classical Roman history and its historiographical literature, with all the validations such a classical reference might imply. Such a process of validation by reference to earlier writings is emphasised by the use in the translation from the Latin, the Declaration's original language, of the word 'loseth'. This is not a grammatical form found in Scots, but it is found in the prestige language of the King James Authorised Version of the Bible. Finally, the inscription on the monument talks of the Declaration having been 'given at Arbroath by the barons, free tenants & the whole community of the kingdom of Scotland in the year 1320'. Certainly, in 1320 one might talk of the 'community' of Scotland, but that meant then in effect the community of magnates including the king. There was no sense in which it might, as it now would, be read as describing the whole population acting together. Yet, the impression given in the context of the Royal Scots monument is of an assertion of a whole Scottish community asserting its independent identity. Layer after layer of versions of, in Harvie's terms, acts 'of remembering', constituting, producing and asserting Scottishness, are embedded in this monument itself and 'written into' the gardens at the centre of Scotland's capital.

Performativity and 'national' enactments

Edinburgh was the site of yet another enactment of a version of 'Scottishness' in the famous 1822 visit of George IV to Scotland, the first visit of a reigning monarch to the northern kingdom in well over a century and a half.

The visit was a highly theatricalised and scenographic event in which ceremonies were stage-managed by Walter Scott working with Daniel Terry of Edinburgh Theatre Royal. Something of its visual impact is captured by J. M. W. Turner's painting, *George IV at the Provost's Banquet in Parliament House, Edinburgh*.[33] The significance of the visit has been much explored in terms of the 'authenticity' of an event which the organiser Walter Scott's son-in-law John Gibson Lockhart described as a hallucination. Unquestionably, there is much to mock in the royal visit which heavily featured tartan. It is not, however, an isolated episode of tartan fantasy, nor is it simply to be regretted as in some sense a creation of 'false' versions of Scottishness.[34] Indeed, it is an interesting debate as to what versions of Scottishness are to be found 'false', as opposed to merely different. The 1822 crossing of boundaries of 'Lowland' and 'Highland' performances of Scottishness during the visit and rewriting of what constituted the imagery and enactment of 'Scotland' is not *ipso facto* false or to be interpreted in a single hegemonic way. Colin Milton has suggested that in 'Scott's view, this dual inheritance equipped the Scots to make a unique contribution to an evolving British identity, one in which the creative tension between "Highland" and "Lowland" values would act as a dynamic principle'.[35] Indeed, there were at once at least two versions of what Highland 'truth' the events might embody. One was promoted by Scott's supporters, led by Sir David Stewart of Garth's Celtic Society of Edinburgh; the other by his opponents, led by the quixotic Alasdair Ranaldson Macdonell of Glengarry and his True Highlanders. What mattered in the event's complex hybridisations was the conscious synthesis of yet other forms of Scottishness. Here, these followed the constitutional inclinations of Scottish Tories like Scott as part of the Hanoverian British settlement when Scotland no longer represented a threat to a British order, half a century after the defeat at Culloden.[36] In this, he sought to elide boundaries between different aspects of Scottish culture and history in a new hybridised performative enactment of Scottishness, however much objected to as 'Celtification' by many at the time and since.

In this perspective, one can apply Kenneth McNeil's aperçu very firmly to the Royal Visit: 'Situated at the very nexus of nation and empire then, representation of the Highlands shifts constantly between Self and Other, making visible the ambiguities, tensions, and ruptures in the formation of national and imperial subjectivities.'[37] As McNeil goes on to argue, in this context, wearing tartan is 'neither a bogus parody nor a faithful expression of some pristine, authentic Highland tradition'.[38] Rather, as Cairns Craig observes,

> If nations are founded not in unity but in exchange, both exchange within a national territory whose boundaries are largely arbitrary, and exchange with cultures that are other to them in time and space, then those bugbears of Scottish cultural history – Lowland Scotland's adoption of the iconography of a Highland Celtic identity and the country's increasing 'Anglicisation' – can be read not as the signs of failed nationhood but as the evidence of a nation which has grasped that its real resources are generated by its capacity for cultural export, translation and assimilation.[39]

Much fun is made of George IV's visit and his corpulently wearing a kilt. To see the performance purely in terms of the visit to Scotland, however, and of a process of tartanisation of Scottish culture – represented as a falsification – is to miss not just these incisive later insights, but a number of contemporary contextual points. The Scottishness to be performed during the visit was both complex and profoundly contradictory. An example of that complex contradiction as different versions of Scottishness were being written is embodied in the adaptation of Scott's *Rob Roy*, presented at the Theatre Royal, celebrating the sometime demonised Highlands and Highlanders, even as Highland clearances took place. Indeed, Alasdair Ranaldson Macdonell of Glengarry of the True Highlanders was at the time clearing tenants from his own land.

Such complex contradiction is surely not rare in most, if not all, expressions of national identity. As the quotation from Craig posits 'nations are founded not in unity but in exchange, both exchange within a national territory whose boundaries are largely arbitrary, and exchange with cultures that are other to them in time and space' so that, at least in Craig's view in

Scotland's case, 'its real resources are generated by its capacity for cultural export, translation and assimilation'. And, one might add, creative contradiction. This can be seen in the ways in which tartan iconography, which Scott appropriated as part of his version of the Lowland/Highland synthesis of an entity expressing Scottishness, becomes an element in a multifaceted dialectic dialogue. Tartan, which had been a symbol of the old Scotland for the Jacobite armies, by the middle of the nineteenth century had become enshrined in the Scottish regiments of the British army, whether Highland or Lowland, the only distinction being that Lowland regiments tended to wear trews as opposed to Highland kilts. The great comedian Tommy Lorne (1890–1935) made comically short kilts a feature of his white-face act, so transporting them into a quasi-Commedia tradition. Scott's Porage [sic] Oats packets would feature a Highland Games athlete – embodying and demonstrating Scottish muscularity and strength – wearing a sports singlet and a kilt in an image which by the 1990s had been adopted as a gay icon. Families might have apparently conflicted, yet open and positive, responses to tartan and the kilt. In my own case, I was dressed solemnly in my grandfather's First World War Black Watch uniform kilt – cut down, of course – for an uncle and aunt's wedding in the early 1950s, a kilt which later I wore for a Coronation year (1953) fancy dress parade. On that occasion, the same kilt, once worn in First World War trenches, adorned a satirical version of a member of the Scottish Republican Army – then for a brief time active in politically motivated vandalism – with a paintbrush for a sporran, a plastic sword, a comic bowler hat and a cardboard brick. One might imagine such ironic performances as the last marked a sceptical view of Scottishness at the time of the Coronation. Yet, when Elizabeth had ascended to the throne in 1952 and the Post Office erected the first pillar box in Scotland with the cypher EIIR that November, it was defaced by tar. A week later, a parcel of gelignite was found in it. In January 1953 it was defaced again, this time with paint and more explosives were deposited. On 12 February, having some days before been attacked with a sledgehammer so that the door had to be taken away for repair, it was blown up. The next day, a Lion Rampant was laid on the ruin. Since then, a special Scottish cypher appears on new Scottish post boxes omitting the regnal number 'II'. In a detail one could not make up, the box stood at the junction of Gilmerton Road with Walter Scott Avenue.

As I began by saying, the ways in which 'Scottishness' is written into existence and performed are not simply matters of written words, however central the act of writing about – and so in a sense creating – Scottishness may be. One example is the apparent effect of the re-establishment of the Scottish parliament in 1999 and subsequent changes in Scottish self-perceptions reflected in the way in which Scottish openness to recognising the diverse nature of its inclusive society and its historic involvement in the slave economy has developed. Since 2000 this has become a live issue both in the literary criticism of such figures as Carla Sassi and Michael Morris and the historiography of Tom Devine and David Alston.[40] The related debate aroused by the Black Lives Matter campaign, further motivated by protest at the murder of George Floyd in Minneapolis in 2020, has led in Scotland, *inter alia*, to the renaming of the David Hume Tower by Edinburgh University – in response to a racist assertion by the great philosopher – and the reworking of the interpretation board for the Melville Monument in Edinburgh's George Square – to draw attention to Melville's involvement in delaying the abolition of slavery by the British parliament at the end of the eighteenth century. The inscription of Scottishness in language, space and performance is indeed complex and contradictory. It is also lively.[41]

Endnotes

1. Thomas Owen Clancy and Barbara E. Crawford, 'The Formation of the Scottish Kingdom', in R. A. Houston and W. W. J. Knox (eds), *The New Penguin History of Scotland* (London: Allen Lane, The Penguin Press, 2001), p. 28.
2. Ulrike Hogg and Martin Macgregor, 'Historiography in Highlands and Lowlands', in Nicola Royan (ed.), *The International Companion to Scottish Literature 1400–1650* (Glasgow: Scottish Literature International, 2018), p. 101.
3. Ibid., p. 109.
4. See, for example, Ian Brown, *Performing Scottishness: Enactment and National Identities* (London: Palgrave Macmillan, 2020), pp. 98–99, from which some material in this paragraph is drawn.
5. Ben Hendry, 'Councillor blasts "Gaelic Gestapo" as region is forced to promote the language', *Press and Journal*, 22 March 2017.
6. Ibid.
7. Robert Crawford, *Devolving English Literature*, 2nd edn [1992] (Edinburgh: Edinburgh University Press, 2000), p. 35.
8. Geoffrey Hunter (ed.), *David Hume: Some Unpublished Letters 1771–1776* (Austin: University of Texas Press, 1960), p. 131.
9. See essays on the 1872 Act and on teaching Gaelic in the nineteenth century in Robert Anderson, Mark Freeman and Lindsay Paterson (eds), *The Edinburgh History of Education in Scotland* (Edinburgh: Edinburgh University Press, 2015), pp. 190–207, 304–25.
10. Scottish Government, 'Scotland's Census: Languages' www.scotlandscensus.gov.uk/census-results/at-a-glance/languages/ [accessed 28 March 2022].
11. National Records of Scotland, 'Scotland's Census, Gaelic Report: Part 1' www.nrscotland.gov.uk/news/2015/scotland's-census-2011-gaelic-report-part-1/ [accessed 28 March 2022].
12. Clark McGinn, 'Vehement Celebrations: The Global Celebration of the Burns Supper since 1801', in Murray Pittock (ed.), *Robert Burns in Global Culture* (Lewisburg: Bucknell University Press, 2011), p. 193.
13. Ronnie Young, '"O what a glorious sight": Performing Identity and the Burns Supper', in Ian Brown and Gerard Carruthers (eds), *Performing Robert Burns: Enactments and Representations of the National Bard* (Edinburgh: Edinburgh University Press, 2021), pp. 85–102.
14. Nigel Leask, '"Their Groves o' Sweet Myrtle": Robert Burns and the Scottish colonial experience', in Pittock (ed.), *Robert Burns in Global Culture*, pp. 172–88 (pp. 181–82).
15. McGinn, p. 194.
16. Ibid., p. 195.
17. Christopher Whatley, 'Contested Commemoration: Robert Burns, Urban Scotland and Scottish Nationality in the Nineteenth Century', in Gerard Carruthers and Colin Kidd (eds), *Literature and Union: Scottish Texts, British Contexts* (Oxford: Oxford University Press, 2018), pp. 240–41.
18. See, for example, Graeme Morton, *Unionist Nationalism: Governing Urban Scotland, 1830–1860* (East Linton: Tuckwell Press, 1999).
19. See, for example, Christopher A. Whatley, 'Burns, Public Ceremonial and Civic Scotland, c. 1796–c. 1914', in Brown and Carruthers (eds), *Performing Robert Burns*, pp. 103–19.
20. Johnny Rodger. 'The Burnsian Constructs', in Johnny Rodger and Gerard Carruthers (eds), *Fickle Man: Robert Burns in the 21st Century* (Dingwall: Sandstone, 2009), p. 60.

21 Johnnie Rodger, *The Hero Building: An Architecture of Scottish National Identity* (London: Routledge, 2017).
22 Rodger, 'The Burnsian Constructs', p. 61.
23 Ian Brown, *Performing Scottishness: Enactment and National Identities* (London: Palgrave Macmillan, 2020), p. 70. This paragraph's discussion is more extensively developed in chapter four of this volume, 'Bards, Britishness, Buildings and Cultural Memory', pp. 57–91.
24 I am grateful to Clarisse Godard Desmarest for pointing out that Thomas Hamilton's inspiration for the Alloway and Calton Hill monuments comes from Stuart and Revett's vol. 1 of *Antiquities of Athens*, published in 1762, the first time the choragic Monument of Lysicrates was introduced, in print, to a British audience.
25 Ibid., p. 72
26 Harvie, *Staging the UK* (Manchester: Manchester University Press, 2005), p. 42.
27 Clarisse Godard Desmarest, 'John Ritchie Findlay (1824–98): Architectural Patron and Benefactor', Proceedings of the Society of Antiquaries of Scotland, 149 (2020), pp. 197–220.
28 John R Gold and Margaret M Gold, *Imagining Scotland: Tradition, Representation and Promotion in Scottish Tourism since 1750* (Aldershot: Scholar Press, 1995), p. 84.
29 For more detailed discussion of this issue, see 'Bards, Britishness, Buildings and Cultural Memory', in Brown, *Performing Scottishness*, pp. 57–91.
30 Jen Harvie, *Staging the UK*, pp. 41–42.
31 See, for example, the chapter cited under note 17 above.
32 G. W. S. Barrow, *Scotland and its Neighbours in the Middle Ages* (London: Hambledon, 1992), pp. 15–16.
33 See: www.tate.org.uk/art/artworks/turner-george-iv-at-the-provosts-banquet-in-the-parliament-house-edinburgh-n02858 [accessed 26 April 2022].
34 The rest of this paragraph draws on and largely repeats an argument first made in my *Performing Scottishness*, pp. 145–46. See also Ian Brown (ed.), *From Tartan to Tartanry: Scottish Culture, History and Myth* (Edinburgh: Edinburgh University Press, 2010).
35 Colin Milton, 'Past and Present: Modern Scottish Historical Fiction', in Ian Brown (ed.), *The Edinburgh History of Scottish Literature, vol. 3: Modern Transformations – New Identities (from 1980)* (Edinburgh: Edinburgh University Press, 2007), p. 117.
36 See Giovanna Guidicini, 'Royal Welcomes in Edinburgh New Town: Portraying Civic Identity in 1822 and 1842', in Clarisse Godard Desmarest (ed.), *The New Town of Edinburgh: An Architectural Celebration* (Edinburgh: Birlinn, 2019), pp. 99–113.
37 Kenneth McNeil, *Scotland, Britain, Empire: Writing the Highlands, 1760–1860* (Columbus, OH: Ohio State University Press, 2007), p. 3.
38 Ibid., p. 80.
39 Cairns Craig, *Intending Scotland: Explorations in Scottish Culture since the Enlightenment* (Edinburgh: Edinburgh University Press, 2009), p. 51–52.
40 See, for example, Carla Sassi, 'Acts of (Un)willed Amnesia: Dis/appearing Figurations of the Caribbean in Post-Union Scottish Literature', in Giovanna Covi, Joan Anim-Addo, Velma Pollard and Carla Sassi (eds), *Caribbean-Scottish Relations Colonial and Contemporary Inscriptions in History, Language and Literature* (London: Mango Publishing, 2007), pp. 131–98; Michael Morris, *Scotland and the Caribbean, c. 1740–1833*:

Atlantic Archipelagos (London: Routledge, 2015); Tom Devine (ed.), *Recovering Scotland's Slavery Past: The Caribbean Connection* (Edinburgh: Edinburgh University Press, 2015); David Alston, *Slaves and Highlanders: Silenced Histories of Scotland and the Caribbean* (Edinburgh: Edinburgh University Press, 2021).

41 This chapter is dedicated to my friend and research colleague Gerry Carruthers, with thanks for his constantly stimulating ideas and fruitful conversation.

2. Lethington, Marie Maitland, and the 'Maitland Quarto': Memorialisation and Performance in Times of 'Troubill' for Scotland

PAMELA M. KING

The surviving literary canon of Older Scots is rich but derives from a very small number of witnesses, all by male authors. Best known are John Barbour (*c*. 1320–1395) and 'Blind' Hary (*c*. 1440–1492) who wrote poems of military exploit inspired by a sense of Scottish identity celebrating the heroic oppressed, and Robert Henryson (?1420–?1500), William Dunbar (?1460–?1520) and Gavin Douglas (1474–1522) were all clerics with little experience of domestic life. The correlative of this circumstance is that we wait for the Reformation to take hold before we find Scottish women like Elizabeth Melville (*c*. 1578–1640) finding their voices in the public sphere. Women are, however, as likely to have composed in Older Scots as they are known to have done in the Gaelic bardic tradition. Recent work has focused productively on the poetry in the so-called Maitland Quarto (Cambridge: Magdalene College, Pepys Library 2553), which is the subject of this paper. Where earlier commentators have read the putative female-authored poems in the manuscript from, for example, critical and codicological,[1] feminist[2] and Foucauldian[3] points of view, the approach here will be different, focusing on the compilation of the manuscript in performative terms and in the real time of a moment in Scottish national history.

In what follows, the line taken will be unapologetically creative, moving away from the decorum of strict evidence usual in literary studies towards the kinds of informed speculation more familiar and accepted in disciplines such as archaeology, or indeed theatrical performance where scholarship customarily takes bearings on the ephemeral from a surrounding ring of contextual information. Hence the scenario constructed here, though research-based, is not proven but suggested. The defence of adopting such an approach is that adherence to established methodologies leaves the history of early women's writing in Scotland blank, despite the absurdity of the notion that before the Reformation women in Scotland did not write. The story here is written into silences from suggestive historical contexts national and familial on one hand, and from close readings of voice on the other.[4]

Sir Richard Maitland of Lethington (1496–1586), whose poetry dominates the manuscript, served as a privy councillor, Lord of Session, and Keeper of the Great Seal of Scotland. Despite his poetic debt to Dunbar, the personal and ethical preoccupations of Maitland's writing revolve around lineage, land and family. His public life was 'devoted to conciliation'.[5] In his negotiations of Border disputes he was commended by the English ambassador. He is also noted for his refusal, however, to capitulate to the English, unlike many of his neighbours, after the Battle of Pinkie in 1547, staying on in his country seat at Lethington, just outside Haddington, although, according to the memorial written by his grandson James, experiencing 'verye great difficulties, having a wyffe, manie children, and ane great familie at the said tyme on his charge during these warres [...]'.[6] John Knox, having dined at Lethington in 1542, said he was '[...] ever civil, albeit not persuaded in religion'. One of his significant strengths was the belief from which he never wavered that religion should never become the main concern of state.[7]

His sons, as we shall later acknowledge, did not follow his advice. Most of his poetry was written in his blind old age, so was composed at home and in the family setting. The manuscript, and a companion folio volume, emanate from his household and its immediate milieu. The Quarto marks his great age and/or anticipates his death, concluding with epitaphs and elegies celebrating him and his wife, who died on his funeral day. Much of Richard Maitland's own poetry, which makes up the bulk of both manuscripts is admonitory but is predominantly social in focus: his concern is more with the decay of family, state, and commonwealth than the fate of the individual soul. His is the voice of the custodian of the law of the land, but also of the father, not standing apart from family and social life, and prepared to admit his own errors.

By the time Sir Richard died, the 'manie children' he defended after Pinkie had been drastically reduced. It seems that four sons died during their minority,[8] and of the remaining three who survived to make their name on the national stage, only the middle one, John, outlived his father. And there were four daughters. His third daughter's name, Marie (c. ?1550–1596), is inscribed twice on the first folio, with the date 1586, the year Sir Richard died, and two poems in the manuscript are addressed to her. Her involvement in the manuscript has been thoroughly explored, precisely because of her role as putative author of the earliest surviving Scottish women's poetry.[9] The whole family is known to have had literary interests. Aside from Sir Richard himself, the manuscript contains poems by his son John (1537–95), and well-known members of their circle, including Alexander Arbuthnot (1538–1583), and Alexander Montgomerie (?1550–1598), and one ascribed to the king, James VI (1566–1625), himself. Thirty-three of the eighty-eight poems in the manuscript are anonymous.

Joanna Martin, the manuscript's editor for the Scottish Text Society, acknowledges the involvement of the Maitland women in the 'composition, compilation, and copying' of the texts within it, but cautions over-enthusiastic seekers for female authors that 'there was a long tradition of ventriloquising the female voice in male-authored lyric poetry in the sixteenth century'.[10] Evelyn Newlyn, on the other hand, argues that where the balance of evidence suggests the possibility of female authorship, the critic should adopt a 'transgressive' reading resisting the assumed probability of male authorship. The current exploration was inspired by Newlyn's cue. She divides the manuscript into six sections, noting that the anonymous poems are clustered at the end of the four 'core' sections.[11] Here we will focus on the nineteen anonymous poems immediately following the one attributed to James VI, not only attending to image, tone, and point of view in isolated poems, but considering the hypothetical mustering and ordering of them as a group, and adding the first one, Poem 68, not previously considered as a candidate for female authorship.

We begin in the middle of the selected group, in order to establish the performative hypothesis. Poem 74, 'In Prais of ane Gentle Woman', indisputably male in voice, and conventional in all respects, ends on an interrogative final two lines,

> I am hir awin: quhat then? It is the onle thing I crave.
> Scho will me not refuus, I knaw. Quhat farther wauld I have?

Taken in isolation, the questions are rhetorical, completing a poem demonstrating how a lady may be won over. The following poem, however, might be read as an answer, by the lady, rendering the questions less than rhetorical, and stating that, given previous treachery in return for trust, she cannot:

> 'Quhen stead is stollin, then steik the stable dure';
> Quhilk causis me full oft to call and cry,
> What fuill, what beast, what simple saull was I! (ll. 6–8)

Poem 75 is the lament of a spurned lover, vigorously exclaiming in the voice of one impotent and undervalued, something later to find similar expression in Poem 79. The speaker in Poem 75 is compared to a hen scratching the knife that 'sould bereve hir lyfe' (ll. 19–20). In a male voice, this homely image would threaten bathos; we hold in mind this image taken from the world of beasts, however.

Poem 76, 'To His Friend', is, in turn, in the voice of a spurned male lover. The matter is conventional in all three poems, but the voice in 74 and 76 imitates that of a man prostrated by unrequited love, striking attitudes of remorse: 'My awin mishap I nothing deime, / O dear to me, and deare againe' (76, ll. 25–26). Poem 75, on the other hand, is more vigorous, more indignant in tone, and more proverbial in register. The confessional 'Not thou, but I, deseruis the pyne' (76, l. 19), answers the wail of protest from the 'schent' woman of (75, l. 4). If one begins to think of the compilation of the manuscript in performative terms, as a collaborative game, perhaps between Marie Maitland and her surviving brother, John, the inclusion of such tit-for-tat sequences of material written as playful exercises in conventional forms is temptingly plausible. The fact that the addressee in both 75 and 76 is an ambiguous 'freind' (*sic*) might support this hypothesis. The term is, of course, applied much more generally in the sixteenth century than in modern usage, but as it embraces lover and family member, as well as friend *per se*, its usage in an imagined sparring game between older brother and younger sister here seems witty.

Poem 77 is a simple piece written in four four-line stanzas 'In Prais of a Gilt Bybill', celebrating a physical Bible as a decorated material object:

> A cot bedect with gold
> And syluer streamis it weiris,
> As just rewaird the maistres gave,
> For love to it scho beiris. (ll. 8–11)

Here the reflection on decorative work, executed or at least commissioned by 'the maistres', and the way in which piety is reverently expressed by the evocation of a small, tactile object, worked with needlecraft, seems perfectly to reflect the marriage of the devotional and domestic which again anticipates the acknowledged territory of Early Modern women's writing. To suggest that 'the maistres' refers to Sir Richard's wife, the mother of the compilers, is completely unsupported, except insofar as the manuscript celebrates the whole family.

Poem 78 returns us to the courtly love theme, and possible game, imitating the voice of the rejected male lover once more, and is followed by 79, 'To Ane Angrie Freinde'. Here the poem opens with an epic simile which is a double female image, drawn again from the world of beasts, as the lioness roars for her whelps, and the turtle dove languishes for her dead mate, going on to assert that all Nature 'Dois seik to keip the thing it loves best [...]' (l. 7). The speaker then rails against Fortune, handing over the power to save a life to the other party: 'And now the hand, that wounded me so soir, / Sall end the lyfe, or ellis againe restoir' (ll. 21–22).

Here we have to choose between reading the poem as an expression of 'real' female impotence, or of the conventional impotence of the male courtly lover; the imagery of the opening simile might suggest the former, especially as the following poem is yet another expression of the condition of rejection, opening with four stanzas of figures of comparison.

Poem 80 appears to be a further rejoinder, as yet again we find the voice of the rejected male lover. We note in passing that the 'rejected male' poems experiment with different structural forms. Poem 82 is a short prayer offering no clue as to the gender of the author, so we pass on to Poem 83, 'To Ane Vnthankfull Freind' which is a bitter attack on a 'periurd and ladye fals' (l. 2), a 'filthie faithless dame', with a 'cruell tygirs hairt' (ll. 18–19). Clearly written from a male point of view, this poem adopts the emphatic tone and animal imagery of the earlier female-voice poems of spurned love. Whether we are looking at two poets in dialogue, with or without role-reversal, or one, probably male, poet adept at ventriloquising the female voice then showing his hand in this poem, are all alternatives of equal possibility. Thereafter Poem 84, 'In Prais of ane Buik Send to his Friend', offers, however, a potential key to the performative imaginary posited above, and adds weight to the argument that the female-voice poems in the exchange are the work of a real woman. The second stanza reflects on the lesson on writing found in the 'buik':

> For thingis of great and high affairs
> In simple style he shawis,
> And als the end of worldlie cairs
> In shape of beastis he drawis,
> Assuir thy self, thairfoir,
> In it of tresoir stoir. (ll. 7–12)

The 'buik' seems to have been offered as inspiration and instruction for an aspirant poet, modelling imagery drawn from the animal world. Might it not have been, given the animals chosen for inclusion in the foregoing 'women's voice' poems, something in the rhymed Aesopian tradition, ubiquitous throughout the late Middle Ages and Early Modern period as schoolbooks for boys, and perhaps just the thing an older brother might give to his bookish younger sister? Thus Poem 84 could be a poem written by an older brother to a younger, literary sister, reminding her of early inspiration for her writing. The possible material circumstances in which the manuscript was compiled surely defend such speculation from dismissal as wholly fanciful.

Poem 85, 'To Your Self', is one commonly cited as likely to be by Marie, because of its appeal to Sappho and (probably) Olympia Fulvia Morata (1526/7–1555), Calvinist convert and biblical scholar, to assist 'Maistres Marie' (l. 9) to become 'poet perfytte'. It is followed by 86 which calls on Diana as 'my muse'. Poem 85, however, also seems to answer Poem 84, as the speaker addresses herself in the third person in the final stanza and coda:

> This buik then bear and beat your branis therein:
> A plesant poet perfytte sall ye be
> And lytill labour lost, the laurel win,
> Adorn's with cumloie croun of poesie [...]

and then:

> For sycophant, for simple saull, for sott,
> Maik weill, mar not, for Momus cair ȝe not.

These two, with the personalised reference to 'Marie' in the first, bear out what the preceding few suggest, which is the ghost of an alternating conversation between a (real) female and a supportive male voice, plausible in the Maitland family context. Contemporary feminist theory offers us the appropriate tools: to return to Evelyn Newlyn's agenda with which she approaches her analysis of Poem 38:

> Poetic structures and strategies with disruption, incompleteness, discontinuity, redirection, and similar complexities may, with other criteria, signal the unexpected woman writer or persona. Additionally, the unconventional employment of rhetoric and language, the use of unusual metaphors and patterns of imagery, and the manipulation of traditional conventions and topoi, all of which can allow meanings to be layered in a poem, are devices a woman poet might use so as to be true to her art and her ideas but to present them in socially acceptable ways.[12]

Moreover, she concludes, 'A second step is to identify, by provenance, history, and association with women, potential manuscripts such as the Maitland Quarto, long associated with Mary Maitland.'

Perhaps that hypothesis is best tested by its alternatives. Reading the section in detail according to performative principles in which the manuscript is the product of a real family collaboration in real time, we find two possibilities. The first, exercising the caution of absolute evidence is that one or more male poets from this literary family wrote poems of unrequited love from both the male and female point of view, adopting a consistent and cunningly constructed female voice in tone and fields of imagery. These were later gathered together by the surviving brother and ordered with the help of his sister in the manuscript, accompanied by one or two accomplished examples in her own hand. The second imagines a context for the compilation of the manuscript as a memorial for Sir Richard, and possibly his wife, by his much and tragically depleted family, in which the collaborators, again probably Marie and John, not only gather poems by their father, family and friends, but engage in, again in real time, or gather from their recent compositional collaboration, a *jeu d'esprit* of competitive writing of conventional love poetry, accompanied by a poem on a 'female' theme, perhaps memorialising their mother, and two recalling the brother's contribution of a book to encourage the sister to join the family poetry-writing habit.

Working backwards from the cluster of poems explored above, we note first Poem 73, a prayer, more elaborate than 81, but in many respects in similar penitential vein as was fashionable in the Scotland of the period. Both prayers may have been written by the same, or different hands, of either gender, but their inclusion is important insofar as they will contribute to the picture of the design of this section overall. Poems 71 and 72 are another pair of conventional lovers' complaints. Poem 71, copied in italic, is written from the male point of view. Poem 72 would be hard to 'gender' without the later poems and remains relatively so but for its appeal to mutual fidelity, a conventional female sentiment acknowledged in, for example, the poetry of Katherine Philips (1632–1664).

Poem 70, which also appears in the Folio Manuscript, echoes sentiments found elsewhere in the manuscript, and particularly in the corpus attributed to Sir Richard. It is a complaint against the decay of the times, and, particularly of civic manhood and the decay of horsemanship. Its rhyming couplets match the subject well, and it could equally well have been written by Sir Richard, or by one of his offspring lampooning their father's complaints about the younger generation.

Poem 69 has been thoroughly and convincingly attributed to Marie by a number of scholars. Sajid Chowdbury explores anagrammatic punning in this poem, concluding that the poem establishes an 'intricate metaphysics of authorship'.[13] Julia Boffey has explored it in the context of its debt to *The Kingis Quair*,[14] while Sarah Dunnigan has focused on its presentation of the 'chaste and beautiful female body'.[15] Since, like Poems 85 and 86, this has been adequately attributed by others, here we move swiftly backwards to the very first in this anonymous sub-section, the much more critically overlooked Poem 68, and a differently focused excursus into the national and family contexts of the production of the manuscript.

Before we do so, however, it might prove helpful to gather more diagrammatically the organisation of this sub-section of the manuscript, which I contend has a particular overall design connected to the intimate family context that inspired the whole, and arguably the product of collaboration:

Poem no.	Subject matter	Point of view
68	Place – Lethington	Individual; valedictory (Marie?)
69	Love vision, derivative	Female – Marie
70	Place – civic	Male; complaint / lampoon – male
71	Love complaint	Male
72	Love complaint	Female?
73	Penitential Prayer	Any individual
74	Love complaint	Male
75	Lover's response	Female (Marie?)
76	Lover's complaint	Male
77	Praise of a Bible	Female (Marie?)
78	Lover's complaint	Male

79	Lover's response	Female (Marie?)
80	Lover's complaint	Male
81	Penitential prayer	Any
82	Prayer of thanksgiving	Any
83	Lover's complaint	Male but mimics earlier female rejoinders
84	Book on composition – gift	Male
85	Poetic endeavour ref. book	Female – Marie
86	Address to Diana as muse	Female – Marie

The sub-section of the manuscript under review mimics in subjects, themes, and range of poetic modes the manuscript as a whole. It also, in its evident symmetries and variety, suggests a context in which its content was planned and assembled in advance of copying. Marie's input of individual poems into it has already been strongly argued by others, and is here tentatively extended by reference to the hypothetical performative construction of the whole in real place, time, and family context. With these explorations in mind, we now turn to Poem 68, the first in the section, an important genre-outrider in early Scots writing, and never satisfactorily attributed, to suggest that it too can be read as the product of a female voice, but one younger than that engaged in the 'game' posited above.

The occasion of the completion of the Quarto manuscript is established as 1586, the year of Sir Richard's death, his son John's elevation to the position of Keeper of the Great Seal of Scotland and Vice-Chancellor to James VI, and Marie's marriage to Sir Alexander Lauder of Hatton. The details of these events are widely recorded and need not be rehearsed here. What we should note, however, is that Sir Richard enjoyed only the final two years of his long life back in his country seat at Lethington, which was restored to the family in 1584. It had been confiscated in 1571, following Richard's son and heir's arraignment for treason, commuted to felony, in the same year. This eldest son's – William – son and daughter were at that time also declared incapable of holding land in Scotland. James, the son, a Roman Catholic living abroad, on being restored to the title in 1584 sold the estate to his uncle, Sir Richard's second and only surviving son, John.[16] It is hardly surprising, in this event, that the Quarto manuscript should include a poem in celebration of Lethington. It is to whom wrote it, and when, that the remainder of this paper is devoted, and that involves in due course a digression into the history of the Maitlands as players on the national stage and targets of Protestant satire, during the troubled years between 1567 and 1571.

Lethington, was renamed Lennoxlove as the result of the vanity of a later owner and has been in the possession of the Dukes of Hamilton since the mid-twentieth century. This poem is heralded in her edition by Joanna Martin as being in the vanguard of the 'country house' genre.[17] Early Modern readers of English poetry will be familiar with Amelia Lanyer's (1569–1645) 'Description of Cooke-ham', written sometime between 1603 and 1609 in honour of Margaret Clifford, Countess of Cumberland, and, of course, Ben Jonson's 'To Penshurst' (1616) and Andrew Marvell's 'Upon Appleton House' (1651).[18] A. A. MacDonald offers the opinion that Poem 68, because of its early date for the genre, 'deserves more attention' and expresses regret that the author is unknown. He further observes that it shares the simple ballad stanza with 'Of the day Estivall' by Alexander Hume (1560–1609).[19]

Joanna Martin in a free-standing article goes further and suggests widening discussion of analogues to other kinds of writing on family lands, citing, for example, the mention of Darnaway at the end of *The Buke of the Howlat*. Geoffrey Whitney's (1548–1601) praise of Richard Cotton's estate at Combermere in 'To Richard Cotton Esquire', printed in his *A Choice of Emblemes* (1586), is another such near-contemporary example. She observes the connections between place and lineage in sixteenth-century Scots chronicle writing, suggesting later in her argument that the entire Quarto manuscript is shot through with concerns, as observed above, of family as inextricably linked with landholding.[20]

It is Martin who also draws attention to Thomas Maitland's elaborate Latin poem in praise of Lethington:

> [...] 'Domus Ledintona' which was printed in *Delitiae Poetarum Scotorum* (1637), and which reflects the taste for neo-Latin poems on country estates which flourished on the continent (especially in the Netherlands and Italy) from the 1560s. Like its Scots equivalent this poem is an extended apostrophe to Lethington, taking in its

peerless architecture, the nobility of its builders, the hospitality it offers visitors, and the evidence it provides of the family's fortitude against the English.[21]

She goes on to note how different the poems are, however, in point of view, particularly as Poem 68 is written by one forced to leave the country seat. Joining the search for an author, I am going to propose that this poem was written by Marie Maitland, following the inclusion of a poem attributed to James VI himself, and fronting-up the anonymous cluster discussed above in circumstances which need some background for those uninitiated in the relevant historical detail.

Marie's celebrated eldest brother, William, was Mary Queen of Scots's sometime secretary. He was George Buchanan's *Chamaeleon*,[22] and also endured satirical attack by Richard Bannatyne, who dubbed him 'Mitchell Wylie' (Machiavelli).[23] He was James Semple's *Bird in the Cage*.[24] His version of his father's refusal of partisanship became a form of political vacillation such that he has only recently been defended as moderate, though he was almost certainly also Machiavellian, if according to more enlightened readings of *Il Principe* than those current in his time.[25] His nineteenth-century biographer, John Skelton, also offers a more even-handed picture of his skills as orator and diplomatist with reference to contemporary sources.[26] In the transition from the regency of Mary of Guise, William Maitland successfully held the peace between outright war with England on the one hand, and the sequestration of Church lands as called for in Knox's *Book of Discipline*. Indeed, it was generally recognised that he was responsible for years of peace and stability in Scotland. He was forced to take action, however, when replaced by David Riccio, as the Queen's tastes favoured Continental appointments. His adherence to Mary's cause became more challenging after she had both lost leverage because she had a male heir and, fatally, became involved with James Hepburn, fourth Earl of Bothwell. Maitland initially deserted her during her period with Bothwell, but he renewed his loyalty as soon as the latter was routed at Carberry, attempting also to reconcile all parties to the new Regent Moray. He parted company with Moray, however, after the latter agreed that Mary should be tried at York for conspiring to murder Darnley. After the Regent was murdered, Maitland finally was unable to hold middle ground and became a partisan of the Queen's party in open warfare with what became the King's party. This time he gained the reputation of being chiefly responsible for Scotland's divided state.[27] In 1570 Maitland was already suffering from a debilitating disease when he was implicated in the conspiracy to murder Darnley, confected from the notorious 'Casket Letters'. As Buchanan, by now his most dangerous enemy, put it in *Chamaeleon*:

> At Sterling the Articles were declared at length, where the *Chamaeleon* was Impeach'd for Treason, as guilty of the Murther of the late King, which griev's him heartily, so that he humbly desir'd my Lord Regent, that the form of the Impeachment might be alter'd, and that he might be accused only of the Troubles that probably should arise from the formentioned Marriage betwixt the Queen and *Norfolk*, which thing he concluded was so firmly contriv'd, that neither Force nor Wit could hinder the performance of it, and believ'd that such an Accusation should be made for his Honour, and make him to be esteem'd for his Wisdom. When he could not gain that point, he obtain'd, against the consent of all the Regent's Friends, that he should be Imprison'd in the Castle of *Edinburgh*, where he wrought against the Nature of the *Chamaeleon*, for there he chang'd the greater part of those in the Castle to his own Colour and Mind, so that the Conspiracy of the Regent's Death, [which] was then executed.[28]

He died in prison of poisoning after the fall of Edinburgh Castle in 1573.

The reason for quoting Buchanan's account in full here is that it gives a precise context for the removal of the Maitland family from their ancestral seat at Lethington and thus a date for the poem. Its inclusion in the much later Quarto collection could be read as memorialising a particularly traumatic moment for the family from a domestic perspective, at a time when they had only recently been restored to their former home.

Youngest brother Thomas died of sickness on his way to Rome in search of papal support for Mary Queen of Scots in 1572. Despite his very short life, he too has left traces of a literary partisan output. He wrote a *jeu d'esprit* in 1570, in which he made fun of the party supporting James VI in his minority and their charges of Machiavellianism against the Queen's supporters.[29] His brother was the politician, but it seems that Thomas was the writer: his status as satirist and queen's partisan is, perhaps best affirmed by a back-handed compliment, as he was George Buchanan's choice as fictional interlocutor in his *De Jure Regni apud Scotos*. Buchanan, by this time a convinced Protestant, wrote this, his most celebrated work, as a dialogue in Latin dedicated to James VI, which was later translated into English in 1689 as *A Dialogue Concerning the Due Priviledge of Government in the Kingdom of Scotland Betwixt George Buchanan and Thomas Maitland*.[30]

During this succession of blows, as his sons played for higher and higher political stakes, the politically less partisan Sir Richard, by then blind, his wife, and almost certainly Marie, were forced to leave Lethington and went into exile at Dundas until Lethington was restored to them in 1584, two years before Sir Richard's death. Their remaining son, John, who became James VI's Lord Chancellor, died in 1595, Marie in 1596.

Returning with more context to Poem 68, we note to begin with that, while Lanyer, Jonson, and Marvell all use the celebration of the country house as a springboard into extolling certain moral and political virtues, Poem 68 is inarguably less intellectually ambitious. It displays a patina of classical learning, but its sentimental message is as simple as its twenty-eight-line ballad stanzas. It is written in iambic tetrameters, rhyming ababcdcd, with most lines end-stopped, generally with a full stop at the end of the fourth. It tidily deploys standard rhetorical tropes, such as repetitio, apostrophe, and the rhetorical question, in the manner of a school-book model. Without wishing to foreground its naïve simplicity as support for a bid for female authorship, that simplicity is an incontrovertible fact. Equally the same want of sophistication can suggest that the poem is a piece of relative juvenilia, and extremely unlikely therefore, to have been written by the mature Sir Richard, or by William – despite the latter's responsibility for the loss. Thomas might be another candidate for authorship, but had already written a tribute to Lethington, and appears to have been a sophisticated writer, despite his youth, and possibly to have favoured Latin. Then there is John – but as we will go on to see, none of this accounts for the fact that the poem also has an identifiably female point of view, established as much by what it does not say as what it does.

We have no record of Marie's date of birth, but we know that John was born in 1537. Given their acknowledged collaboration in the compilation of the manuscript, one might expect them to be close in age. Marie was single much later than her sisters, marrying Alexander Lauder of Hatton in 1586, the same year that her parents died. Her sisters Margaret, Helen and Isabel were at least betrothed in the 1560s. When Marie married, brother John was in his forties. She gave birth to two children in 1587 and 1589, but predeceased her husband by several years, so, we may surmise, this was a late marriage, possibly in her mid to late thirties.[31] Thus, my arithmetic suggests not only that Marie may have been the only daughter still at home when Lethington was confiscated in 1571 but was probably in her late teens or early twenties.

The poem opens with six stanzas on the tradition of poets celebrating place. The first stanza lists classical poets who have celebrated their homes: Virgil's Mantua, Lucan's Corduba, Catullus's Verona, Ovid's Sulmo. The second stanza reflects on how every poet commends a special place thus rendering it world famous. The third and fourth stanzas illustrate the case by citing Greece, Sicily, Parnassus, the sacred fountain of Hippocrene, the river Permessus, and the Vale of Tempe. The argument then suggests that more local places are unworthy of 'dark silence', and the poet would be 'ingrate' and 'vnkynd' not to offer the same chance of immortality through 'eloquence' to another special place.

Far from being a country house, as the reader familiar with the later genre poems might expect, that reader would do well to recall from the outset that the celebrated 'house' was a massive, fortified peel-tower, designed primarily for defence, as Thomas's poem remarks. Its walls – which are three and a half metres thick, with narrow windows, now a single tower – were originally part of a fearsome L-shaped fortress founded in 1345. It is a couple of kilometres outside Haddington, which was occupied by the English forces after the Scots were defeated at Pinkie in September 1547, in the circumstances noted in James Maitland's family memoir cited above. English troops burnt houses belonging to the Maitlands, and, although Lethington itself was damaged, its structure surely also acted as a deterrent. John Skelton describes it thus:

> Even now it is a place where the characteristics of the solitary sheep-walks of the Border dales are appreciated with exceptional vividness [...] the pastoral solitude of the region is not unimpressive [...] Such district as I am describing must have been—three hundred years ago—wellnigh impenetrable. From Soutra to Penshiel there was one track only across the hills which a horseman could ride. The slopes of the Lammermuir were at an early period dense with forest and populous with game [...] ... The wolf and the forest had possibly disappeared before Lethington was born; but, even apart from savage animals and primeval thickets, it is obvious that during an unquiet and turbulent reign, its native valleys must have been well suited for concealment and defence. Within a day's ride of the capital, the sanctuaries of the Lammermuirs, sparsely peopled by clansmen whose fidelity was absolute, were specially convenient to a statesman who had many enemies [...][32]

Moving forward to the final stanzas of Poem 68, starting in the second half of the seventeenth we find:

> Thow hes a thousand plesouris ma
> That my tounge can not tell.
> O happie war he that micht ay
> But troubill in the duell.
>
> And happie art thow sic a place
> That few thy maik ar sene;
> Bot 3it, mair happie for that race

> To quhome thow dois pertene,
> Quha dois not knaw the Maitland [bluid],
> The best in all this land,
> In quhilk sumtyme the honour stuid,
> And worship of Scotland?
>
> Of auld Sir Richard of that name
> We haue hard sing and say
> Of his triumphant nobill fame
> And of his auld baird gray;
> And of his nobill sonnies thrie,
> Quhilk that tyme had no maik,
> Quhilk maid Scotland renoumit be,
> And all England to quaik;
>
> Quhais luiffing praysis maid trewlie,
> Efter that simpill tyme,
> Ar soung in moneye far countrie,
> Albeit in rurall ryme.
> And gif I dar the treuth declair,
> And nane me fleitschour call,
> I can to him find a compare
> And till his bairnis all. (ll. 133–60)

It might be over-interpreting to hang too much on 'but troubill' in the first few lines quoted, except that the last two lines of the fifteenth stanza read: 'And only I rehers the ioy / That I did in the find' (ll. 119–20). The past tense here corroborates the idea that the poem was written by someone leaving, or forced to leave, the celebrated house.

The invocation of the Maitland pedigree refers to an earlier Sir Richard, whose grey beard rather naively supplies the rhyme in line fifty-three. This ancestor's reputation is also invoked in Poem 46, 'Ane Consolatore Ballad to Sir Richard Maitland of Lethington Knicht', also anonymous, but clearly written man to man:

> Richard he was, Richard ȝe are also,
> And Maitland als, and magnanime ar ȝe,
> In als greit age, als wrappit ar in wo.
> Sevin sonnies ȝe had, micht contravaill his thrie,
> Bot burdalane ȝe haue behind, as he.
> The Lord his linnage so enairge and lyne,
> As money hundredth nepotis, grie be grie,
> Sen Richard wes, as hundredth ȝeiris ar hyne. (ll. 121–28)

The consolator refers to Maitland's thirteenth-century ancestor reputed to have established the Maitlands of Thirlestane, pointing out that he established a lineage despite having only one surviving son, or 'burdelane'.

The author of the Poem 68 clearly acknowledges the first Sir Richard's legendary status, with his three sons beside him, defender of Scotland, and invokes the same comparison – except that John is not yet the 'burdelane'. The final two lines 'I can to him find a compare / And till his bairnis all' rule out the likelihood that Sir Richard is the author, as the 'compare' is himself, and 'his bairnis all' seems to refer to his sons William, John and Thomas, which makes it at least improbable that any of them is the author as well as suggesting a *terminus ad quem* of 1572, the year in which Thomas Maitland the youngest son died, a year before eldest brother William.

Having suggested by elimination that Marie might have written Poem 68, we now turn to what it celebrates about Lethington, its true 'country house' poem content, to suggest that, if Marie seems a presumptive step too far, we are at least listening to a young female voice. The eighth stanza begins to anatomise the building:

> Thy tour, and fortress, lairge and lang,
> Thy nychtbouris dois excel,
> And for thy wallis, thik and strang,
> Thou justly beiris the bell.
> Thy groundis deip, and Toppis hie
> Vprysing in the air,

> Thy voltis plesand ar to sie,
> Thay ar so greit and fair. (ll. 57–64)

Its architectural features are listed. They are elements of fortification, including the famous bell, in fact two, still preserved at Lennoxlove, one inside and one outside the tower, to be rung in the event of an attack. But there is nothing of the defensive purpose of the building here; these features are simply 'greit and fair'.

The following two stanzas turn attention to the surroundings:

> Thy work to luik on is delyte,
> So clein, so sound, so evin,
> Thy alryne is a mervall greit,
> Vpreiching to the hevin.
> O quhat plesour is to be their,
> As phoebus dois vpryise,
> To sie the wod and feildis fair,
> Quhilk round about the lyis. (ll. 65–72)

The 'alryne' the walk behind the battlements is here not so much a lookout post or vantage point from which to shoot at besiegers, but a platform from which the surrounding countryside can be admired at dawn, and at dusk:

> O quhat plesour may thair be sene,
> As the dayis lamp dois lout,
> To sie thy medowis fair and grene,
> Quhilk lyis the about.
> O quhat plesour is to be their,
> Quhen as the sone is doun,
> To heir the [bumming] of the air,
> And plesand evenis soune. (ll. 73–80)

What is invoked is not a defensible edifice, but a lofty tower set in surroundings of complete tranquillity. But the speaker seems intent on spending the whole night on the roof before having to leave the place:

> O quhat plesour is thair and ioy,
> Quhen day hes lost his licht,
> To sie the tyme sa calme and coy,
> And silence of the nicht.
> Lang tyme sould I thair remaine,
> Or that I wereit grew,
> And sone sall I desyire againe,
> Quhen I bid thee 'Adiev!' ll. 81–88)

The speaker then moves away from the valedictory, again to marvel at the building in charmingly naïve terms:

> Greit was the work to houke the ground,
> And thy foundation cast;
> Bot greater it was the to found
> And end the at the last.
> I mervell that he did not feir,
> Quha rasit the on hicht,
> That na fundatioun sould the beir,
> Bot thow sould sink for wecht.
>
> Or ellis the air sould not haue tholit,
> So heich for to be persit,
> Nor 3it the erd for to be holit,
> And so deip doun be sersit.
> Then michtie wes that man in deid,
> That first the tuik in hand,
> And in his worke did so proceed,
> That he the maid vpstand. (ll. 89–104)

This is surely a suspiciously wide-eyed view of the building, certainly hard to imagine as having been written by a mature, arms-bearing Scottish aristocrat.

The focus then moves from the outside of the building to the inside. Sadly, no inventories of Lethington survive from the confiscation or restoration to the Maitlands,[33] so we rely on the poem celebrating how comfortable and cosy was this fortress, omitting to mention its defensively critical inner well and dungeon:

> Bot the to plenische and fulfill,
> And mak thy worke compleit,
> Quho so it richt consider will,
> Wes worke of no les spreit.
> They beddis soft and tapeis fair,
> Thy treitting and gud cheir,
> Gif I the treuth wald now declair,
> I wait thow hes no peir. (ll. 105–12)

The following stanza reflects that the poem is unnecessary, as anyone passing by the way can easily see what a splendid place it is. Finally, the speaker goes on to catalogue the pleasures to be found in the immediate environs:

> Thy arbour and thy orchard grene
> I can not pas it by,
> A thing maist semelie to be sene
> Vnder thy wall dois ly;
> Maist plesand place to mak repair,
> Thairin to sit or gang,
> Thy knottis and thy alleis fair,
> Quhilk ar baith braid and lang.
>
> Thy buttis biggit near thame by,
> Sa suire but sone or wind,
> Maist plesand place of archerie
> That euer I ȝit could find.
> Thow hes a thousand plesouris ma
> That my tounge can not tell.
> O happie wart he that might ay
> But troubill in the duell. (ll. 121–36)

Thus we are back where we started. Notwithstanding the masculine pronouns, common enough in the female voice when the subject is indefinite, the preoccupations here seem to be female. Knot gardens, arbours, garden paths, and orchards were the enclosed outdoor spaces in which high-born ladies took the air. And archery, never an exclusively male occupation, could also attract a lady in the sheltered butts of her home. Although it was the English longbow that defeated the Scots at Flodden, by the late sixteenth century archery was well on the way to becoming a social sport for both sexes. We note that nothing is said of the guns that would by then have protected Lethington.

The contention is, therefore, that we look outside the devotional and amorous anonymous poetry in the Maitland Quarto to find the female voice of Marie Maitland, and that this poem, possibly prompted by the confiscation of her home, was preserved until the compilation of the manuscript in 1586. It presents us with a young innocent voice, accustomed to calling a fortified tower her home and finding in it non-military properties which is why it calls to mind the country house celebrations of the English home from years later. In fact, it was Marie's nephew, another John, who was to build on a real country house wing in the seventeenth century, followed by architect William Lorimer in 1912.

The poem unites a strong sense of a peculiarly Scottish space with a female point of view, female as much by omission as inclusion, thus making artful male ventriloquism less likely. Poem 68 also opens, as we have seen, a succession of anonymous poems in the manuscript in which I have suggested we extend the list of poems acknowledged on more secure grounds as being by Marie, and find further active intervention by her older self in dialogue with her surviving brother.

The poem offers a particular kind of occluded national feeling too, as the naïve speaker not only celebrates her home in its rural setting, but also her lineage and its contribution to Scotland's cause historically. The family bred two sons who followed Mary of Guise as Regent then Mary Queen of Scots to the bitter end and to their cost. The voice in this poem, if it is the daughter and amanuensis to her blind father, writes as one deprived of her beloved family home in times when Scotland was internally riven with 'troubill' in which the Maitlands were heavily implicated.

Endnotes

1. Julia Boffey, 'Women Authors and Women's Literacy in Fourteenth- and Fifteenth-century England', in Carol Meale (ed.), *Women and Literature in Britain, 1150-1500*, 2nd edn (Cambridge: Cambridge University Press, 1996), pp. 159-82.
2. Evelyn S. Newlyn, 'A Methodology of Reading Against the Culture: Anonymous Women Poets and the Maitland Quarto Manuscript', in Sarah M. Dunnigan, C. Marie Harker, and Evelyn S. Newlyn (eds), *Women and the Feminine in Medieval and Early Modern Scottish Writing* (Basingstoke: Palgrave Macmillan, 2004), pp. 89-103; Sarah M. Dunnigan, 'Scottish Women Writers c. 1560-c. 1650' in Douglas Gifford and Dorothy McMillan (eds), *A History of Scottish Women's Writing* (Edinburgh: Edinburgh University Press, 1997), pp. 15-43.
3. Sajed Chowdhury, '"Thair is mair constancie in o[u]r sex / Then euer ama[n]g men hes bein": The Metaphysics of Authorship in the Maitland Quarto Manuscript (ca. 1586)', *Textual Cultures* 7 (2012), pp. 50-76.
4. I am grateful to A. A. MacDonald for reading a draft of this article as a rightly sceptical critic of over-enthusiastic speculation, and for the comments which led me to reinforce my defence of the approach.
5. William Blake, *William Maitland of Lethington 1528-1573: a Study of Moderation in the Scottish Reformation* (Lampeter: Edward Mellen, 1990), p. 2.
6. James Maitland, *Maitland's Narrative of the Principal Acts of the Regency, During the Minority; and Other Papers Relating to the History of Mary, Queen of Scotland* (privately printed, 1833), unpaginated.
7. Blake, *William Maitland*, p. 2.
8. Joanna M. Martin (ed.), *The Maitland Quarto: A New Edition of Cambridge, Magdalene College, Pepys Library MS 1408* (Edinburgh: Scottish Text Society, 2015), p. 370, citing *Scots Peerage* V, p. 293.
9. See notes 1-3 above.
10. Martin (ed.), Maitland Quarto, p. 28.
11. Newlyn, 'Methodology'.
12. Newlyn, 'Methodology', pp. 98, 100-01.
13. Chowdbury, '"Thair is mair constancie"', pp. 50-76, 59-69.
14. Boffey, 'Women Authors'.
15. Sarah Dunnigan, 'Undoing the Double Tress: Scotland, Early Modern Women's Writing, and the Location of Critical Desires', *Feminist Studies* 29 (2003), pp. 298-319. See also Jane Farnsworth, 'Voicing Female Desire in "Poem XLIX"', *Studies in English Literature, 1500-1900* 36 (1996), pp. 57-72.
16. John Skelton, *Maitland of Lethington and the Scotland of Mary Stewart*, 2 vols (Blackwood: Edinburgh, 1887), II, p. 430. Despite its early date, Skelton's work remains the fullest account of the background events useful to this study.
17. Joanna Martin, 'The Presentation of the Family in Maitland Writings', in Janet Hadley-Williams and J. Derrick McClure (eds), *Fresche Fontanis: Studies in the Culture of Medieval and Early Modern Scotland* (Newcastle-upon-Tyne: Cambridge Scholars Publisher, 2013), pp. 318-30.
18. See Norbrook and Woudhuysen, *Renaissance Verse*, pp. 414, 420, and 476 respectively.
19. A. A. MacDonald, 'The Sense of Place in Early Scottish Verse: Rhetoric and Reality', *English Studies* 17.1 (1991), pp. 12-27, 25. See also Michael R. G. Spiller, 'The Country

House Poem in Scotland: Sir George Mackenzie's 'Caelia's Country House and Closet', *Studies in Scottish Literature* 12.2 (1974), pp. 110–30. Michael Spiller claims that this is the first Scottish 'country house' poem, written in 1667, a century later than the Lethington poem.
20 Martin, 'Family', p. 320.
21 Ibid.
22 For an English translation see George Buchanan, *Chamaeleon or the Crafty Statesman*, in *Miscellanea Scotica [...]* (London: W. Taylor, printer, 1710), item III, pp. 97–116.
23 Skelton, *Maitland*, I, pp. 321–24.
24 Ibid., p. 230.
25 See Blake, *William Maitland*, passim.
26 Skelton, *Maitland*, I, pp. 322–24
27 Blake, *William Maitland*, pp. 36–40.
28 Buchanan, *Chamaeleon*, p. 116.
29 Mark Loughlin, '"The Dialogue of the Two Wyfis": Maitland, Machiavelli and the Propaganda of the Scottish Civil War', in A. A. MacDonald, Michael Lynch and Ian B. Cowan (eds), *The Renaissance in Scotland: Studies in Literature, Religion, History and Culture offered to John Durkin* (Leiden: Brill, 1994), pp. 226–43, 237.
30 George Buchanan, *De Jure Apud Scotos, or A Dialogue Concerning the Due Priviledge of Government in the Kingdom of Scotland Betwixt George Buchanan and Thomas Maitland* (London: Amazon, Forgotten Books Reprints, 2012).
31 All genealogical information widely available, including Wikipedia.
32 Skelton, *Maitland*, I, pp. 2–3.
33 Here I am grateful to Alison Lindsay of the National Records of Scotland for endorsing my fruitless search.

3. Translating Identities: Tracing the Transfer of a Scottish Origin Myth from Scotland to France c. 1519.

BRYONY COOMBS

In *Historia Gentis Scotorum* of 1527, Hector Boece (*c.* 1465–1536) states that Fergus I

> gatt charteris and euidentis of the crovne of Scottlannd to him and his successouris in this sort; quhilkis charteris war gravin in merbill, with ymagis of bestis in forme of letteris, as wer vsit in thai dayis; syne gaif þe samyn to maist religious preistis, to be obseruit in þair tempillis.[1]

Later, noting that King Rewtha erected monuments to preserve the memory of valiant men, Boece writes 'quhilkis wer engravit ymagerijs of dragonis, wolffis and vther bestis, becaus na inuencioun of letterez was in þai dayis, to put the dedis of nobill men in memory.'[2]

Boece employed the idea of a supposed ancestral link between the Scots and the Egyptians to interpret the carvings on Pictish symbol stones as operating in the manner of Egyptian hieroglyphs; the stones employed to function as memorials to ancient kings in a period that predated the Roman alphabet. This antiquarian approach to explaining the material evidence of an ancient Pictish past, through a fictitious origin myth, was in keeping with developments on the continent. Italian humanists who reconciled their newly discovered ancient objects, with histories penned by classical authors, paralleled what Boece was attempting in his *Historia Gentis Scotorum*. In this Scottish context Boece's *History* sought to make sense of a roughly crafted medieval origin legend by recasting and reshaping it in elegant classical Latin imitating Livy, and thus producing a work that blended history, legend, and material evidence into something more in keeping with its time. John Bellenden's (fl. 1533–1587?) translation of this work into the

Scottish vernacular as the *History and Croniklis of Scotland* (1536) spoke to an intellectual shift towards vernacular histories and made a significant contribution to sixteenth-century Scottish intellectual culture.[3] The *Croniklis* was commissioned by James V (r. 1513–42) soon after he assumed the reins of government in 1528, thus it could be seen as a piece of national propaganda promoted by the newly independent king. Bellenden dedicated his first translation in manuscript form to James V in 1531. This was not, however, the first vernacular translation of a Scottish history, nor were Boece's attempts to explain the visual evidence of ancient Picts the earliest to reconcile the visual and the literary in a Scottish historical sense. The focus of this chapter is to examine a less well-known example of a translation of a Scottish history into a vernacular language, in this case French. This example predates Bellenden's work by seventeen years. Our focus here is the *Liber Pluscardensis*, an abridged and updated version of John of Fordun (*c.* 1320–1384) and Walter Bower's (1383–1437) *Scotichronicon,* translated into French in 1519 by Bremond Domat (fl. 1518–1533). The aims of this chapter are threefold: to explore the specific circumstances of this translation, to argue the case for Domat's source being the Marchmont manuscript in Glasgow, and to examine Domat's use of the visual, as both a propagandic and mnemonic device, in relation to this Scottish history as a didactic text.

The circulation of origin myths and the collective veneration of saints, heroes, and ancient monarchs encouraged a shared sense of national identity in late medieval and early modern Scotland.[4] It encouraged a common sense of the past that could be employed to interpret and understand the present.[5] This is a concept discussed at length in relation to French literature of the period. Chronicles, histories, and romances were all employed as moral exemplars, aids to inciting patriotism, and guides to good government for their late medieval and early modern readers. The case study explored in this chapter allows us to see how Franco-Scottish knowledge networks operated and how concepts of national identity spread. All too often in the literature addressing the interchange of knowledge and information between Britain and the continent, there has been a tendency to lapse into sweeping statements. Generalisations abound supporting the unspecific idea that knowledge most frequently emerged in France, and Italy, eventually filtering through to Scotland. Yet specific studies, such as this, reveal a different picture. Although cultural transfer did occur in this way, it also flowed in the opposite direction. This chapter traces one such example and it is hoped that such work can shift the dialogue away from these generalisations and examine instead how the patronage of Scots on the continent established important networks for knowledge exchange. This study provides important evidence for the transfer of ideas and for the translation of this material into French, and its reworking into a visual format. While the subject of this study is specific, it raises broader questions relating to Scottish national identity at the turn of the sixteenth century. Domat's translation of his source material not only from Latin to French but also into visual form indicates which aspects of Scottish national identity were most highly prized by Scots in France at this time. It also allows us to analyse how a powerful, if fictitious, origin myth was utilised by elite Scots in relation to forging identities and bolstering political power.

John Stuart, Duke of Albany (1482–1536), was the nephew of King James III of Scotland. Born in France, he acted as Regent of Scotland during the minority of James V from 1514 until 1524 and was particularly noteworthy for his love of visual splendour and magnificence. In France, he was an astute patron of the visual arts and of grand architectural projects, such as the Sainte-Chapelle at Vic-le-Comte in the Auvergne.[6] Albany's main architectural achievement in Scotland was the fortification of his principal residence, Dunbar Castle, in the form of a great artillery blockhouse; this was perhaps the first such structure to have been built in the British Isles.[7] Albany was, moreover, an important patron of literary material and the sheer scale and importance of the library that he amassed at his principal residence in the Auvergne is only now coming to light. Two important examples of his manuscript patronage include an *Epistres du Turc*, dedicated to Albany by the French poet and translator Macé de Villebresme, now in the Bibliothèque nationale de France, and a manuscript of Pierre Gringore's *Abus du monde*. This example was apparently commissioned by Albany for James IV but a manuscript that remained in his collection and is now in the Pierpont Morgan Library, New York.[8]

The manuscript copy of the Latin history of Scotland, known as the *Liber Pluscardensis*, translated into French by Domat for Albany, is the only French translation known.[9] The manuscript is today held in the Bibliothèque Sainte-Geneviève in Paris.[10] It is a curious work, with a hastily translated and unfinished copy of the *Liber Pluscardensis* in black ink on paper, with a finely illuminated genealogy of the kings of Scotland, on vellum, appended.[11] Most helpfully, the scribe and artist responsible for this work not only gave the date of 1519 when he undertook the translation but also signed and initialled many passages and poems, identifying himself as Bremond Domat. In relation to this it has been possible to build up something of a picture of Domat's career; attributing at least one other manuscript to him, identifying his later activities in organising triumphal entry ceremonies, and even locating his residence, Maison Domat, in the town of Mirefleurs in the Auvergne.[12] The circumstances surrounding Domat's translation of the *Liber Pluscardensis* for Albany are what concern us here.

The *Liber Pluscardensis* is an abridgement of Walter Bower's *Scotichronicon* and was composed by an anonymous chronicler who stated that it had been compiled at the request of the Abbot of Dunfermline (1444-1468) Richard Bothwell in 1461.[13] Six manuscript copies in Latin are known: one in a private collection, two in Glasgow, one each in Edinburgh, Oxford, and Brussels.[14] One of the versions in Glasgow, now held in the Mitchell Library and often referred to as the Marchmont manuscript, includes extensive passages which have been underlined or highlighted as well as extensive marginal notations. On the flyleaves of this manuscript, furthermore, accompanying a series of Latin verses, are notes providing clear indication that it was in the hands of the French diplomat and herald Montjoie at the turn of the sixteenth century (Figure 1, overleaf).[15] Does this period of French provenance for the Marchmont manuscript provide us with an indication of the source material Domat used for his translation of the text? To answer this, we must consider the motivations behind the commission and the evident need for a visual reworking of this material into an illuminated genealogy. The Scottish records in this regard prove very useful. A note in the Lord High Treasurer's Accounts for 15 October 1506 notes: 'Item, to Johne Beg, messingeir, to pas to Corsragwell, and other places, with writing is to warne of Montjoyis cummyng, ... iiij s.'[16] The presence, therefore, of the French herald Montjoie in Scotland is attested to in the historical record. The account notes that Montjoie visited the Cluniac abbey of Crossraguel and other unspecified places. The account of this visit provides us with documentary evidence within which to understand the inscriptions on the flyleaves.

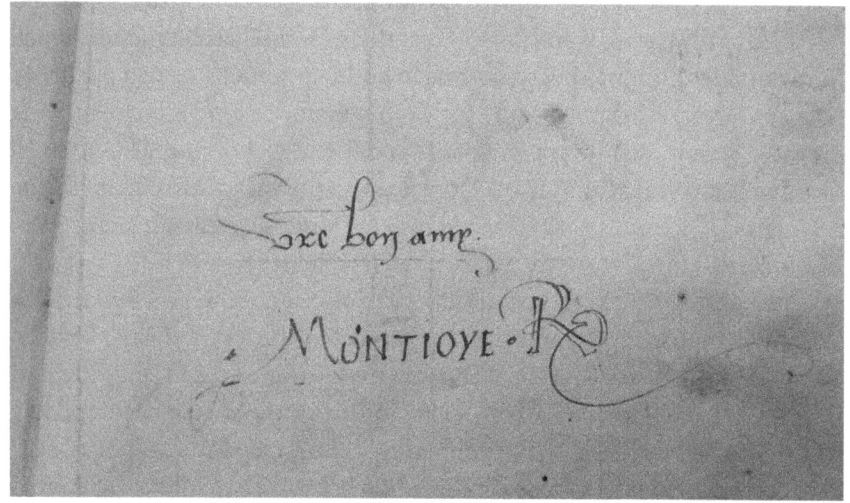

Figure 1

Montjoie was a prestigious French heraldic appointment.[17] The term found its derivation in a rallying slogan or banner for soldiers being called to arms. This was adopted as *Montjoie-St Denis*, war cry of the French troops. In June 1487, such was the disorder in respect of the design of, and rights to, coats-of-arms that Charles VIII created a mareschal d'armes and gave that position to Gilbert Chauveau who was styled as Montjoie roi d'armes.[18] Chauveau can be traced in the French sources as a loyal diplomat for the French kings. He had been engaged on numerous diplomatic missions before his arrival in Scotland and appears to have been the author of a number of written works, including a treatise he composed recording the programme of tournaments to take place in Paris.[19] Described as a man of great presence, eloquence and fearlessness, he was regularly employed on international missions and heavily involved in crusading diplomacy.[20] Gilbert Chauveau certainly visited Scotland in 1506 and, being a figure involved in Venetian politics and crusading diplomacy, was likely known to Albany.[21] The pretext for his visit appears to have been a diplomatic mission from the French king to England, Scotland, and then Denmark.[22] There is evidence to suggest, however, that he used this opportunity to record heraldic material relating to these countries. In the Bodleian Library there is a manuscript which he composed recording the arms of French, Flemish, English, and Scottish nobles: MS. e Mus. 78.[23] The Scottish records are in fact very useful in reconstructing his mission. We know that he visited Dundee and around that time was made a gift of a puncheon of wine.[24] Other later records note gifts of a coat of English russet lined with fox fur and a saddle.[25] On the 13 October 1506 he was given ninety pounds, and his servant nine pounds.[26] Two days earlier, he dined with the king at Holyrood Abbey, for which special occasion 'the copburd' was brought from Edinburgh Castle.[27] The next mention in the Treasurer's Accounts is from April 1507 and coinciding with a Papal embassy to James IV.[28] Another curious entry notes the summoning of a mason, Thom Cuke, to attend the French herald. Then by August, Chauveau received a saddle, perhaps as a farewell gift, and that is the last we hear of him.[29]

We can then ascertain with some certainty that Montjoie was travelling around Scotland in the years 1506 and 1507 and the scribal notes on the flyleaves of the Glasgow manuscript indicate that it fell into his possession, likely at this time. But did this manuscript form the base version from which Domat executed his translation into French? Domat's manuscript opens with the crowned arms of John Stuart, Duke of Albany encircled by the collar of the Order of St Michael in a swirling bouquet of Renaissance-style foliage (Figure 2, overleaf). A banderol encircles the stems bearing the text '*Veritas de terra orta est*' meaning '*truth shall spring from the earth*', a reference to the central theme of the manuscripts, the genealogical tree. Above this hovers the holy dove with a truncated form of Albany's motto '*Sub umbra tuarum*' ('*In the shadow of thy wings*').[30] On the reverse of this page is a fourteen-line poem extolling the virtues of the very magnificent kingdom of Scotland, stating that this solemn work was written to demonstrate how the sovereign and antique kingdom of Scotland was filled with great valour.[31] Below it is signed Domat – the author translator.

Figure 2

Within these lines of verse is a line which reads 'And against Turks often took a lance'. Similarly on one of the flyleaves of the Glasgow manuscript,

Montjoie appears to have noted a line of verse relating to the Great Turk and Pope Alexander VI. Below this is part of a prognostication regarding the political and ecclesiastical tensions between Frederick II and Pope Innocent IV.[32] This reference to the Turks is not found in the other versions of this text and perhaps this provides some indication of the inspiration behind Domat's opening poetic composition for Albany. We are on firmer ground, however, with a textual comparison between the two manuscripts; not only does Domat's manuscript contain the preface and prologue, which are found only in Montjoie's manuscript and one other, but a careful comparison of the texts apparently reveals Domat's workings as he translated the text from one manuscript into the other. Throughout the Glasgow manuscript many passages of the *Liber Pluscardensis* are underlined, and the corresponding margins contain a plethora of hastily penned notes. These sections most often relate to people, places, and dates. Furthermore, if we compare them to Domat's work in the Paris manuscript we find a direct comparison in the sections that are highlighted. For example, corresponding lines in each manuscript are underlined throughout. In one comparative example the lines read '*Albion in terris rex primus germine Scotis ipsorum turmis rubri tulit anna leonis Fergusius fulvo Ferchard rugientis in arvo. Christum ter centis ter denis prefuit annis*', which translates as 'The first king of Scottish descent in the lands of Albion, Fergus son of Feredach bore on his arms amid his hosts, a red lion roaring on a yellow field. Three hundred and thirty years before Christ'. In each manuscript the exact same words are underlined. It seems likely, therefore, that Domat was specifically interested in references to Fergus, within the context of the antiquity of Scottish kingship.[33] Fergus, it is noted here, reigned three hundred and thirty years before Christ. Further underscoring his interest in this section, Domat appears to have added the note '*Arma regis Scotorum*' and drawn a very quick sketch of some arms above.[34] This appears to be a hastily penned reminder by Domat during the translation process to remind himself to include the arms of Scotland in relation to this section and sure enough in the Paris manuscript this is what he does in a very grand manner at the opening of book II (Figure 3, overleaf).[35] Here the royal arms of Scotland are accompanied by a banderol bearing the text '*Vivat felix in eternum*' and they herald the start of the book that contains the aforementioned description of the royal arms. This is a section, furthermore, that Domat felt was important enough to highlight in the illuminated genealogical tree that he later appended to the text. Here next to an illumination depicting Fergusius, Domat reiterates this information and crucially he includes the fact that this ancient king of Scotland had lived 330 years before Christ (Figure 4).[36]

Figure 3

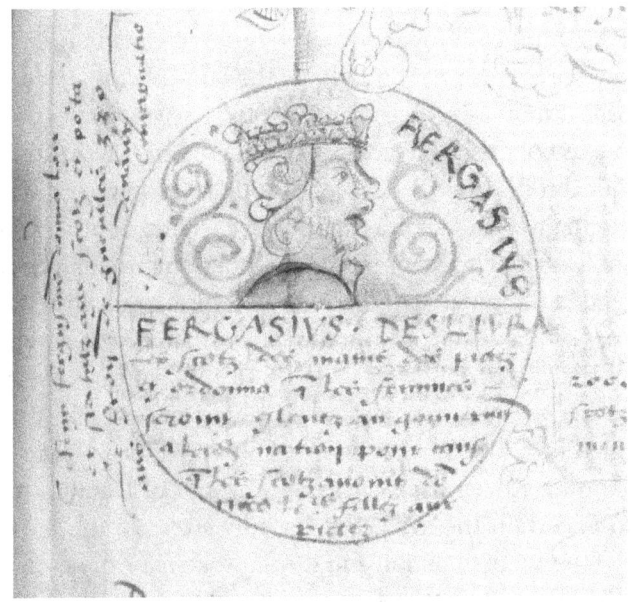

Figure 4

Figure 5

If we consider another comparison, and there were many more to choose from, we can see that Domat underlined the same phrase – '*Scoti de Scota, de Scotis Scocia tota*' – in each manuscript.[37] The translation, in context, illustrates the emphasis placed on Scota rather than Gaythelos as the first king and queen of Scotland, according to Fordun in the Scottish origin myth. It highlighted in this way that the Scots and Scotia derived their names from Scota.[38] This is a point that Domat then visually emphasised in his appended illuminated genealogy, with his extraordinarily fine illuminations of Gaythalos and Scota accompanied by their progeny and potted histories of their lives (Figure 5).[39] We find this pattern repeatedly in a comparison between the two works, the same sections of text underlined or highlighted by a note in the margin, and this information assimilated into the illuminated genealogical tree at the end of Domat's translation. Furthermore, certain themes are repeatedly stressed: the antiquity and autonomy of the Scottish nation and the unbroken line of descent through an ancient lineage of Scottish kings.

From the textual evidence we can be confident that Domat did indeed use the Glasgow manuscript to make his translation, underlining key passages and names to help him organise his work, and to highlight areas that he thought important to include in the illuminated genealogy. It is always exciting to establish a connection like this between two manuscripts and the workings in each of these texts tell us a great deal about how the work was undertaken, and what Domat's (or Albany's) intentions and priorities were. The inclusion of a hastily sketched coat of arms, for instance, provides interesting visual evidence for the working process in action. We may, furthermore, delve deeper into the circumstances surrounding this translation of knowledge from Scotland to France. In the notes made by Montjoie in the flyleaves of the Glasgow manuscript we find a series of lines describing Edward III's justification for assuming the royal arms of France. This is followed by a French man's retort; so, an English propagandic poem with a French parody in reply.[40] This would constitute important literary matter, of course, for the interests of a French herald. But underneath and a little separate from this we find the Latin maxim, '*Qui tenet teneat possessio valet*, translating as '*Possession is nine points of the law*', signed below, '*your true friend, Montjoie*', evidence perhaps of how the manuscript fell into Domat's hands?[41] Did Montjoie 'borrow' this manuscript without permission? We are left to speculate, but one reading might be that either Domat or, more likely, Albany was being addressed here by their true friend Montjoie, and that the recipient of the manuscript understood the true context of this tantalising line, suggesting the advantage of being in possession of disputed goods.

Having looked, therefore, at the circumstances surrounding this translation and migration of a Scottish origin myth to France, we might now consider just what Domat did with this material, and why. Domat is a fascinating figure. We can attribute to him at least one other manuscript now in the Hague, again a work dealing with genealogical material and including a very interesting self-portrait where he holds a banderol declaring 'unless what we do is useful our glory is in vain', signed with a capital letter D (Figure 6, overleaf).[42] Indeed the didactic application of Domat's translation and reworking of his material seems clear: evidently the utility of knowledge was at the heart of this commission. Throughout his translation of the *Liber Pluscardensis*, he includes his initials and his name, visually declaring a sense of self-assurance or pride that is noteworthy.

The translation is also highly embellished: opening initials are decorated with heraldic and emblematic devices used to highlight the magnificence of the royal house of Scotland in general, and Albany, as Regent, in particular. On folio 47v, for instance, a tree-like 'P' is embellished by a lion rampant, and on folio 73r an ornate 'L' bears the banderol '*Vive Scoce Terre Jolie et son Regent Duc Dalbanie*.' The botanical theme of the growing genealogical tree extends throughout. This theme finds its culmination in the finely worked genealogical diagram appended, which is introduced by a statement of intent. The initial letter of this statement bears the royal arms of Scotland before it proceeds to explain how Domat composed the genealogy to 'clarify and resolve the very illustrious and ancient lineage of Scots to that end that every noble prince descended from this line may apprehend the true source and origin of their lineage'. Domat stresses that few kingdoms can claim

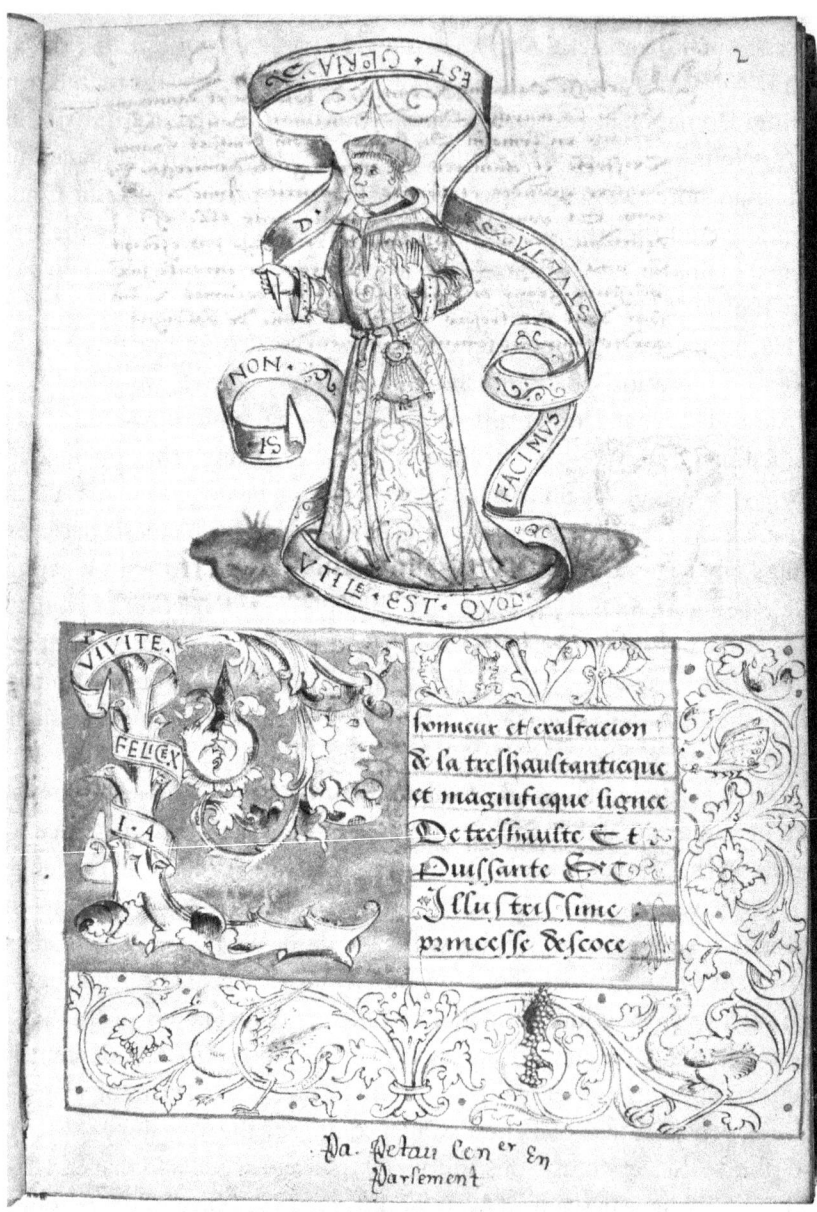

Figure 6

such an ancient line of descent as that of Scotland which here is traced back 330 years before the advent of Christ.[43] Within this illuminated genealogical tree certain themes are stressed; the concept of pre-ordained kingship, and the interceding of figures, objects or events that stress the divinely ordained nature of inherited kingship. For instance, in the eighth roundel under a slightly comic representation of Simon Brer, the text reads

> Simon Brer came third from Spain to live in Hibernia and Scotland and he brought the chair of marble which he had drawn from the sea and had it put next to the most eminent place, to crown the kings. He did prowess and beautiful deeds.[44]

Franco-Scottish relations are also stressed throughout; in the forty-third roundel, showing King Achaius, we are told that he came to power in 787 and reigned for thirty-two years. His brother was the noble Gilmour the Scot, who fought against the infidels with Charlemagne. He was renowned for marvellous prowess and was the motive for the first friendship between Kings of France and Scotland.[45] In visual terms the pseudo-portraits are characterised using fantastic apparel and elaborate headwear to suggest their remote and exotic past as well as to allude to great heroes of other nations such as ancient Greece or Rome. Some figures are clad in a more contemporary form of Italianate armour again employed to suggest their invincibility. The roundel depicting Selbach forty-second king of Scots, for instance, claims that he is noted for his warmongering and correspondingly depicts him in a type of elaborate zoomorphic pageant helmet perhaps influenced by those seen in Italy.[46] The illustrated genealogy appended to Domat's translation of the *Liber Pluscardensis* appears to have been an original invention. In no other versions of the text do we find such illustrations although in copies of the *Scotichronicon* we do find some schematic genealogical diagrams.[47] It is therefore likely that Domat adapted a French tradition to meet the needs of his patron. As such Domat appears to have concerned himself primarily with the medieval concept of likeness in which images played a crucial part in mnemonic systems. When used in this way physiognomic likeness was not crucial to the success of the image. Domat's concern was with reflecting what the reader was told in the text accompanying each image and providing a memorable visualisation that would allow Albany to commit his ancestry to his memory. Domat likely drew on aesthetic ideas current on the continent such as we see employed in a near contemporary illuminated genealogy of the paternal line of Charles V now held in Brussels.[48]

In conclusion, the case study explored of the Montjoie manuscript in Glasgow, and Domat's work in Paris, provides important evidence for the transfer of literary material and intellectual ideas from Scotland to France – the opposite direction to that which we are more accustomed to studying the flow of ideas. The translation of that material into French, and its subsequent reworking into visual form, is crucial for understanding Albany's motivations during this period. Albany's principal interests in the *Liber Pluscardensis* were both in promoting the prestige of Scotland on the continent and enhancing his own illustrious reputation as newly appointed regent of Scotland. This study provides us with important material for understanding Scottish national identity and Franco-Scottish knowledge networks. It allows us to move away from the types of sweeping generalisations I mentioned at the beginning and determine how information moved between Scotland and Europe, in what direction, and why. It allows us to really see how knowledge was obtained, and in this case perhaps taken without permission, and how it was manipulated and employed to further specific political agendas. The visual material, furthermore, prompts us to consider the value placed on the visualisation of concepts, in the form of emblems, arms, devices, and effigies in order to elucidate and promote complex ideas regarding sovereignty, lineage, autonomy, and pre-ordained kingship. Details, of course, remain unclear and we are left to ponder if Montjoie's true friend was really John Stuart, duke of Albany, or the more enigmatic Bremond Domat.

To end it is worth stressing the importance of Domat's French translation of the *Liber Pluscardensis* and speculate on the agency of this text. Albany was an influential figure with regards to Scottish culture in the early sixteenth century. As a pan-European noble he was a catalyst for the movement of ideas between particularly Scotland, Italy, and France. He commissioned significant artworks in Italy and discussed military fortification ideas with important Italian Renaissance architects. He founded one of the most significant religious foundations in early sixteenth-century France in the form of a Sainte-Chappelle at Vic-le-Comte and, significantly, he retained his interest in the governance of Scotland.[49] It is likely that Albany instructed Gilbert Chauveau to obtain a work of Scottish history on his visit so that Albany could quite literally do his homework before taking up the reins of Scottish governance in 1514. In all likelihood his first visit to Scotland impressed upon him the need to learn more about his ancestral homeland and to understand the pantheon of historical figures so central to a notion of Scottish national identity. Domat's translation, but also his illuminated genealogy, did just this. It provided a short, engaging and visually stimulating work to assist Albany in committing these important figures to memory. It is likely, furthermore, that Albany may have brought this work with him on one of his two later visits to Scotland. If this was the case one wonders what influence it had on the young King James V, to whom no doubt he would have shown it. Was it, therefore, Albany and Domat's project of 1519 that inspired James V to commission Bellenden to perform the same service for him? Albany certainly held great influence over the young king, and this was likely another manifestation of that influence. That Albany placed such importance in being able to read the history of Scotland in his native French, and that he desired the work to be committed to memory using images, has not until now been acknowledged. The employment of imagery not only aided Albany's understanding and recollection of important historical figures, but also made them more present. The anachronistic use of contemporary forms of costume and armour gave them credibility or at least a semblance of authenticity and thus in a similar way as in our opening example with Boece's attempts to reconcile the visual evidence with the literary, Domat imaginatively employed a visual aid to Fordun and Bower's historical argument. As the old adage goes, seeing is, after all, believing. So, ideas of national identity and a pantheon of

Individualised and recognisable ancestors was central to this national project in securing a unified history. Both Domat and Boece understood the value of employing the visual in this endeavour. Understanding ideas surrounding Scottish national identity stems back to this period and, thus, central to our understanding of Scottish identity was Scotland's relationship with France.

Endnotes

1 *The Chronicles of Scotland, compiled by Hector Boece, translated into Scots by John Bellenden, 1531*, eds R. W. Chambers and Edith C. Batho, 2 vols (Edinburgh: Scottish Text Society, 1938–41) [hereafter Chron. Bellenden], I, p. 45; John McQueen, 'The Renaissance in Scotland', in G. Williams and R. O. Jones (eds), *The Celts and the Renaissance, Tradition, and Innovation* (Bath: University of Wales Press, 1990), p. 52.
2 Chron. Bellenden, I, p. 67.
3 *History and chronicles of Scotland*, New York, Morgan Library and Museum, MS M.527.
4 Carol Edington, 'Paragons and Patriots: National Identity and the Chivalric Ideal in Late-Medieval Scotland' Image and Identity', in D. Broun, R. J. Finlay and M. Lynch (eds), *The Making and Remaking of Scotland through the Ages* (Glasgow: John Donald, 1998), pp. 69–82.
5 Collette Beaune, *The Birth of an Ideology, Myths and Symbols of Nation in Late-Medieval France* (Oxford: University of California Press, 1985); R. E. Asher, *National Myths in Renaissance France, Francus, Samothes and the Druids* (Edinburgh: Edinburgh University Press, 1993); Elisabeth Morrison and Anne Hedeman, *Imagining the Past in France, History in Manuscript Painting 1250–1500* (Los Angeles: Getty Museum, 2010).
6 For Albany see: Marie W. Stuart, *The Scot who was a Frenchman* (Edinburgh: William Hodge and Co, 1940); Elisabeth Bonner, 'Stewart, John, Second Duke of Albany (*c.* 1482–1536)', *Oxford Dictionary of National Biography*, 2004; Bryony Coombs 'The Artistic Patronage of John Stuart, Duke of Albany 1518–19: The "Discovery" of the Artist and Author, Bremond Domat', *Proceedings of the Society of Antiquaries of Scotland* 144 (2014),

pp. 277–309; Amy Blakeway, *Regency in Sixteenth Century Scotland* (Suffolk: Boydell & Brewer, 2015); Bryony Coombs, 'The Artistic Patronage of John Stuart, Duke of Albany, 1520-30: Vic-le-Comte, the last Sainte-Chapelle', *Proceedings of the Society of Antiquaries of Scotland* 147 (2017), pp. 175–217; Bryony Coombs, 'John Stuart, Duke of Albany and his contribution to military science in Scotland and Italy, 1514-36: from Dunbar to Rome', *Proceedings of the Society of Antiquaries of Scotland* 148 (2018), pp. 231–66; Ken Emond, *The Minority of James V, Scotland in Europe, 1513–1528* (Edinburgh: John Donald, 2019).

7   Coombs, 'John Stuart, Duke of Albany', 2018, pp. 231–66.

8   *Epistres du Turc, Translated from Latin into French, by Macé de Villebresme* (1515), Paris, Bibliothèque nationale de France (BnF), fr. MS 12406; Pierre Gringore, *Les Abus du Monde*, New York, Pierpont Morgan Library, MS M.42. For recent work on these manuscripts see: Bryony Coombs, 'Les Abus du Monde: A French Manuscript Produced for James IV of Scotland ca. 1509, Pierpont Morgan, MS M.42,' *Scottish Historical Review* (2021), pp. 109–128; Bryony Coombs 'John Stuart, Duke of Albany, and the transfer of ideas between Scotland and the continent, 1509–1536', in Dirk H. Steinforth, Charles C. Rozier (eds), *Britain and its Neighbours* (London: Routledge, 2021).

9   The *Liber Pluscardensis*, while based on Bower's *Scotichronicon*, includes several passages written in the first person as eye-witness accounts. The first five books follow Fordun's *Chronica Gentis Scotorum* and the work up to James II is indebted to Bower. The remainder of the work is due, it is noted, to one whose name will appear at the end of the sixth book. This promise is unfulfilled in the surviving manuscripts. Skene proposed an identification with Maurice Buchanan. Mapstone proposed Gilbert Hay as a possible candidate. William F. Skene, *The Historians of Scotland VII: Liber Pluscardensis* (Edinburgh: Edmonston and Douglas, 1877), pp. xix–xxiii; Marjorie Drexler, 'The Extant Abridgements of Walter Bower's Scotichronicon', *Scottish Historical Review* 61 (1982), pp. 62–74; Sally Mapstone, 'The Scotichronicon's First Readers', in B. Crawford (ed.), *Church, Chronicle and Learning in Medieval and Early Renaissance Scotland* (Edinburgh: Mercat Press, 1999), p. 4.

10 Paris, Bibliothèque Sainte-Geneviève (BSG), MS 936.

11 The illuminated tree begins with Galahel, the first king of Scotland, and his wife Scota. Far from the 'very coarse miniatures' described by Thomas Innes in 1729, the illuminations are finely, if hastily, executed. Thomas Innes, *A Critical Essay on the Ancient Inhabitants of the Northern Parts of Britain or Scotland*, 2 vols (London: W. Innys, 1729), pp. 633–34. Innes was the vice-principal of the Scots College, Paris, so would have had ample opportunity to examine the manuscript.

12 For château Mirefleurs, see: Jean-Baptiste Fouilhoux, *Fiefs et châteaux forts relevant de la Comté d'Auvergne (Capitale Vic-le-Comte)* (Clermont-Ferrand: G. de Bussac, 1926); Coombs, 'The Artistic patronage', pp. 277–309; Coombs, 'Vic-le-Comte', pp. 175–217.

13 Details of the provenance of the chronicle come from the author's prologue and internal evidence. See note 9.

14 Skene, *Liber Pluscardensis*, pp. xv–xvi, n. 2. Skene lists six surviving manuscripts of the *Liber Pluscardensis* written in Latin: (1) MS Glasgow College [Glasgow, University of Glasgow Archives and Special Collections, MS Gen 333]. A signature indicates that it belonged to Archbishop William Scheves; (2) MS Advocates' Library [Edinburgh, National Library of Scotland, Adv.MS.35.5.2]. Perhaps a copy of the Glasgow MS; (3)

MS Cavers, copied in 1696 [private collection]. Perhaps a copy of the Glasgow MS; (4) MS Bodleian [Oxford, Bodleian Library Special Collections (Bod), MS Fairfax 8]; (5) MS Marchmont [Glasgow, Mitchell Library, Marchmont MS 308876]. Perhaps a copy of the Bodleian MS. It contains a *praefacio* and *prologus* and a table of contents for the first book which were probably copied from a now lost leaf of the Bodleian work; (6) MS Bibliothèque Royale, Brussels (KBR) [MS 7396]. Perhaps a copy of the Bodleian MS. It also contains the *praefacio* and *prologus* contained in the Marchmont MS. Skene surmises that our Paris manuscript was copied from the Marchmont manuscript.

15 Skene first noted that a poem on the flyleaf of the Paris manuscript mentions the Scots combat against the Turks suggesting that this may relate to similar notes on the Marchmont MS. Skene, *Liber Pluscardensis*, xv–xvi, n. 2. Supporting this view see: R. Somerville, 'Translation of the Liber Pluscardensis', *Scottish Historical Review* 25 (1928), pp. 377–78.

16 Sir James B. Paul (ed.), *Accounts of the Lord High Treasurer of Scotland*, 13 vols (Edinburgh: H. M. General Register House, 1901), III, p. 350 [Hereafter: *TA*, iii].

17 On Montjoie see: Charles F. Du Cange, *Glossarium mediae et infimae latinitatis*, 10 vols (Graz: Akademische Druck-U, 1954) IV, pp. 185–88 (which cites at length from a manuscript written by Le Fèvre); Paul Adam-Even, 'Cris d'armes des rois chrétiens', *Archivum Heraldicum* 58 (1954), pp. 35–38. For Chauveau see: Robert Gaguin, *Les Gestes Romaines* (Paris: Antoine Vérard, 1508); Jehan le Feron, *De la primitive institution des roys, herauldz et poursuivans d'armes* (Paris: Maurice Menier, 1555), f. 39r; Philippe Contamine, 'Office d'armes et noblesse dans la France de la fin du Moyen Age', *Bulletin de la Société Nationale des Antiquaires de France* (1996), pp. 310–22.

18 Paris, BnF, MS Dupuy 755, fol. 43–47v; G. de Montgrand, Le Comte Godefroy, *Armorial de la Ville de Marseille: recueil officiel dressé par les ordres de Louis XIV* (Marsellie, 1864), xvii, 27; Contamine, 'Office d'armes', pp. 319, 322.

19 *La publication des Joustes publiees a Paris a la table de marbre par Montjoye premier heraulx darmes du roy de France. Le mardy. XV. jour de Janvier Mil cinq cens et. xiiii* (1515), BnF, Rothschild 2119 [IV, 3, 238].

20 *TA*, iii, p. 350; Jean Brittain and James Brown, '"And uther placis": two French ambassadorial missions in Ayrshire', *Scottish Local History Journal* 94 (2016), pp. 1–14.

21 Chauveau had been a herald for the Duke of Bourbon and became Lord of Vomeau in Bourbonnais, receiving the honour of knighthood from the emperor of Constantinople. The fiercely competitive nature of Chauveau is illustrated in a 1499 account which claims he travelled almost non-stop for a distance of approximately nine hundred kilometres: 'Among the heralds of our kings, that of Louis XII, named Gilbert Chauveau, is the most remarkable; because he jealously wanted to be the first to advise the King of the capture of Milan, he came to the Château of Amboise, where the king was, in less than three days, and nearly died at his feet [...]'. C. Leber, *Collection des meilleurs dissertations, notices et traités particuliers relatifs à l'histoire de France* (Paris: G. A. Dentu, 1838), XIII, p. 396; René de Maulde-la-Clavière, *Diplomatie au temps de Machiavel* (Paris: E. Leroux, 1892), I, pp. 434–35, n. 2.

22 *TA*, iii, pp. lxx, lxxv, 385–86.

23 *Shields of arms by the French royal herald Montjoie*, Bod MS. e Mus. 78.

24 *TA*, iii, pp. lxxv, 342.

25 *TA*, iii, p. 319.
26 Ibid., p. 349.
27 Ibid.
28 Ibid., p. 384.
29 Ibid., p. 411.
30 Psalm 85.11. '*Veritas de terra orta est, et iustitia de caelo prospexit*': 'truth is sprung from the earth and justice has looked down from heaven'. Albany's motto translates as, 'In the shadow of thy wings', taken from Psalms 17.8 of the Vulgate Bible: '*a resistentibus dexterae tuae custodi me ut pupillam oculi sub umbra alarum tuarum proteges me*', which translates as 'From those who resist your right hand, preserve me as the apple of thy eye. Protect me under the shadow of your wings'. For enamel plaques and coins displaying the same device see: Coombs, 'The artistic patronage', p. 2014.
31 Bremond Domat, *Chronique d'Écosse & généalogie des rois d'Écosse*, BSG, MS 936, f. 2v. 1519.
32 Charles H. Haskins, 'Latin Literature under Frederick II', *Speculum* 3.2 (1928), pp. 129–51; Similar Latin verse appears at the back of Bod MS Ashmole 1437.
33 Compare Domat, *Chronique d'Écosse*, MS 936, f. 25v. 1519 and MS Marchmont 308876, f. 19r.
34 '*Albion in terris rex primus germine Scotis ipsorum turmis rubri tulit anna leonis Fergusius fulvo Ferchard rugientis in arvo. Christum ter centis ter denis prefuit annis*', MS Marchmont, f. 19r.
35 Domat, *Chronique d'Écosse*, BSG, MS 936, f. 19v. 1519.
36 Domat, *Chronique d'Écosse*, BSG, MS 936, f. 257r. 1519.
37 Compare Domat, *Chronique d'Écosse*, BSG, MS 936, f. 14v. 1519 and MS Marchmont 308876, f. 11r.
38 *Scotichronicon by Walter Bower*, ed. D. E. R. Watt, 9 vols (Aberdeen: Aberdeen University Press, 1993) I, p. 67.
39 Domat, *Chronique d'Écosse*, BSG, MS 936, f. 256vr. 1519. We are told that 'Galahel first king of Scotland, reigned 24 years. He was a sage prince. He conquered a quarter of Spain and Scotland in these happy years. He divided his Kingdom in three parts and founded the edifice Brigantie. Reigned [virtuously (?)]', and for Scota, 'Scota, his wife, daughter of King Pharaoh, the last in Egypt. From whom Scotland took its name. After the death of her husband, she conquered Hibernia, after which she named her first son and reigned 28 years' [the author's translation].
40 When Edward III assumed the arms of France, he explained his claim to them in these Leonine verses. A French man replied in the verse below. George Puttenham, *The Art of English Poesy, A Critical Edition* (London: Cornell University Press, 2007), p. 103.
41 Meaning that ownership is easier to maintain if one has possession of something and difficult to enforce if one does not.
42 Bremond Domat (Self-portrait), *Généalogie de Madame Anne de la Tour, princesse de l'Écosse*, Den Haag, Koninklijke Bibliotheek, KB.74.G.11, f.2r. 1518.
43 Domat, *Chronique d'Écosse*, MS 936, f. 256r. 1519 [Author's own translation].
44 Domat, *Chronique d'Écosse*, MS 936, f. 257r. 1519 [Author's own translation].
45 Domat, *Chronique d'Écosse*, MS 936, f. 259r. 1519 [Author's own translation].

46 Ibid. This is close in design to an Italian helmet: Milan or Brescia, *c*. 1550. The Met, New York, 29.17.
47 For example, see the genealogical tree with pictorial heads of Scottish kings from Malcolm Canmore and Margaret to James II in the *Scotichronicon*, Edinburgh, University of Edinburgh Special Collections, MS 186, f. 345r.
48 *Triptych with the paternal line of Charles V*, KBR Albert Ier, MS 14569.
49 Coombs, 'Vic-le-Comte', pp. 175–217; Coombs, 'from Dunbar to Rome', pp. 231–66.

4. 'Losing its religion'? Scottish Literature and Confessional Identity

GERARD CARRUTHERS

Problematic sectarianism in Scottish culture begins with the Reformation and opposition between Protestants and Catholics. However, we might find elements of a sectarian theme earlier in 1320, as the nobles of Scotland send a letter to the Pope which becomes known as 'The Declaration of Arbroath'. This attests to the orthodox Christian nature of Scotland, asking that the Holy Father recognises this fact in the face of English imperial predation and their foreign implication that Scotland is less a part of Christian civilisation in its independence. As part of the same strategy of Scottish nation-building, John Barbour (c. 1320–1395) produces his epic poem *The Brus* (c. 1375) about King Robert the Bruce and adapts a long-standing European Romance depiction of strife between Christians and Muslims, transposing this to become the Scots versus the English during the fourteenth-century Wars of Independence. One of the first cultural blasts in the emerging Reformation landscape occurred when Benedictine priest Ninian Winzet (1518–1592) accused the fiery apostle of reform John Knox (1514–1572) of preferring English 'speech and thinking' as opposed to his native Scots.[1] Early during the Scottish Reformation, in 1565, appears the 'Gude and Godlie Ballatis', a publication which translates Scots vernacular secular songs to religious use, overlaying the sensual often with sacred expression and so a harbinger of a more puritanical aesthetic in Scotland. The drama, *Ane Satyre of the Thrie Estatis* by David Lyndsay (c. 1490–1555), from its 1540 early royal court version at Linlithgow to its 1552 Cupar and 1554 Edinburgh full public versions, has often been seen as a great anti-Catholic Scottish text. It provides, certainly, a contemporary pan-European critique of power abuses, mocking, for instance, the sale of plenary indulgences; however, theologically, Lyndsay was in many ways perhaps not all that far removed in his central faith tenets from the old faith.[2] Interestingly, his play was mutably inspirational in mode, being reprised a century and a half later by Episcopalian Archibald Pitcairne (1652–1713) in his *The Assembly, or Scotch Reformation* (1691) which savagely satirised the General Assembly of the Presbyterian Church of Scotland. Increasingly, in a comfortably Protestant nation, *Ane Satyre of the Thrie Estatis* came to be seen as a canonical national as well as, or even more than, a confessional text. This status was highlighted by its use as a cornerstone feature of the early Edinburgh Festival, with expurgated Scots, in 1948 and subsequently 1973 and 1985, and in an unexpurgated 2018 workshop version edited by Ian Brown.

As Pitcairne's work attests, the seventeenth century, as elsewhere in the British Isles and across Europe, was an unsettled, tendentious period in religious terms. In Scotland inter-Protestant tension and violence was as intense as anything (paradoxically) in the more familiar, later divide between Protestants and Catholics. Related to British dynastic tensions around the Scottish-cradled Stewart/Stuart dynasty, during the 1670s and 1680s 'The Killing Time' (a term bestowed by Robert Wodrow (1679–1734) in his *History of the Sufferings of the Church of Scotland* (1721–22)) saw the Scottish Covenanters harshly persecuted by an at-the-time Episcopal-led Protestant Church of Scotland. The Covenanters had thought with the signing of the Solemn League and Covenant (1643) that they had secured a future Presbyterian form of church-government for the whole of the British Isles, something that increasingly slipped from their grasp as the Wars of the Three Kingdoms and related civil wars ensued down to 1688. 1668–69 saw the 'Glorious Revolution' which finally deposed the Stuarts with their High Anglican and even Catholic predilections. The brutality of the Killing Times is recalled in the Whig-Presbyterian novel of the early nineteenth century, which includes James Hogg's *The Brownie of Bodsbeck* (1818), showing the Covenanters in heroic light. Presbyterian Hogg's novel was in part a rejection of another fiction, *The Tale of Old Mortality* (1816) by Episcopalian-sympathetic Walter Scott (1771–1832), which depicted a fanaticism in the covenanting cause that repelled Hogg.[3] Appearing in the work of both Hogg and Scott, John Graham of Claverhouse (1648–1689), fierce opponent of the Covenanters in the southwest of Scotland was known alternatively as 'Bluidy Clavers' by his enemies or 'Bonnie Dundee' by his supporters. He features as a hero in one text in the *Choice Collection of Serious and Comic Scots Poems* (1706–11), an anthology of largely Episcopalian and even Catholic-inclined allegiances around the desire for a restored House of Stuart. Anthologies such as this assumed as axiomatic the aesthetically denuded sensibilities of the Presbyterian Whigs, largely sympathetic to the new British dynasty from 1689 with its deposition of the Catholic King James II (and VII) and the ascendancy to the throne of King William III of Orange and his wife Mary, James's daughter. Like Claverhouse, another confessionally contentious figure, James Graham (1612–1650), first marquis of Montrose, initially a covenanter, later a supporter of Charles I in the Wars of the Three Kingdoms, is a figure who fascinates across four centuries of Scottish verse and fiction.[4]

John Graham of Claverhouse died at the Battle of Killiecrankie in 1689, as part of the Jacobite Rising seeking to defend James II. One hundred years later Robert Burns (1759–1796) celebrated that effort in his song 'The Braes o' Killiecrankie' (1789), which has become a staple of the modern Scottish 'folk' canon. Opposed though these things were, both Jacobitism and Covenanting have become strong Scottish cultural signifiers (the use of the term 'covenant' being prominent in the campaign for the establishment of the Scottish parliament at Holyrood in the late twentieth century). Jacobitism, associated more often with Episcopalianism and Catholicism, might appear odd in the mouth of a Presbyterian-born poet like Burns. However, his ancestry in the Jacobite heartlands of Aberdeenshire partly explains this expression as well as a romantic and polemical deployment of these cultural politics. Burns identifies with the Moderate Party (more theologically liberal) in his own day, as opposed to the Popular Party (more theologically conservative) in Scottish Presbyterianism, and Jacobitism is particularly an anathema to the latter. However, Burns, despite a preferential option for Jacobitism throughout his writing career, can also celebrate the more toughly Calvinist Covenanters, by the 1790s re-reading these following the French Revolution as defenders of conscience and political liberty.[5] Identification, then, with different 'sects' is possible within the corpus of the one writer, Burns, who personally had sympathy with a number of Scottish Catholics. This perhaps makes him appropriately the national 'bard', the celebrator of promiscuous Scottish identity. A poet who influenced Burns was Rev. John Skinner (1721–1807), an Episcopalian priest at Longside in Aberdeenshire who complained in his 'Jezebel once Queen of Israel' in 1746 about the persecution of his flock and faith (tainted by association with Jacobitism) by local land-magnate Lady Kinmundy.[6] Rather nicely, this poem is loosely a source for Burns's 'Address of Beelzebub' (1786), a satire implicitly defending Catholic Highlanders against the exploitative Earl of Breadalbane.

The early eighteenth century – with ongoing Jacobite agitation and the 1714 establishment of the Hanoverian royal dynasty in Britain following closely on from the Glorious Revolution – remained a time of cultural, confessional wars as well as very real physical intimidation including the burning of Skinner's chapel by Lady Kinmundy. During the eighteenth century, the philosopher and historian David Hume (1711–1776) in his *History of England* (1754–61) decried the fanaticism of the seventeenth century in the British Isles, including the Scottish Covenanters. Strong agnostic or even atheist as he was, he also famously rejected the Catholic idea of miracles, a strong element of anti-Catholic derision in post-Reformation Scotland. However, his fellow Scottish Enlightenment intellectual and friend Adam Smith (1723–1790) with his idea of 'sympathy', or entering into the psychology of people and identities very different from one's own, as well as the work of Scottish Enlightenment historians including Hume, created a generally revisionist undertow which created a different cultural atmosphere. Renewed interest in the Covenanters through the long eighteenth century, sparked by the likes of Wodrow and even the hostile Hume, meant that there was much to read and re-imagine in the Whig-Presbyterian novel of the early nineteenth century, or earlier in Burns's poem already alluded to. At the other end of the sectarian spectrum, we have the rather strange case of Mary, Queen of Scots, the deposed and executed Catholic Stuart monarch whose rise to iconicity through the nineteenth century warrants some explanation. Important here is the powerful influence of eighteenth-century antiquarian William Tytler (1711–1792). His *Inquiry Historical and Critical into the Evidence against Mary Queen of Scots* (1759) was a piece of scholarly revisionism that helped begin the propulsion of the Stuart queen into the romantic national icon that she has become today. If not necessarily a 'nationalist' in modern parlance, Tytler, in explicitly opposing previous work that cast Mary in a bad light by David Hume and William Robertson (1721-1793), presented a narrative of long historical English predatoriness against Scotland and its dirty tricks, including opportunistic Protestantism, to undermine the Stuart dynasty from the time of James V to that of his daughter Mary.[7] Tytler, known personally to Burns, is a direct influence on his writing of Jacobite songs as well as several texts sympathetic to Mary Stuart.

The eighteenth century and perhaps the Enlightenment in general had a double effect. While there was much decrying of previous religious strife, read as dependent often on abstruse points of scriptural principle, there was also, as seen in work by Burns, Hogg and others, a great deal of overlapping confessional and dynastic cultural fodder to be imaginatively channelled. One of the most strikingly ambidextrous cases here concerns the Aberdeenshire Catholic priest, biblical scholar and poet Alexander Geddes (1737-1802). In his 'Epistle to the President, Vice-Presidents, and Members of the Scottish Society of Antiquaries, on being chosen a Correspondent Member' (1792), he defends the efficacy of the Scots language as against English. In the process he celebrates Knox's usage of Scots (so contradicting Ninian Winzet) and as part of his national patrimony lays claim to Knox, as well as the story of Andrew Melville, the Presbyterian reformer of the late sixteenth century who was harshly censured by the Episcopalian-inclined James I. He likewise salutes the Catholic poet, Alexander Montgomerie and Gavin Douglas, Catholic Bishop of Dunkeld:

> Do bot compare each nation's phrase
> In BESS'S and in MARY'S days,
> Is English prose mair orthodox
> Than that of Kennedy an' Knox?
> Does Melvil's story muddier flow
> Than those of Holinshed an' Stowe?
> Are Barclay's rimes mair tight an' terse

> Than Lindsay's or Montgomery's verse?
> Does Spencer, deathless bard, precel
> The peerless Bishop o' Dunkel?[8]

Elsewhere in his text, he also praises Archibald Pitcairne, exemplifying again Geddes's ability to lay claim quite comfortably to the diverse religious traditions of Scotland. Geddes's ecumenism in the service of a national cultural agenda, however, does not pertain in the nineteenth century. The lawyer, antiquarian and poet William Motherwell (1797–1835) does more than anyone to import the anti-Catholic Orange Order to Scotland from Ulster in the 1820s and 1830s. In an age of potential leftist revolution, Motherwell was looking to bind a non-radical, loyalist working class as part of the British, Tory imperial project. Amid his right-wing populism Motherwell also anthologised Scottish song and was active in the growth of the 'Burns Movement', part of the explanation for the strong right-wing accents in Burns circles down to the present day. Through this association, Burns has often been seen as a poet somehow antipathetic to the values of Catholicism, which has nothing to do with his actual views or his work.[9]

Prior to the first large wave of Irish immigrants to Scotland during the 1840s, these already formed a steady trickle, to which in part Motherwell was responding. However, the resentment against the Catholic Irish in the country on sectarian grounds is arguably less virulent earlier in the century. A traditional horror towards Catholicism is ventriloquised through the character of Rev. Micah Balwhidder, minister of a fictional Ayrshire parish in *Annals of the Parish* (1821) by John Galt (1779–1839). Balwhidder's flock, however, are not in accord with their pastor's militant outlook, as he tells us in his diary for 1804:

> the Mass, which, with all its mummeries and abominations, was brought into Cayenneville by an Irish priest of the name of Father O'Grady, who was confessor to some of the poor deluded Irish labourers about the new houses and the cotton-mill. How he had the impudence to set up that memento of Satan, the crucifix, within

my parish and jurisdiction, was what I never could get to the bottom of; but the soul was shaken within me, when, on the Monday after, one of the elders came to the Manse, and told me, that the old dragon of Popery, with its seven heads and ten horns, had been triumphing in Cayenneville on the foregoing Lord's day! I lost no time in convening the Session to see what was to be done; much, however, to my surprise, the elders recommended no step to be taken, but only a zealous endeavour to greater Christian excellence on our part, by which we should put the beast and his worshippers to shame and flight [...][10]

A little earlier, and in similar weaving context, the Irish Catholic incomer could even be celebrated by Paisley poet Alexander Wilson (1766-1813). In his poem 'Hollander, or Light Weight' (1790), which landed its author in the real-life libel court, Wilson saluted a 'brave Hibernian boy' who had stood up to a worker-defrauding mill-owner.[11] And Scottish literature in the same area continued to reflect sympathy for Irish (majority Catholic) radical political aspirations, even after the fearful 1790s period of the United Irishmen (an organisation, to which Wilson was partial, which included Presbyterians as well as Catholics). For instance, another poet, John Mitchell (1786-1856), in his 'A Braid Glow'r at the Clergy' (1843) wrote favourably of the maverick Presbyterian minister Patrick Brewster (1788-1859), proponent of Chartism who also welcomed to his parish Daniel O'Connell, 'the great liberator' who did so much to advance the cause of Catholic emancipation in Ireland. Satirically, Mitchell has an ill-disposed narrator address Brewster:

> Wi' Dan O'Connell, too, ye dined,
>   A man that's lang been working
> To get our kirk and state disjoin'd,
>   Tho' it should be by Burking.
> An' weel ye ken that rascal rude
>   Is doing a' he can, sir,

> To prove a Catholic's as good
> As ony ither man, sir—
> O! dool this day.[12]

Even as Mitchell's text demonstrates a countermovement to the anti-Catholicism that was developing through the growing power of the Orange Order, its reference to 'burking' (suffocation) recalls the Irish 'body-snatchers' (actually murderers), William Burke (1792–1829) and William Hare (1792 or 1804–after 1829). Burke and Hare had both come from Ulster to work as 'navvies' on the Union Canal and their names are strongly etched within the litany of bogeymen of Scottish, indeed, British popular history. Their infamous Edinburgh trial of 1829 revealed their murdering of vulnerable, derelict people to order to provide cadavers for the anatomy room. The pair were far from the only dubious suppliers of the dead for dissection in this period, but theirs are the names which have most infamously survived and their existence undoubtedly contributed to the virulent stereotype of the criminal, untrustworthy, drunken Irishman (Burke and Hare drank heavily prior to all of their crimes) that grew in Scotland and elsewhere during the nineteenth century.

Several waves of 'Celticism' onwards from the mid-eighteenth century (seen most famously in the 'Ossian' controversy) inflect British, indeed European cultural history. A similar predilection is seen again in the late nineteenth century in the 'Celtic Twilight' movement in Ireland and also Scotland. In Ireland this saw, for instance, the Protestant poet W. B. Yeats (1865–1939) become a nationalist proselytiser on behalf of a majority-Catholic population desiring independence from Britain. In Scotland, Celticism was less directly charged with confessional-national impetus, being more of a generally aesthetic disposition. We see evidence of this in the fashion for the Celtic Cross used as a burial marker for the most douce Presbyterian citizens in Edinburgh and Glasgow from the 1880s (and down to the present day). Part of this wider 'fashion' includes the foundation and naming of Celtic Football Club in 1887–88 to counter the severe hardship of the Irish (and other poor) in the east end of Glasgow. The brainchild of Brother Walfrid (Andrew Kerins, 1840–1915) of the Marist Order, who took his cue from the earlier foundation of another football club by the Irish in Scotland, Hibernian Football Club in Edinburgh, in 1875. The presence of the latter becomes a key cultural signifier in the work of Irvine Welsh.

Ironically, even as Christopher Murray Grieve, 'Hugh MacDiarmid' (1892–1978), largely deplores what he takes to be an ethereal, unrealistic Celticism, his literary pseudonym is derived from a Celtic/Gaelic stream of culture he believes, along with Scots, to represent the genuine, traduced essence of Scottish identity. As part of his own pan-Celtic predilection, he wished that (largely Catholic) Irish immigration into Scotland might accelerate by way of providing a healthy cultural infusion.[13] He also flirted with the idea of becoming a Catholic himself.[14] The leader of Scottish literary modernism was, however (as throughout his life), an often rather uninfluential cultural voice. More typical of this time was the anti-Irish campaign that sat at the centre of the outlook of the Church of Scotland, whose Church and Nation Committee produced the report *The Menace of the Irish Race to our Scots Nationality* (1923).[15] Colleagues of MacDiarmid's in the Scottish literary 'renaissance' of the 1920s and 1930s likewise swam against the tide of anti-Irishness and anti-Catholicism. The most outspoken of these was Thomas Macdonald, 'Fionn Mac Colla' (1906–1975), formerly a teacher in a United Free Church school in Palestine, who became a founder member of the National Party of Scotland and a convert to Roman Catholicism. His novel *The Albannach* (1932) features the Irish priest Father O'Reilly, a cultural exemplar to the central protagonist Murdo Anderson from the Presbyterian Gàidhealtachd, who meets this mentor when a student at the University of Glasgow. The finely written novel depicts a landscape, a culture and an outlook on life in Scotland depressingly beaten down by Calvinist negativity.[16] Mac Colla's other novel published to some approval in his lifetime, *And the Cock Crew* (1945), depicts a nefarious Scottish church largely complicit in the great cultural trauma of the Clearances.

Of a piece with MacDiarmid's and Mac Colla's religious politics are the views of Edwin Muir (1887–1959), who might be thought of as something of a 'crypto-Catholic', sympathetic to Catholicism throughout his lifetime but never becoming a member of that church. Muir's reading of the historic trajectory of Scottish culture was one of spiralling ruin brought about by the displacement of Scots with English as the language of cultural authority, for which he blamed the English Bible, tightening union with England, and Scottish pursuit of material wealth in the context of the British Empire. As if this were not enough, Muir reads Calvinist Scotland as essentially aesthetically barren, promulgating all of these views in his *Scott and Scotland: The Predicament of the Scottish Writer* (1936), which 'proved' that authentic Scottish literature was impossible. Muir's denial of the possibility of literary revival and assertion that the only option for the modern Scottish writer was to write in English greatly angered his erstwhile ally, MacDiarmid (although he too was now writing his major work in English). Muir's travel-book *Scottish Journey* (1935) is as bleak and as well-written as anything by Mac Colla. It depicts a Scotland blighted by the aforementioned cultural catastrophes and the related Industrial Revolution. Pointedly, one of the few bright spots Muir finds as he traverses the nation is the Marian shrine at Carfin in Lanarkshire, built through the indefatigable will of (often unemployed) Irish and Scottish miners from 1922 under the direction of an English-born priest, Monsignor Thomas Taylor (1873–1963). Of a piece with the outlook of *Scott and Scotland* and his other writings, Muir's poem 'Scotland 1941' (1943) depicts an organic medieval Scotland (an independent kingdom, loyal in religion to Rome) enervated of community and imagination by Knox and leading Covenanter Alexander Peden (1626–1686) who wore a rather grotesque mask (rather like the face of a sinister hooded crow, Muir implies) by way of disguise:

> We were a tribe, a family, a people.
> Wallace and Bruce guard now a painted field,
> And all may read the folio of our fable,
> Peruse the sword, the sceptre and the shield.
> A simple sky roofed in that rustic day,
> The busy corn-fields and the haunted holms,
> The green road winding up the ferny brae.
> But Knox and Melville clapped their preaching palms
> And bundled all the harvesters away,
> Hoodicrow Peden in the blighted corn

Hacked with his rusty beak the starving haulms.
Out of that desolation we were born.[17]

Forming his views in the early part of the twentieth century, Muir (like Mac Colla) tended to over-read Calvinism as cognate in outlook with the totalitarian views of the post-First World War European political landscape.[18] Identification of a damaging puritanical Calvinism at work in Scotland had previously been read (but without the recommendation to Catholicism) in *The House with the Green Shutters* (1901) by George Douglas Brown (1869–1902) who suggested in this novel that the intensely practical, engineering, entrepreneurial and imperial Scot was a product of Reformation and a related exceptionalist Britishness. This anticipated in a way *The Protestant Ethic* (1904 and 1905 but not translated into English until 1930) by German sociologist Max Weber (1864–1920) which argued for a particular affinity between the supposed individualistic theology of Calvinism and the outlook of Capitalism. One of the other things that Brown's novel did was to lampoon the 'Kailyard' school of Scottish fiction particularly successful in the 1880s and 1890s. In its attention to the small-scale confines of Scottish rural parish, such fictions have often been read as wilfully evasive of the wider, increasingly urban realities of late nineteenth-century Scotland. Critique of Kailyard, along with dislike of Scottish Calvinism, was a pronounced expressive part of those who desired what they took to be a newly courageous look at Scottish culture in the literary renaissance of the early twentieth century. Many of the Kailyard writers, including the hugely successful J. M. Barrie (1860–1937), came from the theologically conservative part of the Scottish kirk which had become the Free Church of Scotland during the 'Disruption' of 1843, when a third of the Church of Scotland walked out of the mainstream church, asserting the right of local parishioners to appoint their ministers (as opposed to the 'patronage' in a more centralised control of this process, led by local landowners of the 'Moderate' wing of the church). It is possible to argue that one of the things 'Kailyard' does is exemplify, *contra* the views of Muir and others, Scottish Calvinism's strong investment in community rather than individualism, but literary criticism has been slow to proffer a more generous approach to the Kailyard and its confessional context.[19]

Following the likes of Muir, Scottish critics tended to take a highly querulous, secular view of religion in Scottish literature. David Craig, for instance, in his *Scottish Literature and the Scottish People, 1680–1830* (1961), was rather puzzled that nineteenth-century Scottish fiction should be so concerned with what he took to be, even by then, largely superseded debates about abstruse points of theology. Also, somewhat curiously for an avowed Marxist, Craig identified an ultimately self-defeating verve in Scots poetry of the eighteenth century (including, most famously, Burns) which he called the 'reductive idiom', a satirical outspokenness (as part of the extended democratic expressiveness of Calvinism) he claims to be at odds with what he implies to be a properly mature literary sensibility and expression.[20] For Craig, what was happening was not so much Muir's identification of puritanical 'censorship or suppression as the bringing out, by Calvinism, into full potency of a native trait which itself tended to thwart or curtail imagination'.[21] Part of the reason for Craig's sweeping critical generalisation (and the same applies to Muir) is their Anglocentric reliance on the notion of a more or less unbroken, properly developed tradition of literature as England is assumed to have. Following the critical predilections of T. S. Eliot above all, it is assumed by such critics that Scotland's problematic, ruptured history (although not any more so than England's in fact) cannot encompass a full, or in Muir's terms, 'homogenous' literary tradition.[22] In fact, the attempt to posit this lost cultural homogeneity required Muir entirely to ignore the third major literary language of Scotland with its own great 'tradition' and contribution to the writing of Scottishness, Gaelic. Discussion of a Scottish literary tradition has to take account of at least three languages – besides Gaelic, Scots and English – while any definition of a literary tradition that cannot accommodate such a range of languages in a Scottish, or any other, multilingual context is itself flawed.

It took a long time for modern Scottish criticism to begin to move beyond its extremely secular and culturally nationalist (meaning mainly the idealisation of unproblematic tradition) tendencies. Cairns Craig in *The Modern Scottish Novel: Narrative and the National Imagination* (1999) argues for a more positive creative dividend resulting from Scottish literature in a

Calvinist context. In particular, he suggests that the idea of 'fearful selves', based on the strong Calvinist sense that the deceitful and discombobulating Devil is abroad in the world, is very useful.[23] This is the key background to what is often seen as the greatest of all Scottish novels, James Hogg's *The Private Memoirs and Confessions of a Justified Sinner* (1824). Here someone, vouchsafing his own salvation due to the Calvinist doctrines of the elect and of predestination, perpetrates the most vile crimes, 'knowing' that he has been chosen to go to Heaven by God at the beginning of time. Inspired by Robert Burns's 'Holy Willie's Prayer' (1785), a satire of the extreme Calvinist mindset, true-believer Hogg implies in his text that conscience and morality ultimately count, in fact, for the Calvinist as much as anyone else. Published in 1947 with an introduction by French critic, Andre Gide, Hogg's novel was, in a sense, re-tooled for the post-Auschwitz world as a critique of the fanatical mind. Already a strong contributor to the nineteenth-century Gothic sensibility (influencing, *inter alia*, the Brontës), *Confessions of a Justified Sinner* took on a new lease of life for twentieth-century Scottish literature, providing direct inspiration for other 'justified sinner' depictions in *The Cone Gatherers* (1955) by Robin Jenkins (1912–2005), *The Prime of Miss Jean Brodie* (1961) by Muriel Spark (1918–2006) and *The Fanatic* (2000) by James Robertson (b. 1958) among others, all, as Gide's interest implies, taking Scottish themes and offering a problem that is universally applicable. As we examine Scottish literature without recourse to the dogmatic, over-secularised manner that pertained for much of the twentieth century, older Scottish texts are also retrieved in more benign Protestant reading contexts.[24] For instance, Scottish Protestant literary aesthetics can be suggested in one of the most influential of all western poems, *The Seasons* (1726–30) by James Thomson (1700–1748), where the strong empirical, or realistic observational, lens over nature might be seen to reflect the desire for the unadorned quotidian. More importantly, perhaps, the assumption of critics such as Muir and David Craig that literature emerges from supportive historic and cultural contexts ought to be questioned. Work by Burns, Scott and Hogg, reflecting Scotland's Protestant controversies exemplifies *de facto*, one might say, creative capital from contested confessional circumstances.

Following in the thematic tradition of explosive Calvinist repression in his novel *Witch Wood* (1927) is another sincere Presbyterian (indeed a man very active as a kirk elder), John Buchan (1875–1940). Set in the seventeenth century amid that period's fraught and fractious contest over preferred dynastic and confessional settlement, *Witch Wood* shows humans using the Devil as well as God for their own selfish ends (even as they are not necessarily aware of their own motivations). A novel with profound things to say about human nature (including spirituality), it is a well-written, brilliantly paced story very obviously making creative capital from the tragic effects of Scottish history. It is rather odd but nonetheless necessary that such a statement of good creativity from unpropitious events has to be made so emphatically in the context of the historical trajectory of Scottish literary criticism.

The gentle mockery of Scottish Catholic-phobia by John Galt just over a century before is added to by J. M. Barrie in more comically robust fashion in his late novella *Farewell Miss Julie Logan* (1932). Locked down in a wintery glen, the young minister Adam Yestreen (whose surname means 'yesterday evening' in Scots) falls in love with a Jacobite ghost, Julie Logan, a strange reality he implicitly realises and with which he accommodates himself. It is only when she reveals herself to be a Catholic, however, that he comes close to letting her drop into a burn and the relationship ends. Barrie's *reductio ad absurdum* happens amid a novel that reflects on Scotland's entangled confessional identities; however, even as a 'historical' novel, it was also timely at a highpoint of anti-Catholic sectarianism in Scotland. It appeared less than a decade after 'The Menace of the Irish Race' report and at a time when The Protestant Action Society and the Scottish Protestant League began to make longstanding political gains in local council elections in Edinburgh, Glasgow and elsewhere. Their 1933 founder John Cormack (1894–1978), a councillor for South Leith, forged strong links with British Fascism (founding at one point 'Kormack's Kaledonian Klan') and led the 'Morningside Riot' in 1935, when twenty thousand PAS adherents stoned, spat at and jeered ten thousand Catholics gathered for a Eucharistic Congress. Among many other aggressions, his movement besieged the parish of

Scottish writer-turned-priest Father John Gray (1866–1934), threatening his mutilation.[25] A poet of the *fin de siècle* period, Gray was author of the pioneering novel *Park* (1932) and is, personally, a strong element in the composite model (not least in his name) for Oscar Wilde's *The Picture of Dorian Gray* (1890). He is a part of Scottish Catholic creative literature still today under-attended to.

Scottish literature of the twentieth century has been an effective voice in mocking populist anti-Catholicism, among the most famous texts here being 'King Billy' (1963) by Edwin Morgan (1920–2010). It sums up the ignorance, pathos and toxic masculinity (albeit also incorporating, one might argue, the author's gay gaze) of 1930s Glasgow anti-Catholic gang leader Billy Fullarton (styled 'King Billy' for King William of Orange). The Orange Order of which Fullarton was an adherent remains a potent rabble-rousing hate group through the twentieth century and into the present. Peter McDougall (b. 1947) deals with this situation in his play *Just Another Saturday* (1975), turned into a powerful BBC television production, as does Alan Spence (b. 1947) in a short story of brilliantly painted domestic and public tension, 'Its Colours They Are Fine' (1977). The 'heyday' of Scottish sectarian violence in the 1930s also demonstrates its notoriety in the massively popular BBC TV series *Peaky Blinders* (in 2019), set in early twentieth-century Birmingham with the appearance of members of Fullarton's gang as purveyors of far-Right mayhem. Less dramatic religious culture clashes – indeed deeply embedded 'routine' bigotry – find encapsulation frequently in modern Scottish writing. We might point to the reference to 'gangs of midden-rakers from Blackhill [a 'notorious' Catholic area of Glasgow]' in *Lanark* (1981) by Alasdair Gray (1934–2019). The novella *Another Time, Another Place* (1983) by Jessie Kesson (1916–1994) is about the strange-seeming Catholic ways of Second World War Italian prisoners of war in the north-east of Scotland.[26] Both of the latter two examples have found great acclaim as they clearly and profoundly set out realities of cultural perplexity. Scottish literary canon formation, however, in its homogenising, secular-Protestant predilections, has unthoughtfully tended to overlook (or sometimes facilely absorb) Scottish Catholic experience and writing.

Andrew O'Hagan (b. 1968) has written of the seeming absence in his formative years of literature from his own Irish-Scottish Catholic background:

> There were no novels in the new library [in Kilwinning, Ayrshire] written by Scottish Catholics. If the novel was thought to be the great social form, and Scotland was thought to be a progressive society, where were the Catholic novelists? There were converts – Muriel Spark – but that wasn't the same. Where were the novels of those millions of people, who had travelled out of Ireland, who had played into an industrial revolution, who had drunk, and prayed, and talked, and loved, and died here? Where were they? The millions of lives.[27]

Coming out of that apprehension in the same year is a helpful anthology, *Across the Water: Irishness in Modern Scottish Writing*.[28] More generally, Scottish Catholic writers have, like their Protestant counterparts, written, and had a successful reception, of their variegated cultural experience such as in the play by Ann Marie Di Mambro (b. 1950) *Tally's Blood* (1990), dealing with Catholic Italian experience during the Second World War and a hit at Edinburgh's major Traverse Theatre. More typical Irish-Catholic experience runs throughout the sardonic, witty and often hilarious action of another modern part of the Scottish theatre canon, The 'Slab Boys' trilogy (1978–82) by John Byrne (b. 1940). Perhaps least self-consciously of all in its Catholic 'background', *Trainspotting* (1993) by Irvine Welsh (b. 1958) features a cast of working-class Hibernian FC supporters who make easy assumptions about Scottish Protestant culture responding, in effect, to the tribalism shored up by the likes of the Orange Order.

Among the 'converts' as alluded to by O'Hagan, George Mackay Brown (1921–1996), taught and very much influenced by his fellow Orcadian Edwin Muir, is a writer who frequently deals with the workings of grace in his fiction and poetry. Grace, or the workings of God on the margins, is a suitably analogous theme for Mackay Brown in his highly conscious status as a writer operating confessionally (as well as geographically, based as he was in Orkney) not from the mainstream of Scottish culture. Like Mackay Brown, Muriel Spark frequently wields, as in *The Prime of Miss Jean Brodie*, a dissenting Catholic outlook on the world as she views Protestant Scotland (and indeed Britain). However, both writers too in their Catholicism seek to countermand not so much Protestantism but materialism, which in their view has lost sight of a divinely ordained universe. In its very secular agenda of prioritising 'condition of Scotland' texts for much of its history, Scottish literary criticism, arguably, has not been much minded to take seriously works of a religious or spiritual nature.

Endnotes

1. Jane E. A. Dawson, 'The Two John Knoxes: England, Scotland and the 1558 Tracts', *Journal of Ecclesiastical History* 42.4 (October 1991), p. 576.
2. For a discussion of Lyndsay's beliefs, see D. W. B. Somerset, 'The spirituali movement in Scotland before the Reformation of 1560', in *Scottish Reformation Society Historical Journal* 8 (2018), pp. 1–43.
3. See Valerie Wallace and Colin Kidd, 'Between Nationhood and Nonconformity: The Scottish Whig-Presbyterian Novel and the Denominational Press', in Gerard Carruthers and Colin Kidd (eds), *Literature and Union: Scottish Texts, British Contexts* (Oxford: Oxford University Press, 2018), pp. 193–219.
4. See Catriona M. M. Macdonald, 'Montrose and Modern Memory: The Literary Afterlife of the First Marquis of Montrose', in *Scottish Literary Review* 6.1 (Spring/Summer 2014), pp. 1–27.
5. See Burns's 'The Solemn League and Covenant', in James Kinsley (ed.), *The Poems and Songs of Robert Burns* (Oxford: Oxford University Press), p. 803.
6. David Bartie (ed.), *John Skinner: Collected Poems* (Peterhead: Buchan Field Club, 2005), pp. 86–89.
7. See especially Tytler's 'Introduction' to his *Inquiry* (London and Edinburgh: Caddell and Creech, 1790), pp. 35–74.
8. Alexander Geddes, 'Epistle to the President, Vice-Presidents, and Members of the Scottish Society of Antiquaries, on being chosen a Correspondent Member', in *Archaeologia Scotica* 1, p. 448: journals.socantscot.org/index.php/arch-scot/article/view/378 [accessed 19 June 2022].

9   See Gerard Carruthers, 'Responses to Peterloo in Scotland, 1819–1822', in Michael Demson and Regina Hewitt (eds), *Commemorating Peterloo: Violence, Resilience and Claim-making during the Romantic Era* (Edinburgh: Edinburgh University Press, 2019), pp. 120–39. At the anecdotal level, the present author wrote about Burns's warm relationships with contemporary Catholics, to be phoned by a journalist to tell him there was grumbling in response by several individuals in the largely Catholic village of Croy in Lanarkshire who saw Burns as a poet 'hostile' to their faith. In the Catholic parish at Croy, instead of a Robert Burns Supper, they stage annually a Tommy Burns Supper in tribute to a favourite Celtic FC player (1956–2008).
10 John Galt, *Annals of the Parish*, ed. Robert Irvine (Edinburgh: Edinburgh University Press, 2020), p. 149.
11 A. B. Grosart (ed.), *The Poems and Literary Prose of Alexander Wilson*, 2 vols (Paisley: Alex Gardner, 1876), II, p. 63.
12 Tom Leonard (ed.), *Radical Renfrew* (Edinburgh: Polygon, 1990), p. 150.
13 Hugh MacDiarmid, *Albyn: Or Scotland and the Future* (London: Kegan Paul, Trench, Trubner), p. 69.
14 Scott Lyall, *Hugh MacDiarmid's Poetry and Politics of Place: Imagining a Scottish Republic* (Edinburgh University Press: Edinburgh, 2006), p. 41.
15 See Stewart J. Brown, '"Outside the covenant": the Scottish presbyterian churches and Irish immigration 1922–1938', *Innes Review* 42 (1991), pp. 19–45; and David Ritchie, 'The civil magistrate: the Scottish Office and the anti-Irish campaign, 1922–29', *Innes Review* 63.1 (2012), pp. 48–76.
16 For the author's explicit ideological purpose here see the foreword (pp. i–viii) to the 1971 edition of *The Albannach* (Edinburgh, Reprographia). See also *Move Up John* (Edinburgh: Canongate, 1994) for Mac Colla's most polemically direct view of a life-denying Calvinism and a more life-positive Catholicism.
17 Peter Butter (ed.), *The Complete Poems of Edwin Muir* (Aberdeen: Association for Scottish Literary Studies, 1991), p. 100.
18 See, for instance, Edwin Muir, 'Bolshevism and Calvinism' (1934), in *European Quarterly* 1.1, pp. 7–9.
19 For a compelling revisionist approach here of the 'genre' as against traditional critical narratives of Scottish Literature, see Andrew Nash, *Kailyard and Scottish Literature* (Amsterdam: Rodopi, 2007).
20 David Craig, *Scottish Literature and the Scottish People, 1680–1830* (London: Chatto & Windus), p. 83.
21 Ibid., p. 75.
22 See Gerard Carruthers, 'The Rise of Scottish Literature', in Carruthers, *Scottish Literature* (Edinburgh: Edinburgh University Press, 2009), pp. 4–28.
23 Cairns Craig, *The Modern Scottish Novel: Narrative and the National Imagination* (Edinburgh: Edinburgh University Press, 1999), pp. 37–74.
24 A good starting point here is David Mullan and Crawford Gribben (eds), *Literature and the Scottish Reformation* (London: Routledge, 2009).
25 For a treatment that covers Protestant Action generally, see Tom Gallagher, *Glasgow: The Uneasy Peace* (Manchester: Manchester University Press, 1987); see also the same author's 'Protestant Extremism in Urban Scotland 1930–1939: Its Growth and Contraction', in *The Scottish Historical Review* 64.178 (Oct 1985), pp. 143–67.

26 Alasdair Gray, *Lanark* (Edinburgh: Canongate Classics, 2002), p. 122.
27 Andrew O'Hagan, 'Into the Ferment', in T. M. Devine (ed.), *Scotland's Shame: Bigotry and Sectarianism in Modern Scotland* (Edinburgh and London: Mainstream, 2000), pp. 26–27.
28 Jim McGonigal, Donny O'Rourke and Hamish Whyte (eds), *Across the Water: Irishness in Modern Scottish Writing* (Glendaruel: Argyll Publishing, 2000).

5. Collective Identities and the *Other* in Scottish Jacobite Songs

KRISTEL VAN SOEREN

Introduction

Songs, and popular protest songs in particular, are essential sources for the study of national and cultural identities in any given society. They can tell the stories of marginal groups and individuals that oftentimes are overshadowed or dismissed by the more dominant historical narratives. In the present study, songs are defined as anything that is sung, a combination of text and tune. Music, according to Martin Stokes, plays a significant role in the formation of identity because it makes people recognise identities, places, and what sets them apart.[1]

Songs can be used not only to distinguish the Self from the Other but also to maintain this distinction.[2] This becomes overtly clear in the study of Jacobite song culture. Jacobites were the supporters of the exiled Stuart kings after 1688. To help the Stuart king regain the throne, they plotted and executed several uprisings against the British state between 1688 and 1759. The last major uprising culminated in defeat at the Battle of Culloden in 1746. Jacobitism was a threat to the British state, therefore the production, dissemination, and consumption of Jacobite material – including songs – could lead to arrests and prosecutions.[3]

Although Scottish Jacobite songs have gained some scholarly attention in the fields of literature and history, research has mainly tended to focus on issues of dating and authorship rather than the contents, meanings, and functions of the songs themselves. Moreover, when Jacobite songs are subjected to research, they are often regarded as *texts* rather than songs. I argue that studying both the text and tune is essential as often the tunes themselves already carry cultural, national, and collective identities. In some cases, a text can explicitly address a group's norms and values. In terms of tunes, melodies can express a group's identity because of the cultural associations attached to them.[4]

By considering both text and tune, the meanings and associations that the eighteenth-century audience attached to the songs will be revealed. It is these associations, and sometimes testimonies, that are usually ignored in dominant historical narratives. Moreover, songs, especially in the form of broadsides, were vehicles of mass communication.[5] Their accessible form enabled them to reach all layers of society – not just the layer whose material has been historically deemed 'archivable'.

In this chapter, I examine through the case study of two specific eighteenth-century Jacobite songs, 'Wherry Whigs Awa' and 'The Highland Laddie', how notions of the Self and the Other are conveyed in songs and discuss expressions of national identities. I discuss how collective identities were articulated in these songs. These songs were chosen because of the period in which they circulated, the way they convey the Jacobite cause, and because they both contain common Jacobite themes. Although both songs contain these elements, they do so in a distinctive manner, which gives a clear idea of the broad range of Jacobite song culture. Within Jacobitism, songs were one of the most crucial mechanisms to spread the movement's sentiments and strengthen the bonds within the cause.[6]

I argue that the emphasis on loyalty and the active and conscious distinguishing from the Other helped to strengthen the feeling of collective identity and thus played an indirect but significant role in forming a Scottish national identity.

Setting the tone

In the study of early modern songs, and in particular Jacobite songs, some crucial aspects in terms of production and circulation must be kept in mind. Early modern songs were mostly contrafacts. This means that the poet took an existing tune, often one that was already familiar to the audience, and placed it under a new set of lyrics.

Writers of songs would frequently pick particular tunes as musical settings because the audience already had certain cultural and emotional associations with certain tunes.[7] These associations would then serve as a foundation that would reinforce the new lyrics. A tune could literally 'set the tone' for the meaning of the text.

Because of the frequent use of contrafacts, it was common to hear several songs with the same melody. It needs to be kept in mind that, due to oral transmission, variations of one song would have circulated. Although most songs were printed in this age, paradoxically, and despite being printed, the songs were altered when sung, and so, in the context of early modern song culture, the print mechanism allowed ballads to be changed again and again as in the oral tradition where it would be altered nearly every time it was sung.[8] Hence the variations.

In the study of Scottish Jacobite songs, one needs to be aware of the cultural transmission of songs between England, Scotland, and Ireland. Songs did not stop at the border, and it is sometimes challenging to figure out where the origin of a song lies. As Mary Ellen Brown observes in her chapter on balladry in early modern Scotland, 'the song and literary cultures of Scotland and England share many exemplars', reminding us that 'national borders do not limit the free circulation of art'.[9] Furthermore, it must be kept in mind that the aim of Jacobite poets was not to 'compose' the most beautiful musical pieces but rather to convey their message and spread their cause.

Because of the fugitive nature of Jacobite songs and the cheap material on which they were printed, the majority of these songs have perished.[10] The reason that part of the repertoire still exists today is due to the popularity of the songs, not only during the decades of the Jacobite risings but especially later in the eighteenth and nineteenth centuries. Jacobite songs were collected by people interested in the conservation of Scottish culture. James Hogg collected Jacobite songs in the early eighteenth century, for example. These collectors would sometimes also make a song up and include them in the collection. Because of these practices, we now have collections of contemporary Jacobite songs, fake or 'invented' songs, and Jacobite-inspired songs composed by poet-composers such as Robert Burns. Merging these different types of repertoires in research is problematic as contemporary Jacobite songs were created with a completely different purpose than the Jacobite-inspired songs that were composed decades later.[11]

Collective identity

In the early modern period, a variety of means could be used to identify a person or a group. These means could be coats of arms, seals, other insignia, and portraits.[12] Jacobite identity was expressed by symbols such as the Royal Oak, white roses, the blue bonnet, and after 1745, the Highland dress.[13] To present themselves as Stuart adherents, Jacobites in the early eighteenth century would publicly wear oak leaves on 29 May, which of course was a celebration of the Restoration in 1660. Furthermore, they would wear white roses on 10 June to celebrate the birthday of King James III.[14]

Most significant, these celebrations and expressions of identification were combined with the public chanting of ballads to tunes that were ingrained with Jacobite resistance.[15] The connection between song and identification is strong. Expressions of identity can even be found in purely a melodic line. When Jacobites were not sure about the nature of some individuals in their company, or when there was a threat, the melody would be whistled or played on a bagpipe.[16] The tune would then be recognised by Jacobites as support, resistance, and a means of identification, but to the outsiders, it was just a tune.

In a broader sense, collective identity can be found in collective memories, a shared past, shared language, or shared cause in the case of the Jacobites. Jacobite poets consciously used the story-telling functions of music to shape their image of the nation and the cause.

This becomes clear in the use of mythology and the recreation of national heroes by poets: an example of this can be found in the song 'Wherry Whigs Awa'. This practice of drawing on mythology and heroic figures was common in poetry in the British Isles. According to David Aberbach, by recreating national heroes, poets can 'give hope in victory, wisdom in failure, and unity in defeat. Songs instil pride in national accomplishments even when the nation is defeated and powerless.'[17]

All of these characteristics can be found in Scottish Jacobite songs, especially songs that deal with lost battles and songs that lament the Stuart king's absence. Mythical history is used by poets to establish a collective or national identity. In 'The Highland Laddie', and other Jacobite songs that present the Stuart kings as heroic figures and songs that deal with national symbols, the poets emphasised the pride and hope of the nation. Drawing on these aspects of collective identity could 'enable the nation to hold together and resist oppression'.[18] The differences between Scottish Jacobites and the Whigs were emphasised in poetry and songs. This cultural defence mechanism was used by the Jacobites as a political and military tool.[19] This is a common phenomenon. According to Aberbach, 'when independence is threatened or lost, whether because of foreign invasion or internal wars or disasters', poetry will reach a peak.[20] Songs can indeed be seen as arms in battle.

'Wherry Whigs Awa'

The anti-Government sentiment of the Jacobites is unmistakably present in the song 'Wherry Whigs Awa' which is dated around 1743.[21] The word 'whurry' and its variants 'wherry', 'whirry', and 'furich' appear in several eighteenth-century Jacobite songs. The uncommon verb's origin is a combination of Scandinavian and Old English, namely 'whirr' and 'hurry' and carries the meanings: 'to carry off, drive away, hustle along, expel with force'.[22] As 'awa' is Lowland Scots for 'away', the dominant message of the song is 'drive the Whigs away!' The poets of this song have drawn on collective memory, a shared past, and aspects of language.

The tune of this song was likely composed for the occasion and was thus not a contrafact. Paula McDowell has found evidence that a song called 'Awa Whigs Awa' was chanted during Jacobite risings in 1715, however, this evidence is only textual.[23] The lack of musical evidence has some implications. It is uncertain that the tune was used for more than one song and there is a chance that the tune was used only for 'Wherry Whigs Awa' and its variations, possible including 'Awa Whigs Awa'. The only eighteenth-century fragment of the tune 'Wherry Whigs Awa' available is held in the Scottish Catholic Archives in a manuscript of Scottish violin tunes (see Example 1).[24] Occasional tunes, as I would call them, are not loaded with cultural associations as popular contrafact tunes are. This, in combination with scarce archival evidence, makes it more challenging to perform an in-depth musical analysis.

COLLECTIVE IDENTITIES AND THE *OTHER* IN SCOTTISH JACOBITE SONGS

Example 1: 'Wherry Whigs Awa' in C Major', Scottish Catholic Archives

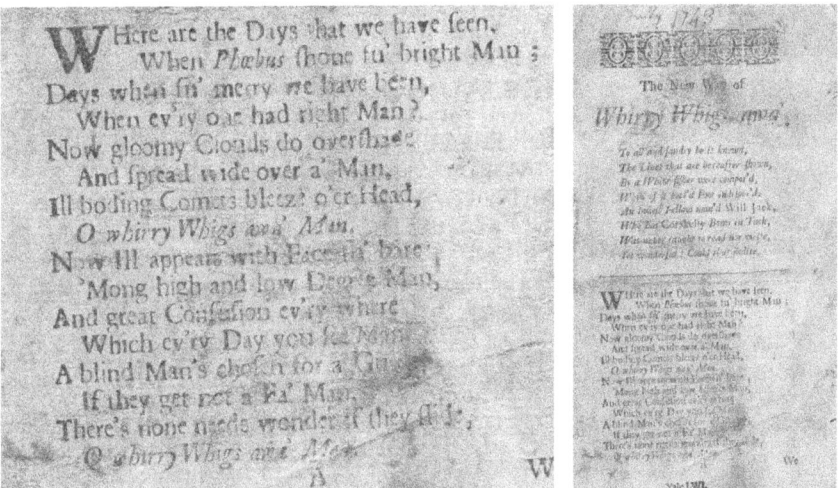

Example 2: 'Wherry Whigs Awa'', Walpole Library, Yale

This version of the song, as can be seen in Example 2, was found in the Lewis Walpole Library at Yale. What is interesting is that it mentions 'The New Way of Whirry Whigs awa'' as the title. This implies that there has been an older version, which would tie in with the evidence presented by McDowell, but further investigation of earlier versions lies beyond the scope of the current chapter.

Analysis

The 1743 version of 'Wherry Whigs Awa' consists of two verses. As can be seen in Example 3, in the first verse, the poet recalls a collective memory and the Jacobites look back at better times, a glorious past. The poet then illustrates a more depressing picture of the situation. The 'gloomy clouds' that overshade the nation can be read as a metaphor for the British government and the suffering they brought upon the Scottish Jacobites.

Wherry Whigs Awa

Where are the days that we have seen,
When Phoebus shone so bright, man;
Days when so merry we have been,
When ev'ry one had right man?
Now gloomy clouds do overshade
And spread wide over a' Man,
Ill-boding comets blaze o'er head,
O whirry Whigs awa Man.

Now ill appears with face so bare,
'Mong high and low degree man,
And great confusion ev'ry where
Which ev'ry Day you see Man
A blind man's chosen for a [...]
If they get not a fa' Man,
There's none needs wonder if they slide,
O wherry Whigs Awa Man.

Example 3: Wherry Whigs Awa

Looking at how the Self is conveyed, it becomes clear that especially in the first four lines, the collective is mentioned. 'We' is important here; it can be seen as a rhetorical tool. As Renée Vulto has pointed out in her work on early modern song cultures, by using the first-person plural pronoun 'we', the person who sings the song can automatically represent the voices of the entire group to which he or she belongs.[25]

As can be seen in the second line of the song, the poet mentions 'Phoebus', which is another name for the god Apollo in Greek and Roman mythology. It was common for Jacobite poets to refer to the Stuart kings as mythological figures.[26] James III, for example, was often referred to and painted as Hercules and Phoebus Apollo, as is the case here. Presenting the Stuarts as heroic figures from mythology would grant them authority. It would emphasise the Jacobite belief that the Stuarts were kings by divine right.[27] Although the Other is not mentioned explicitly, the metaphors the poet uses can be seen as references to the Whigs and the British government, and in particular, the sorrow their laws and actions had caused. See, for example, the 'gloomy clouds' and 'ill-boding comets' in the first verse. The last line in verse two, 'O wherry Whigs Awa Man', could be read as a stirring protest message against the British government. It can be concluded that in 'Wherry Whigs Awa', the Self is presented as the faithful nation loyal to a heroic mythological figure. The Other is presented as bringing doom over the nation. In this song, collective identity is formed on collective memories of a shared past and by addressing the suffering to which many Scottish Jacobites could relate. Through encouraging messages, a feeling of togetherness or brotherhood is conveyed.

'The Highland Laddie'

'The Highland Laddie' is arguably most familiar as a song by Robert Burns. The present study, however, focuses on a version that was contemporary to the Jacobite period. The song 'Highland Laddie' comes from the most popular Jacobite song groups, namely the 'Bonnie Highland Laddie' group. Several versions of the song were circulating in the eighteenth century. Originally, the songs represented Scotland as the woman-nation lamenting and praising her lover, the Highland 'laddie'.[28] Disguising their political sentiment in the form of a love song was a trick the Jacobite poets often played. To the unexpectant ear, the song would just sound like a sweet love song, but insiders would immediately recognise it as a Jacobite song.

In these songs, Prince James Francis Edward Stuart and Prince Charles Edward Stuart were both presented as patriotic Highlanders. The tune to which the lyrics are set dates from at least 1678.[29] It is an older tune that likely was loaded with cultural associations. The tune is also known under the title 'If thou'lt play me fair play', which is the first line in this version, and thus likely in older versions as well. This melody only needed to be whistled and Jacobites would immediately recognise it as Jacobite activism.[30]

Adjusted version of the tune 'The Highland Laddie', as given in William Donaldson's *The Jacobite Song: Political Myth and National Identity* (Aberdeen: Aberdeen University Press, 1988)

II.

The time shall come when their bad choice,
Bonny Laddie, Highland Laddie.
They will repent, and we rejoice;
Bonny Laddie, Highland Laddie.
I'd take thee in thy Highland Threws,
Bonny Laddie, Highland Laddie.
Before the Rogues that wear their Blues.
Bonny Laddie, Highland Laddie.

III.

Our torments from no cause do spring,
Bonny Laddie, Highland Laddie.
But fighting for our lawful King;
Bonny Laddie, Highland Laddie.
Our King's reward will come in time,
Bonny Laddie, Highland Laddie.
And constant Jenny shall be thine,
Bonny Laddie, Highland Laddie.

IV.
There's no distress that earth can bring,
  Bonny Laddie, Highland Lassy.
But I'd endure for our true King;
  Bonny Laddie, Highland Lassy.
And were my Jenny but my own,
  Bonny Laddie, Highland Lassy.
I'd undervalue Geordie's Crown.
  Bonny Laddie, Highland Lassy.

Example 4: 'The Highland Laddie', from *A Collection of Loyal Songs*

Analysis

Musically, this song uses a lot of repetitive phrases and is syllabic (one syllable per note), which made it easier to sing along to. As can be seen in Example 4, the melody is accessible, and the catchiness of the refrain likely added to the song's popularity.

This version of 'The Highland Laddie' comes from *A Collection of Loyal Songs*, a Jacobite songbook that was printed in 1750, four years after the last uprising.[31] On the face of it, this is a love song involving a Highland couple, but the political dimension of the song is obvious.[32] The first three verses present the woman's perspective, and the fourth and last one presents the man's perspective. The pair was supposed to get married in the near future, but because the Highland laddie had to fight for the cause, the wedding was postponed. The bride does not mind waiting; for her, too, the cause comes first.[33] In the second verse, the woman expresses criticism of other Highland women, who betray the Stuarts and marry George's adherents. The bride warns them, and her tone is urgent yet hopeful: she knows that they will regret their choices once the Stuart king returns to the throne. The line 'I'd take thee in thy Highland trews, before the rogues that wear their blues' could be interpreted in different ways, with one being the vow of marriage. She will proudly marry a Highland Jacobite, regardless of the repercussions it can lead to. What can be seen here is a fusion between love, gallantry, and the Jacobite cause which was already implanted in the popular mind before

93

the last rising.[34] The song is hopeful and can only lead to a happy ending: the Laddie gets the Lassie; the Stuart gets the throne.

In terms of collective identity, this song draws on national symbols such as the Highland dress, Highlander characters, and the mention of 'Jenny'. The Highland dress in this and many other songs represents the pride of the nation and the Self as distinguished from the Other. Another important element of collective Jacobite identity is loyalty to the Stuarts and the cause. This is strongly evident in verse 4: 'There's no distress that earth can bring, but I'd endure for our true King.'

Conclusion

The songs 'Wherry Whigs Awa' and 'The Highland Laddie' exemplify how collective identities, the Self, and the Other were addressed in Jacobite songs. As shown in this chapter, collective identities were articulated by addressing common Jacobite themes such as the absent monarch and heroic Highlander, but also by using national symbols such as the Highland dress, and by drawing on the collective memories of a shared, glorious past. Placing these themes on a tune that had specific Scottish cultural associations would have reinforced the message of the text.

Where the Other was presented as destructive, the Self was often portrayed as loyal and legitimate with a heroic figure as ruler by divine right. Rallying messages such as 'Wherry Whigs Awa!' brought a sense of unity when these songs were sung collectively. By addressing the shared history, whether myth or reality, poets formulated a collective memory that gave the Scottish Jacobites hope in times of distress.

Makers of Jacobite songs were skilful poets that knew how to trigger emotional reactions from listeners. The most powerful aspects of the songs were the sentiments that made people identify themselves with the messages and the narratives expressed in the songs. This could be the feeling of belonging, triggered by the shared suffering expressed in 'Wherry Whigs Awa', but also the human experiences of the Highland couple in 'The Highland Laddie', and the way their lives were affected by the ongoing struggle. Many people would have been able to identify themselves with these characters and, consequently, would become more compassionate regarding the cause.

Finally, having looked at these two songs, one might wonder how they functioned in the active fight for the Jacobite cause. The study of Jacobite songs enables us to see the bigger picture in terms of collective identity and its importance for the Jacobite cause. Singing together was one of the main activities undertaken by Jacobites. Even though as a group they could not always fight the cause in public, by singing together their bond was continuously strengthened. Research on early modern song cultures has pointed out that especially in times of political unrest, singing together would strengthen the bonds that were necessary to maintain the collective identity of a group.[35] For these Jacobites, according to Simon Frith, 'making music isn't a way of expressing ideas; it is a way of living them'.[36] When Jacobites could not actively fight for the Cause, singing together would substitute for the physical fight. I would thus argue that the performance practice of Jacobite songs should be seen as the embodiment of collective identity of Scottish Jacobites.

Endnotes

1 Martin Stokes (ed.), 'Introduction', in *Ethnicity, Identity and Music: The Musical Construction of Place* (Oxford: Berg Publishers, 1994), pp. 1–28 (pp. 5–6).
2 Ibid.
3 Doron Zimmerman, *The Jacobite Movement in Scotland and in Exile, 1746–1759* (Basingstoke: Palgrave Macmillan, 2003), p. 1; Paula McDowell, '"The Manufacture and Lingua-facture of Ballad Making": Broadside Ballads in Long Eighteenth-Century Ballad Discourse', *The Eighteenth Century* 47.2 (2006), pp. 151–78 (p. 156).
4 Louis Peter Grijp and Dieuwke van der Poel, 'Introduction', in *Identity, Intertextuality, and Performance in Early Modern Song Culture*, ed. Dieuwke van der Poel, Louis Peter Grijp and Wim van Anrooij (Leiden: Brill, 2016), pp. 1–39 (p. 8).
5 Patricia Fumerton and Anita Guerrini, 'Introduction: Straws in the Wind', in Patricia Fumerton, Anita Guerrini and Kris McAbee (eds), *Ballads and Broadsides in Britain, 1500–1800* (Farnham: Ashgate, 2010), pp. 1–9 (p. 1).
6 Kristel van Soeren, 'Political Sentiments in Disguise: Scottish Jacobite Songs between 1700 and 1750' (unpublished Bachelor's thesis, Utrecht University, 2019), p. 25. studenttheses.uu.nl/handle/20.500.12932/33045
7 Una McIlvenna, 'Ballads of Death and Disaster', in Jennifer Spinks and Charles Zika (eds), *Disaster, Death, and the Emotions in the Shadow of the Apocalypse, 1400–1700* (London: Palgrave Macmillan, 2016), pp. 275–94 (pp. 277–78).
8 Peter Burke, *Popular Culture in Early Modern Europe* (Farnham: Ashgate, 2009), p. 173.
9 Mary Ellen Brown, 'Balladry: A Vernacular Poetic Resource', in Ian Brown et al. (eds), *The Edinburgh History of Scottish Literature: From Columba to the Union (Until 1707)*, vol. 1 (Edinburgh: Edinburgh University Press, 2006), pp. 263–72 (p. 264).
10 Murray Pittock, 'Scottish Song and the Jacobite Cause', in Ian Brown et al. (eds), *The Edinburgh History of Scottish Literature: Enlightenment, Britain and Empire (1707–1918)*, vol. 2 (Edinburgh: Edinburgh University Press, 2006), pp. 105–09 (p. 106).
11 See, for example, Carol McGuirk, 'Jacobite History to National Song: Robert Burns and Carolina Oliphant (Baroness Nairne)', *Eighteenth Century* 47.2–3 (Summer/Fall 2006), pp. 253–87.
12 Valentin Groebner, *Who Are You?: Identification, Deception, and Surveillance in Early Modern Europe*, trans. Mark Kyburz and John Peck (New York: Zone Books, 2007), p. 11.
13 Pittock, *Inventing and Resisting Britain: Cultural Identities in Britain and Ireland, 1685–1789* (Basingstoke: Macmillan, 1997), p. 112.
14 Daniel Szechi, *The Jacobites: Britain and Europe, 1688–1788* (Manchester: Manchester University Press, 2019), p. 51.
15 Szechi, p. 51.
16 Pittock, *Inventing and Resisting Britain*, p. 113.
17 David Aberbach, 'Myth, History and Nationalism: Poetry of the British Isles', in Athena Leoussi and Steven Grosby (eds), *Nationalism and Ethnosymbolism: History, Culture and Ethnicity in the Formation of Nations* (Edinburgh: Edinburgh University Press, 2006), pp. 84–96 (pp. 94–95).
18 Aberbach, pp. 84–96 (p. 95).
19 Pittock, *Inventing and Resisting Britain*, p. 111.
20 Aberbach, pp. 84–96 (p. 84).

21 Lister M. Matheson, 'An Early Jacobite Song on the Battle of Inverurie', *Scottish Studies Review* 8.2 (2007), pp. 36–53 (p. 42).
22 Matheson, pp. 36–53 (p. 42).
23 McDowell, pp. 151–78 (p. 159).
24 Anonymous, 'Wherry Whigs Awa in C Major', Scottish Catholic Archives opac.rism.info/search?id=806630953&View=rism [accessed 10 April 2022].
25 Renée Vulto, '"De Duivel Schoptse voor haar kont. Hoezée, Hoezée, Hoezée!" Het lied als agitator in Nederlandse Twisten, rellen en protesten, 1780–1820', *Jaarboek De Achttiende Eeuw* 52 (2020), pp. 127–39 (p. 133).
26 Pittock, 'Scottish Song and the Jacobite Cause', pp. 105–09 (p. 107).
27 Pittock, *The Invention of Scotland: The Stuart Myth and the Scottish Identity, 1638 to the Present* (London: Routledge, 1991), pp. 4, 52.
28 Pittock, 'Scottish Song and the Jacobite Cause', pp. 105–09 (p. 106).
29 James Hogg, *The Jacobite Relics of Scotland: Second Series*, ed. Murray Pittock (Edinburgh: Edinburgh University Press, 2003), p. 512.
30 Pittock, *Inventing and Resisting Britain*, p. 113.
31 'Highland Laddie', *A Collection of Loyal Songs, Poems, &c.* ([Raglan], 1750), pp. 33–34.
32 Pittock, *The Invention of Scotland*, p. 46.
33 William Donaldson, *The Jacobite Song: Political Myth and National Identity* (Aberdeen: Aberdeen University Press, 1988), p. 59.
34 Donaldson, p. 60.
35 Vulto, '"Waer vriendenmin gaet, hand aen hand, met liefde voor het Vaderland" Het zingen van politieke liederen als verbindende praktijk in het Nederlandse revolutietijdvak (1780–1815)', *TVGESCH* 133.4 (2020), pp. 617–38 (p. 619).
36 Simon Frith, 'Music and Identity', in Stuart Hall and Paul Du Gay (eds), *Questions of Cultural Identity* (Los Angeles: SAGE, 1996), pp. 108–27 (p. 111).

6. Napoleon and Ossian: Celtomania and the Construction of French Nationhood

CLARISSE GODARD DESMAREST

In April 1799, Joséphine de Beauharnais bought the Malmaison, a manor house and small estate in Reuil near Paris, from the Le Couteulx du Molay family for 225 thousand francs.[1] With its wheat fields, vineyards, and forests,

Figure 1. View of Malmaison from the entrance, engraving by Jean-Baptiste Chapuy, 1807. Courtesy: Bibliothèque nationale de France.

the estate was intended to be a rural retreat for Joséphine and her husband, Napoleon Bonaparte. Though charming, however, the existing house was hardly grand enough to be a suitable residence for a man who was not only one of France's greatest military heroes, but soon to be – following the establishment of the Consulate after the coup of 18 Brumaire and Napoleon's subsequent appointment as First Consul – the country's effective head of state. With no residence other than the Palais des Tuileries allocated to him, the Malmaison became the second residence of the chief of state, and it had to be comprehensively remodelled for its new role. The work was supervised by Bonaparte's favourite architects, Charles Percier and Pierre Fontaine – who had been recommended by Jacques-Louis David and Jean-Baptiste Isabey – who went on to be employed to transform the house between January 1800 and July 1802. Amongst the most important elements of this first tranche of works was the redecoration of the ground floor salon (dubbed the 'golden salon'), the house's principal reception room.[2]

Figure 2. Malmaison's 'Salon doré', or 'salon de compagnie'.
Courtesy: RMN-Grand Palais (musée des châteaux de Malmaison et de Bois-Préau) / Gérard Blot.

From the beginning, the decoration of the salon was to be based around a series of specially commissioned paintings. Four landscape painters of established reputation (Bidauld, Taunay, Dunouy and Thibault) were given commissions for one painting each, while two brilliant young talents, Anne-Louis Girodet-Trioson (1767–1824) and François Gérard (1770–1837), were given commissions for a further two, larger paintings. The landscape painters were clearly expected to produce landscapes, but the subjects for the paintings by the two young history painters, both pupils of Jacques-Louis David, proved more difficult to define. It was initially proposed that all the artists should portray Bonaparte's recent victory at Marengo, but this theme was soon abandoned. Girodet was then asked to paint a 'tableau d'agrément' (a light subject). Instead, he chose to take his subject from political actuality, the unsuccessful plot against the life of Napoleon that took place on 3 Nivôse/22 December 1800. However, Girodet was advised by Percier to abandon this subject too. While Girodet was thus floundering, his contemporary and rival Gérard managed to identify and secure approval for his own subject. It was to be drawn from Scottish literature and would show the bard Ossian evoking ghosts on the shore of the Lora.

Girodet must soon have become aware of Gérard's proposed subject, and this in its turn seems to have determined him, too, to take on an Ossianic theme.[3] The subject chosen did not, nevertheless, entirely abandon the more contemporary concerns that he had previously sought to represent: his painting would show the protagonists of the Ossian poems alongside their modern French equivalents, the fallen heroes of Napoleon's recent campaigns. The two paintings were installed in 1802 in the salon, a finely proportioned room (over forty-nine square metres in area) that the Jacob brothers had lined with fine mahogany panelling. The paintings were hung in pride of place on the fireplace wall, on each side of an elaborate white marble chimneypiece with hardstone (*pietra dura*) inlay (the gift of Pope Pius VII).[4] Girodet received twelve thousand francs for completing his painting in January 1803, and the two paintings remained at Malmaison until 1810.

Gérard's painting (H: 180.5 cm/W: 198.5 cm) presents the bard Ossian in his desolate, blind old age, with his harp echoed by celestial harps,

Figure 3. *Ossian evoking ghosts on the shore of the Lora* by François Gérard, 1801–02. Courtesy: RMN-Grand Palais (musée des châteaux de Malmaison et de Bois-Préau) / Daniel Arnaudet.

producing music that evokes the ghosts of his dead family. His father Fingal, wearing his winged helmet, appears on the right with his mother Roscrana, with their warriors behind them, only the tips of their spears visible. On the left, his son Oscar and daughter-in-law Malvina. A romanticised Highland landscape and castle features behind them. This is the only painting on an Ossianic subject by Gérard, and though it presents the major protagonists of the Ossianic corpus, it does not represent a specific episode from the poems. The painting was also executed rapidly and its style is closer to that of a sketch than to a landscape painting. This all suggests that Gérard's primary aim was to evoke the spirit of the poems rather than to present a sustained pictorial narrative.

The situation could hardly be more different with Girodet's painting, which is self-evidently more complex and ambitious. *Ossian and his warriors welcoming in their aerial realm the shades of the French heroes* (H: 192.5 cm/W: 184 cm), also referred to as the *Apotheosis of the Heroes*, is clearly intended to be a major history painting. It is difficult to avoid the impression that Girodet was consciously seeking to ensure that his painting outshone Gérard's painting in every conceivable respect: in composition, in the density, variety and postures of the figures it contains, in the complexity of its symbolism, and in the finesse of its surface finish.[5] Several preparatory sketches also survive, including one on wood panel now kept in the Louvre (H: 34 cm/W: 29 cm, inventory reference: R.F.2359).[6] Its composition is almost identical to that of the finished painting, showing how meticulously he planned his commission.

When exhibited at the Salon de l'An X in 1802, the painting's complexity meant that it had to be accompanied by a long description by the artist detailing the identity of the figures.[7] Leading Girodet scholar George Levitine has combined this information with that contained in the titles of a series of contemporary lithographs of details from the painting, the *Collection de Têtes d'Étude* by Girodet's student Jean-Baptiste Aubry-Lecomte (1797–1858), to identify both the overall iconographic scheme and almost all the main figures.[8] In contrast to Gérard's relatively conventional depiction of a scene during the lifetime of the bard, who is evoking the shades of his ancestors but remains himself very much alive, Girodet transposed all his figures into the afterlife and, implicitly, to his own time.[9] There are two main types of figure: characters drawn from the Ossianic corpus (primarily on the left) and the French soldiers who had lost their lives in battle during the wars of the Revolution and first Republic (towards the right). In the centre of the composition, we see Ossian embracing General Desaix, a leading general in the Egyptian campaign who later lost his life at the battle of Marengo against Austria in 1800.[10] Behind Desaix stands a veritable pantheon of French generals: Kléber (immediately to the right of and behind Desaix), Caffarelli-Dufalga (looking to the right and holding a flag with his left hand),

Figure 4. *Apotheosis of the French heroes* by Anne-Louis Girodet de Roucy-Trioson, 1801–02. Courtesy: Musée National du Château de Malmaison, Rueil-Malmaison, FrancePhoto © Photo Josse/Bridgeman Images.

Marceau (wearing the cylindrical hat of the hussars), and also Hoche, Dugommier, Joubert, Dampierre, Championnet, Kilmaine, Marbot, and Duphot. In addition, two other military figures feature in the composition: the first grenadier of the Republic, La Tour d'Auvergne (behind the flag held by Caffarelli-Dufalga, his back turned to the spectator) and, allegedly, the drummer Joseph Bara. The remaining French soldiers – such as the grenadiers, sappers, dragoons, chasseurs, hussars and cannoneers – can only be identified by their uniforms.[11] The items held by the generals symbolise French victories over the Turks and Austrians: Desaix and Kléber hold aloft a trophy of Mameluke weapons and armour, and Caffarelli-Dufalga a Turkish battle flag, while the background is dominated by an Austrian standard, immediately adjacent to the figure of Victory who floats above the generals. With her left hand, she bears a caduceus, a symbol of peace, and with her right she holds the palms and laurels that are the reward of victory. Above her rises a cockerel, the symbol of France. Behind the main central figure group, we see a large body of French troops, and further troops – drinking, riding, hunting or pursuing the maidens of Morven – fill the centre middle ground.[12]

The second major figure group, the Ossianic characters, can be further subdivided into two groups, differentiated by the way they react to the arrival of the French warriors. The first consists of the former inhabitants of Morven, the area of north-western Scotland associated with Ossian's own people. Ossian (purported author of the Ossianic poems and the last of Morven's royal line) stands, as we have seen, at the centre, reaching out to grasp Desaix's shoulder with his right hand. Ossian stands just in front of his father Fingal and son Oscar, who wear winged and crested helmets respectively. Like the French generals, they and their men, too, bear trophies of war, evidently seized from the Roman legions whom they are described as having fought in the poems. Behind and above Fingal and Oscar stand Ossian's grandfather Comhal and finally, in the upper left corner, his great-grandfather Trenmor, with crown and sceptre. Around them cluster many of Fingal's most celebrated comrades in arms, including Cuthullin, king of Dunscaith, between Comhal and Fingal; Morar immediately above the head of Comhal; and Crugal, 'whistling a bellicose tune', immediately to the left of Comhal.[13] The two harp-playing maidens immediately below Fingal are the wives of Ossian and Oscar, Everallin and red-haired Malvina. They lead the other maidens of Morven in welcoming the French with music, flowers, wreaths and libations.[14]

The second group of Ossianic figures represent the people of Lochlin, which was, according to Macpherson, the ancient Scottish name for Scandinavia and North Germany. Starno, their king, is in the lower left corner wearing a crowned helmet and with a skull hanging from his belt. At the extreme left of the picture, just above Malvina and Everallin, we see his son Swaran, his followers Cormac and Clothel, and his ally Foldath. The inhabitants of Morven and Lochlin were enemies, and in contrast to the welcome Ossian's people give to the French, they react to their arrival with anger. However, two of their maidens, Lorma and Agandecca (daughter of Starno), join the maidens of Morven, and they are only just saved from Starno's wrath by a French dragoon, who is poised to decapitate him.[15]

Above their heads, an eagle, the symbol of the Austrian Empire, flies in fright at the sight of a cockerel, representing, of course, France. The cockerel's wing shields a dove of peace, which has just escaped the eagle's grasp.[16] The remainder of the picture is filled by innumerable ethereal figures bathed in celestial light. Girodet wrote that he had to invent the costumes and the arms of the Caledonian warriors and be guided only by analogies because Macpherson was vague in the poems. Ossian is dressed in the garment of the barbarians, the helmet of Oscar has a classical character and those of Fingal and Cuthullin are almost medieval. The red-haired maidens are an obvious, clichéd reference to the Celts.

As Levitine has argued, the painting's complex iconography must be read in the contemporary context of the signing of the Treaty of Lunéville by the French and the Holy Roman Emperor Francis II in February 1801.[17] The Treaty followed on from Austrian defeat at Marengo, that battle itself clearly referenced by Desaix's prominent position in the painting, and brought to an end nearly a decade of warfare in Continental Europe. The cost of peace to the Emperor was recognition of substantial territorial gains by France from the lands of the Holy Roman Empire and the Hapsburg domains in Italy. The French heroes, it would seem, are being rewarded for the sacrifices that paved the way for the profitable peace with Austria.

In this context, it seems probable that the violent and implacable men of Lochlin should be read as representatives of the last remaining impediment to the pacification of Europe – the British. This interpretation seems to be borne out by the naval waves found on their leader Starno's helmet, an allusion to British sea power. Moreover, the threatening aspect of the men of Lochlin reminds us that Great Britain had not yet been brought to the negotiating table. It seems that in this context, the men of Lochlin should be seen as proxies for the United Kingdom's continuing resistance to French power.[18]

Levitine's interpretation is, on its own terms, generally convincing; however, this chapter argues that there is a further layer of symbolism underlying Girodet's painting: this extends the allegory further in order to explore the fate of Empires, and in ways that implicitly relate the nationalities of those involved to the ethnic identities of the protagonists of the Ossianic corpus. This deeper symbolic agenda, I wish to suggest, highlights the way that the growing demand for national identity and autonomy in the later eighteenth and nineteenth centuries posed specific challenges in Napoleonic France, where the claims of French unity and national destiny had to be reconciled with the need to forge a cohesive identity for Napoleon's burgeoning, multi-ethnic empire. If this interpretation is valid, it can contribute, at the very least, to complicating orthodox views about the relationship between ethnicity, modernity and politics in the formation of modern nation-states, and may even suggest that the strong current of theoretical and historiographical bias towards studying nation-states and nationalism has distorted our view of the past in potentially significant ways.

The foundation for this case is to be found in the striking unconventionality of Girodet's iconography, which has few direct predecessors or obvious parallels. It does clearly draw on more orthodox classical models showing military heroes being conducted to Parnassus to be received by the gods, and Victory with her caduceus is a clear reference to that pictorial tradition. Yet in notable contrast to such imagery, it is striking that the representatives of Gallic heroism are not being received by the gods from on high, but are being embraced as brothers by the Celtic heroes of ancient Caledonia. It seems that we are being told something about the relationship between the ancient inhabitants of Scotland and the modern inhabitants of France. Similarly, we are implicitly being invited to see a similar parallelism between the struggles of the men of Morven and those of Napoleonic France. Whereas the ancient Scots had lost their lives in the struggles against Ancient Rome and with the north German and Scandinavian raiders from

Lochlin, the modern Gallic heroes had lost theirs in battles with their modern heirs: on the one hand, the successors of the ancient Roman empire, that is to say the Holy Roman Empire, which laid to the heritage of the western Roman Empire, and the Ottoman empire, which had taken over the eastern Roman Empire; and on the other hand, the men of Lochlin's heirs, that is to say the modern English descendants of the Anglo-Saxon and Scandinavian invaders of 'South Britain'.

Indeed, it possible to go further and see in Girodet's painting a vision of the putative future defeat of the English at Napoleon's hands. The crowns of oak leaves being borne by the maidens of Morven at the lower right of the painting can plausibly be interpreted as those destined for the Gallic heroes of future victories against the English 'oak'. Implicitly referring to the idea that the Celts outclassed and predated the Anglo-Saxons, Girodet seems to be suggesting that it was only a matter of time before Gallic virtue would defeat the modern rulers of Albion.

Such implicit equivalences become both more convincing and more legible when placed in a wider historical context of growing interest in eighteenth- and early nineteenth-century France in the Celtic identity of pre-Roman Gaul. The scholars who pioneered the study of France's Celtic origins were reacting against legendary accounts derived from chroniclers from the early Middle Ages such as Gregory of Tours (in *Decem Libri Historiarum*, sixth century AD) and, especially, those that drew on *The Chronicle of Fredegar* (c. 660). Fredegar provides us with a legendary narrative of French origins that focuses on the Frankish invaders who took control of the province of Gaul after the fall of the Roman Empire, tracing their ancestry to the diaspora of Trojans that followed the fall of Troy to the Greeks. According to Fredegar, the first king of the Franks was Priam. After the Trojan War, the ancestors of the Franks left Troy for Macedonia or Phrygia. Fredegar says that this group later had a king called Francio, from whom they derived their name. Under Francio, the Franks settled between the Rhine, the Danube and the sea, having travelled through Asia and fought with many peoples. The Franks eventually settled on the Rhine. The Franks were briefly subjugated by the Romans after the death of Francio, but were quick to shake off the Roman yoke.

Historian George Huppert points out that the Trojan pedigree not only gave a distinguished ancient provenance for the Franks but also established their kinship with the Romans, who traced their ancestry to Aeneas, who was, according to Virgil, a Trojan who left Troy after its fall and made his way to Italy, where he established the line of kings who would eventually found Rome.[19] In this way, the Franks were able to imagine themselves as the legitimate successors to the Romans as rulers of Gaul.

The credibility of these fabulous tales of Trojan origins began to be systematically questioned in the sixteenth century. At this time the self-conscious expansiveness of royal power under Francis I and his successors, the growth of Protestant belief, and the development of humanism led to a search both for justifications of 'absolute' monarchy and for grounds to oppose it. In both cases, there was a shared assumption that historical precedent could help define the relative power that should be exercised by the monarchy, aristocracy and judicial and representative institutions such as the *parlements* and the Estates General.

The most influential early contribution was made by the jurist François Hotman, whose *Francogallia* of 1573 helped define the direction of all subsequent debate.[20] For the Protestant Hotman, writing in the wake of the St Bartholomew's massacre, it was necessary to defend the 'people' against an all-powerful and potentially oppressive crown. Hotman's starting point was complete rejection of the myth of the Trojan origin of the Franks. This cleared the ground for him to assess the legitimacy of the new 'absolute monarchy' in relation to the alleged customs and 'national' characteristics of the peoples that played a role in the emergence of the French state: the earliest Gallic inhabitants, their Roman conquerors, and the Frankish warriors who took control of the Roman Gaul in the early medieval period. For Hotman, the Gauls were characterised by a deep-rooted love of freedom and a corresponding commitment to popular sovereignty: even where Gallic provinces were ruled by kings, they were chosen by the will of the people and subject to law. There was a 'common council for all Gallia', which was the ultimate arbiter of law and policy. The ancient principles of liberty and popular sovereignty had been absorbed into the Roman government of Gaul and then descended unbroken to Hotman's own day. In Hotman's account, the Franks were not of Trojan but Germanic origin, sharing the Gallic commitment to liberty, and were originally invited by the Romans to act as defenders of Gaul. The kings of the Franks were consequently, in Jacques Barzun's pithy formulation of Hotman's vision, 'the protectors of the Gauls, and the guarantors of their liberties'.[21]

Ironically enough, in the later seventeenth and early eighteenth centuries the power of the Bourbon monarchy resulted, at least in appearance, in something of a scholarly regression of knowledge, as questioning the Trojan origins of the French monarchy came to be seen as an act of *lèse-majesté*. In the background, however, opposition to Louis XIV's mode of government once again drove renewed interest in the origins of France's ancient constitution.

In the eighteenth century this debate became increasingly polarised between 'Germanists', who saw the ancient constitution of France as essentially Frankish in origin, and 'Romanists', who stressed the continuing influence of the Gallo-Roman period. The founding father of the Germanist school was Henri de Boulainvilliers, comte de Saint-Saire (1658–1722). Boulainvilliers came from the ancient French military or 'sword' nobility and believed the status and political influence of his order was under threat from Louis XIV's bureaucratic and authoritarian state. His political philosophy centred on the conquest of Roman Gaul by the Franks, a Germanic nation. Whereas for Hotman the tradition of liberty came from the Gauls, for Boulainvilliers it was properly the characteristic of their Frankish overlords. These Franks, in accordance with the customs described by Tacitus in his *Germania*, elected their kings and decided important issues through popular assemblies. Tacitus praised the moral simplicity of the Germans, their love of freedom, generosity, frankness and individuality. According to Boulainvilliers, since the French nobility were the direct descendants of the Frankish conquerors, the true French constitution was therefore based on a powerful nobility in which the king was *primus inter pares* – first among equals – and in which the nobility acted – through their 'right of conquest' – as the political representatives of the French nation. Though it might seem to be a symptom of aristocratic arrogance, this theory was not, it should be stressed, primarily intended to legitimate the position of the nobility over the third estate, but rather to defend the rights of the ancient nobility against the Crown's alleged encroachments on their status and prerogatives.

Other writers also sought a more 'constitutional' approach to government but were less inclined to dismiss the role of Roman Gaul in establishing the principles and values that were to be the foundation of the French state. In the view of these 'Romanists' (including the Abbé Dubos),[22] the Romans had brought the advantages of civil law, good government and high civilisation to France, and the Franks had simply taken the place of the Romans as the ruling class. The moment when representative modes of government were lost was not, then, with the advent of the Romans, but when the coming of the Emperors began to corrupt the Roman Republic.

This debate developed dramatically after the Revolution, but very much within the broad framework established by the Germanists and Romanists. Somewhat ironically, it was the ideas of the Germanists that proved to be of particular relevance to the Revolutionaries: initially intended to support the authority of the ancient nobility, the idea of a Frankish conquest of the Gauls was readily adapted to provide moral justification for the overthrow of the old order. In this new perspective, the revolt against the nobility could readily be justified as the return of political power to the Gallic people from the oppressive Frankish nobility. It was in these terms that the well-known civil servant and administrator Baron Étienne Dupin (1767–1828) argued that France should, once again, become Gaul: 'Magnanimous people, regaining your liberty, take back your glorious name. You are Gallic.'[23] Similar ideas were taken up by the Abbé de Sieyès, who contributed to a fundamental shift in the self-representation of the French nation by developing them into a cohesive historical and sociological framework for interpreting the Revolution. For him, political rights belonged to a citizen because he worked and not because he owned property; it was through political commitment that men formed a nation. For him, the nobility was an alien body, a parasite. Echoing Hotman's *Franco-Gallia* ('kings are made for the people and not the people for kings'), for Sieyès the downtrodden Gauls had finally taken their revenge upon the Frankish oppressor. Although, as Matthew D'Auria has noted, he 'conceded that by relinquishing their privileges noblemen could become part of the nation, this required an unconditional acceptance and subjection to the will of the Third Estate'.[24] For Sieyès, the nation once rid of the nobility would be at peace with itself and composed of individuals contributing to the general wealth through their labour. Thus, in the course of the 1790s, the Germanist school became, in effect, the source of a new Gallicist interpretation of French history.

This growing interest in Gallic origins was given a further boost in 1796 by the publication of the popular *Origines gauloises*, written by the Breton antiquary and later officer in the Napoleonic army, Théophile Malo de La Tour d'Auvergne (1743–1800). This is the same La Tour d'Auvergne, it should be pointed out, who features in Girodet's painting, a remarkable measure of his prominence in Napoleonic France as both a scholar and a soldier. His scholarly reputation was built on his uncompromising argument for the continuity between the moral and physical character of the Celts, 'our ancestors', and the identity of the people of modern France. The Gauls, he argued, should be recognised for their virtues – bravery, frugality and love of freedom – and it was those same virtues that had led to the military success of the new French Republic. No less significantly, he added a substantial epilogue to his work in which he sought to show that the Gallic language – as preserved in the speech of his native Brittany – was the most ancient language of Eurasia, and the ultimate source of all the other great ancient and modern languages.

The methods of analysis he used were, even by contemporary standards, laughable, and his conclusions bizarre. Mystified, the modern French historian Jean-Yves Guiomar has understandably remarked 'The renown of La Tour d'Auvergne is completely astonishing; he was a soldier of worth, certainly, but by no means exceptionally so, and a scholar of the second rank'. No doubt rightly, he ascribes the author's success to the 'high favour that Celticism enjoyed under the Consulate'.[25] In fact, La Tour d'Auvergne's work was actively promoted by Sieyès, a highly influential figure in the Revolutionary government who would in due course become one of the five Directors who governed France; the sponsor of the coup of 18 Brumaire that brought Napoleon to power as First Consul; and thereafter, albeit briefly, an interim second consul.

In this context, it may not be a coincidence that the publication of the *Origines gauloises* was nearly contemporary to the first references in the historiography to Napoleon's enthusiasm for Ossian, the Celtic bard who extolled the virtues of a warrior society. Daniel Van Tieghem quotes from the *Mémoires* of Mme de Chastenay, who recalls a conversation with Bonaparte about Ossian, in May 1795. He also refers to a letter of March 1796 mentioning Ossian and melancholy addressed by Bonaparte to Joséphine, three days after he had left for Italy.[26] On the outward journey to Egypt, on board *The Orient*, Bonaparte read Homer's *Odyssey* with Arnault, his librarian, and declared that he preferred Ossian to Homer. Among the Ossianic poems which Bonaparte kept by his bedside, his favourite was *Temora*. He later carried a copy of the poems on the battlefield. Bonaparte's Ossianic predilections are further revealed by his indignant response to the opera singer François Lays's polite refusal to sing his *hauts faits* during the Egyptian campaign: 'As for Lays, I am vexed that he refuses to follow us, he might have been our Ossian; we need one, we need a bard, who would in case of need sing at the head of our columns'.[27] The poet Nepomucène Lemercier famously declared that in 1800 Bonaparte adopted Ossian as his favourite poet because Homer and Virgil were already taken (by Alexander and Augustus respectively). That same year, a medallion portrait of Ossian featured in the library at Malmaison, among the frescoes of those of the great authors, ancient and modern, whom Bonaparte appreciated, alongside such figures as Homer, Voltaire and Plato. At this time, the decor was primarily guided by Bonaparte's tastes, as he resided at the Malmaison until the autumn of 1802 when he settled into his official residence as First Consul at Saint-Cloud; thereafter, Malmaison and its remarkable gardens which contained exotic plants were shaped by the empress who lived there until her death in 1814.[28]

Bonaparte's enthusiasm for Ossian may have reflected a genuine literary predilection for Macpherson's poetry. But it should be remembered that he was already ruthlessly ambitious and deeply pragmatic in his pursuit of power and influence. Everything he did was related to what was dominant in his mind: politics and warfare. It could even be argued that he was incapable of considering literature apart from his own immediate reality and could consequently see the aims of an author only in relation to his own.[29] What was it, then, that motivated Bonaparte's obsession with Ossian when he was, first and foremost, a man of action?

A clue to the answer can be found in the close coincidence in time between the publication of *Origines gauloises*, the growth of Bonaparte's interest in Ossian, and his first campaign in Italy. Italy seems to have had special significant for Napoleon and, following his conquest of the peninsula, he maintained particularly close personal and political relationships with the so-called Italian Republic centred on Milan of 1802–05. With the establishment of the Empire, he then transformed the 'Republic' into his personal 'Kingdom of Italy'. This evidence of affinity is not surprising given that Napoleon, as a Corsican, had more in common, culturally and linguistically, with Italy than he did with France.

There is therefore a case to be made that part of the appeal of Celticism for Napoleon reflects the universalising agenda of La Tour d'Auvergne, with its claim that Gauls, Romans and Franks, their many conflicts notwithstanding, were ultimately united as common heirs to a shared Celtic past. This deep past was therefore peculiarly suited to providing a rationale for a new kind of polity that, by drawing on the claim that Celtic culture was the cradle of all the great languages and civilisations, would bring together all these long-separated peoples and cultures into a coherent and harmonious whole.

In this vision, the Celtic homeland of Gaul – in spite of the valour of its warriors – was never sufficiently unified to resist the conquest of their own better organised ethnic cousins, the Romans. The Romans had been succeeded by another people, the Franks, who were also ultimately Celtic in origin. Their retention of ancient warrior values had enabled them to produce a second founder of the western Roman Empire in the person of Charlemagne. Now, however, with the Gallic people of France unified in the wake of the Revolution, they were able to reassert their primitive virtues and become the nucleus of a new Empire that would embody once again the might of Rome, but under the leadership of its reborn Celtic *fons et origo*.

It is not difficult to imagine the potential utility of such an ethnology for the leaders of the Directoire and the Consulate, and Napoleon in particular, as the Revolutionary Wars went from being wars of defence to wars of conquest. The Celtic past – still so mysterious that a history painter as scrupulous as Girodet found himself having to invent the costumes and arms of his Ossianic heroes and heroines – was a venerable but conveniently blank canvas into which could be projected a great unifying imperial project that would once again bring together Gauls, and Franks, and their Roman 'cousins' in a single polity, a conscious revival of the common Gallic root from which they were held to have sprung. The potential appeal of such a project for a French general and political leader who was ethnically Italian, should, moreover, be obvious. Girodet's painting, then, can be seen as a great pictorial celebration of the re-unification of the Celtic nations, under *the aegis* of Napoleonic France. Napoleon, then, in this view appears as the leader of the new Roman Empire that has now been revived by the efforts of the Gauls' modern descendants.

That Napoleon was indeed thinking along these lines is strikingly evidenced only a few years later. It seems unlikely to be a coincidence that in the same year that Napoleon was preparing for the formal establishment of a new French Empire of which he would be the Emperor, Joséphine once again used her cultural power to promote the cause of the Celts. On 31 March 1804, a new *Académie celtique* was founded under the future Empress's patronage. According to its statement of direction, the *Académie celtique* would explore the Gallic origins of France and present rational, historical arguments. Prefiguring later nineteenth-century scholarship on folklore and popular traditions, the *Académie* intended to collect survivals of ancient Celtic civilisations and hoped to disentangle druidic religion from Christianity, discover the origin of religious beliefs, tales and popular traditions, as well as clarify national antiquities and monuments, not just in France but across the new Empire.[30]

Such seemingly innocent antiquarian concerns should not, however, distract from the new institution's deeper purpose. In the words of André Burguière, the *Académie* was distinguished by the fact that

> In place of imputing a Gallic origin to folkways in order to bring to light from this heritage the things that made the French people

distinctive, it sought at all costs to rediscover an original universal culture that predated Greco-Latin civilization.[31]

Its first secretary was Éloi Johanneau, the heir to La Tour d'Auvergne's extensive library and continuator of his literary and archaeological interests. He was therefore the nearest thing to La Tour d'Auvergne's appointed successor as the leader of French Celticism, and he explicitly justified the new academy's existence in terms that sustained the fantasy of Celtic unity: 'nearly all the peoples of Europe are descendants of the Celts, almost all are children of la Celtique: newly reunited, they nearly all form again today a single great family under one federative government.'[32] At this time, he claimed,

> when the French have demonstrated themselves so worthy of their ancestors, when, for the last ten years, Napoleon has led us from victory to victory [... and] is bringing their vast Empire back to life, it has become more interesting to amass the facts that Illustrate the history of its ancient inhabitants.[33]

The Imperial commitment to Celticism is further evidenced in the wider cultural activity of the period. In the same year as the new *Académie*'s foundation, the composer Jean-François Le Sueur had a notable hit with his opera 'Ossian ou les Bardes', which attracted Napoleon's favour and gained Le Sueur the cross of the Legion of Honour. And it is equally striking that Cesarotti, who had translated Ossian into Italian in 1763, was especially favoured by Napoleon and in his turn flattered the Emperor by calling him the 'Emperor of the Celts'.

Nevertheless, the Roman heritage, not least in the field of warfare and politics, was not easily dismissed. The veneration of ancient Rome was shared by many leaders of the Revolution including Napoleon himself. During his expedition in Egypt (1798), he pointed to the Romans as examples for his soldiers to follow and considered himself as a successor to Scipio and Caesar. As emperor of the French, king of Italy, master of Rome, overlord of the Pope, protector of the Federation of the Rhine, Napoleon succeeded the German emperors as heads of the Holy Roman Empire (a title which had lapsed in 1806). He was then heir to Charlemagne, and through Charlemagne, the heir of all the former Caesars. And so, it was the work of the old Caesars that he attempted to reproduce through an analogy of imagination, situation and character, but in a very different Europe.[34] But the particular value of the Celticist narrative, as constructed by La Tour d'Auvergne and Johanneau, was its potential to absorb, rather than displace, the classical Roman values that retained such cultural prestige.

Of course, as Girodet's painting implicitly acknowledged, the great hold-out against Napoleon's expanding empire remained the rival British empire. Is it too much to suggest that implicit in the Ossianic tales, as interpreted by Girodet, is yet another unifying narrative that would have had distinct appeal for Napoleon? It is worth recalling the terms in which the *Académie celtique* would later defend the authenticity of Macpherson's 'translation'. Those Englishmen who doubted Macpherson were motivated not by dispassionate scholarship but by jealousy that derived from the Scottish rediscovery of their ancient bardic culture and the Celtic Homer in whom it was personified. It is worth remembering that in the years around 1800, French sympathy with the Scottish Highlands continued to be shaped by recollections of the ancient alliance between France and Scotland and, more recently, by French efforts to protect and support the Jacobite dynasty. The events of the '45 remained within living memory, and with them the close links between France and Scotland. In this eulogy of Gallic, Highland culture which the Ossianic corpus embodied, France becomes the new repository of Celtic culture and the potential deliverer from Anglo-Saxon oppression of the living heirs of Scotland's Celtic past.

How else, in the event of French subjection of Britain, would Napoleon articulate its incorporation within the French Empire except as the reunification of Gauls with their Celtic brethren of Scotland and Ireland, the modern representatives of the ancient inhabitants of the British Isles? If this is the case, then it would seem that Girodet's deepest message is that it would not be long before France and Scotland, Gallia and Caledonia, would come together in brotherhood once again, liberated from Anglo-Saxon oppression thanks to the Emperor of the Celts.

By using the Celtic myth, then, Bonaparte was able to construct a unifying narrative that transcended a potentially troublesome multi-ethnic and multi-linguistic reality. Celtic culture, in the vision of the Revolutionary and Imperial Celticists, offered a common ancestry that could strengthen perceived kinship among the Empire's many component peoples, rally support for an ever-expanding multinational Empire, and help forge it into a cohesive, multi-ethnic community. This was both retrospective – in unifying the polities already conquered by Napoleon – and prospective, by uncovering commonalities between the Empire and yet to be conquered territories, including, most notably, the British Isles.

My analysis has shown, therefore, the significance of Girodet's painting for the reconceptualisation of not just of the French state, but of the French Empire as the contemporary heir of Celtic Gallia. In doing so, it offers additional evidence in favour of the importance of cultural productions for forging political identities. In this respect, my analysis accords with Anthony D. Smith's emphasis on history and culture as fundamental components of modern nationalism, as against the more economistic and technologistic interpretations offered by the pioneer scholars of nationalism, Ernest Gellner and Benedict Anderson, with their emphasis on mass print publication as the precondition for the emergence of the modern national state.[35]

At the same time, however, this study points to a dimension of the cultural formation of the modern state that has been rather neglected as a result of an understandable but somewhat restrictive focus on the nation-state. There is a danger that this focus may distract attention from appropriately sustained consideration of the ways that complex multi-national polities that have sought to accommodate ethno-linguistic and cultural diversity. While it is easy to regard such polities as lessons in failure – the ethnic conflicts of the 1990s were ultimately built, after all, on the ruins of the Hapsburg and Ottoman Empires – it should be remembered that multi-ethnic polities had previously enjoyed a long history of success. Until the emergence of the modern national state, the superpowers of Europe were almost all 'composite monarchies' that derived their unity from common loyalty to a ruling dynasty rather than real or imagined ethnic uniformity. Had it not been for the shock of the First World War, moreover, it is quite possible that the Habsburg empire would have survived in some form or another far into the future, enabling its model of cohabitation of cultures, languages and peoples to become an alternative to the ethnic nationalism that became increasingly dominant over the nineteenth and twentieth centuries. Similarly, had Napoleon been content to maintain the Peace of Amiens and avoid further warfare, it is by no means impossible that Celticism might have flourished as the official ideology of an enduring multi-national Empire in Western Europe. No less significantly, we should not entirely forget the United Kingdom, a multi-national polity that reached its apogee of unity and confidence at just the moment ethnic nationalism was becoming a force to be reckoned with in the rest of Europe. While Ireland sought and obtained its independence long ago, and the relations between Scotland and the rest of the Union is undoubtedly under stress at present, the British state represents yet another model that presents a fascinating, if inevitably impure, counter-example to the ethno-nationalisms that have been the focus of recent scholarship.

Girodet's painting, then, is a fascinating embodiment of a specific moment in French history when the Celtic past was reimagined as a potential source of unity through diversity, rather than unity through uniformity. It reminds us that ethnic nationalism is not the only model for modern statehood, and that forms of multi-ethnic and multi-level belonging are available for historical study. The value of this kind of study, moreover, has never been more apparent than now, when the Russian invasion of Ukraine has brought into focus competing and now conflicting visions of political belonging in Eastern Europe – some inherited from the Soviet past, some from deeper pan-Slavic ideologies, others from the aspiration to attain a new European identity. It is surely time to give the same care and attention to the study, empirical and theoretical, of multi-national polities, as to their ethnic nationalist equivalents.

Endnotes

1. Bernard Chevallier, *Malmaison, château et domaine, des origines à 1904* (Paris: RMN, 1989), p. 39.
2. E. J. Delécluze, *Souvenirs de Soixante années* (Paris: M. Levy, 1862), p. 48, quoted by P. Van Tieghem, *Ossian en France*, 2 vols (Paris: F. Rieder, 1917), II, p. 142.
3. P. A. Coupin, *Œuvres posthumes de Girodet-Trioson, peintre d'histoire*, 2 vols (Paris: Jules Renouard, 1829), I, pp. xv–xvi.
4. Chevallier, *Malmaison*, pp. 66, 84.
5. The competition between the two artists transpires in the campaign launched in the press; The *Journal des Débats* (2 Messidor An X) always raised Girodet above Gérard.
6. Sylvain Bellanger, *Girodet 1767–1824*, exhib. catalogue (Paris: Gallimard and Musée du Louvre, 2005), pp. 240–41.
7. Girodet, *Œuvres Posthumes de Girodet-Trioson, peintre d'Histoire; suivies de sa correspondance; précédées d'une notice historique, et mises en ordre par P. A. Coupin*, 2 vols (Paris: J. Renouard, 1829), II, pp. 291–95.
8. George Levitine, *Girodet-Trioson: An Iconographical Study* (New York and London: Garland Publishing, 1978), pp. 175–95.
9. Levitine, *Girodet-Trioson*, p. 181.
10. Ibid., p. 175.
11. Ibid., p. 176.
12. Ibid., pp. 176–77.
13. Ibid., p. 178, quoting from Girodet, *Oeuvres posthumes*.
14. Levitine, *Girodet-Trioson*, pp. 178–79.
15. Ibid., pp. 179–80.
16. Ibid., p. 180.
17. Ibid., p. 188.
18. Ibid., pp. 190–91.
19. G. Huppert, 'The Trojan Franks and their critics', in *Studies in the Renaissance* 12 (1965), pp. 227–41.
20. The most comprehensive overview of theories of national ethnic identity under the *ancien régime* remains Jacques Barzun, *The French Race: Theories of its Origins and their Social and Political Implications Prior to the Revolution* (New York: Columbia, 1932), which is the basis for the account presented here; for the pre-revolutionary period and the nineteenth century, Matthew D'Auria's recent *The Shaping of French National Identity* (Cambridge: Cambridge University Press, 2020) offers a rich and well-judged analysis that uses its findings to question current theories of national identity and nationalism.
21. Jacques Barzun, *The French Race*, p. 80.
22. Ibid., pp. 167–83.
23. Matthew D'Auria, *Shaping of French National Identity*, p. 242.
24. Ibid., p. 273.
25. Jean-Yves Guiomar, 'La révolution française et les origines celtiques de la France', *Annales historiques de la Révolution française* 287 (Janvier-Mars 1992), p. 70.
26. Van Tieghem, *Ossian en France*, II, pp. 4–5. 'Bonaparte me parla des poèmes d'Ossian, qui lui inspiraient de l'enthousiasme' in *Mémoires de Madame de Chastenay*, I, p. 284.

27 'Quant à Lays, je suis fâché qu'il ne veuille pas nous suivre, c'eût été notre Ossian; il nous en faut un, il nous faut un barde, qui dans le besoin chante à la tête des colonnes.' Antoine Vincent Arnault, *Souvenirs d'un sexagénaire*, 4 vols (Paris: Dufey, 1833), IV, p. 35.
28 Bernard Chevallier, pp. 35, 44.
29 Frank George Healey, 'The Literary Culture and Opinions of Napoleon I' (unpublished doctoral thesis, University of Birmingham, 1954), p. 122.
30 Eloi Johanneau, 'Prospectus: Breton, Gallois, Gallique, les Trois Dialectes les plus pures de la langue Celtique', *Mémoires de l'Académie Celtique* 2 (1808), pp. 3-4.
31 André Burguière, 'L'historiographie des origines de la France; Genèse d'un imaginaire national', *Annales. Histoire, Sciences Sociales* 58 (2003), p. 48. Burguière quoted in Michael Dietler, '"Our Ancestors the Gauls": Archaeology, Ethnic Nationalism, and the Manipulation of Celtic Identity in Modern Europe', in *American Anthropology* 96 (1994), p. 588.
32 E. Johanneau, 'Discours d'ouverture sur l'établissement de l'Académie Celtique', in Société Nationale des Antiquaires de France, *Mémoires de l'Académie celtique, recherches sur les antiquités celtiques, gauloises et françaises publiés par l'académie celtique dédiés à sa majesté l'impératrice et reine*, 8 vols (Paris: Dentu, 1807), I, p. 42.
33 Quoted in H. Senn, 'Folklore Beginnings in France, the Académie celtique: 1804-1813', *Journal of the Folklore Institute* 18.1 (1981), pp. 23-33.
34 Hippolyte Taine, *Les origines de la France contemporaine* [1986] (Paris: Robert Laffont, 2011), pp. 1290-01.
35 E. Gellner, *Nations and Nationalism* (Ithaca: Cornell University Press, 1983); B. Anderson, *Imagined Communities: Reflections on the Origin and Spread of Nationalism* (London: Verso, 1983); A. D. Smith, *Nationalism and Modernism: A Critical Survey of Recent Theories of Nations and Nationalism* (London and New York: Routledge, 1998).

7. Transatlantic 'Scott-land': Re-locating the Late Waverley Novels within a Transatlantic Discussion

PAULINE PILOTE

Scotland had closed the last page of her history as a power among the nations. With a national life and sovereignty merged and lost in the union with Great Britain, there remained from the past a story unsurpassed for brilliancy, full of situations the most glorious, and illuminated by rare heroisms. [...] When Scotland had lost its distinctive nationality, it was necessary that all these, its rich store of history and legend, should pass by the wand of art into imperishable forms of beauty. [...] [T]he work that had waited for the hand that could accomplish it was fairly done by Walter Scott; the great chiefs and warriors of ancient Scotland will always be seen and estimated as they appear in his pages.[1]

These lines from an 1872 issue from the *Harper's New Monthly Magazine* celebrating Walter Scott's (1771–1832) centenary are representative of the general discourse on the legacy of Walter Scott through the nineteenth century. The author, Moncure D. Conway, like many of his contemporaries, envisages Scott as the champion of Scottishness, the man who managed to pass on Scotland's history and traditions, after it had been integrated into the United Kingdom. Yet, this magazine is an American publication, inviting us to consider Scott, and his close relationship with romantic nationalism and Scottish identity, on a transnational, transatlantic scale. Indeed, Scott's popularity was tremendous in the United Kingdom, but also in Europe and beyond, across the Atlantic, his poetry and novels meeting the general enthusiasm of many American readers.[2] His poetry and Waverley Novels (1814–32) circulated far and wide across Europe and North America, thereby exporting beyond the borders of the UK their representation of Scottish history.

Such an endeavour found a particular echo with American readers, who saw Scott as the defender of 'national life and sovereignty', so much so that they took lines from *The Lady of the Lake* (1810) to shape 'Hail to the Chief', a patriotic hymn sung in the War of 1812 against the English.[3] Scott thus became not only a paragon of Scottishness, but also a champion of national construction, at a time when such an issue was very much in the minds of the Americans in the decades following their independence and into the Jacksonian era (1824–48). Throughout the nineteenth century, in a context of growing patriotism, the American public repeatedly called for a similar writer who would transfer to the United States Scott's representation of a past grandeur and share his ability to shape a romantic view of the nation: the US Congressman and orator Rufus Choate (1799–1859), for example, observed, 'a series of North American or New England Waverley Novels would be eminently valuable auxiliaries to the authoritative written history of New England and of North America'.[4]

If Choate here called for a writer who would emulate Walter Scott and create American versions of the Waverley Novels, others at the same time tried rather to appropriate Scott himself and Scott's popularity: if many claimed through the nineteenth century that Scott had met a particular reception with American readers, different and more intense than the enthusiasm of his European readers, there were some voices that sought to give the US credit for their own role in the very shaping of the Waverley Novels. An 1856 issue of *The Living Age* exemplifies this view: in an article entitled 'Were All "The Waverley Novels" Written by Sir Walter Scott?', the anonymous author questioned the very authorship of the Waverley Novels. Founding the analysis on an unexplained secret in the correspondence between Walter Scott and his brother Thomas, then living in America, and on the presence of 'wigwams' as mentioned in *Rob Roy* (1817), the article concludes that Thomas – and not Walter – wrote, or at least participated in the writing of, some of the Waverley Novels.[5]

Such comments, although rare, invite one to re-think the initial close link between Walter Scott and this 'Scott-land'[6] that he had shaped and championed for these nineteenth-century readers. They reveal, beyond the particular interest the American public took in the Waverley Novels, that the versions of Scottishness delivered in his historical novels actually incorporated some foreign features and were shaped by images and references borrowed transnationally. Here, the wigwams in *Rob Roy* serve to describe the houses of some Highlanders,[7] resorting to a vocabulary associated with widely disseminated descriptions of Native Americans.

Here, Scott borrowed from representations that circulated at the time in the United Kingdom. Although he had never crossed the Atlantic, Scott was familiar by the time he wrote *Rob Roy* with writings about North American Indians, since he had read Indian stories in magazines and newspapers, was aware of the accounts of his countrymen who had emigrated to North American (after all, within the British Empire, many Scots had encountered Native Americans, not least as missionaries were sent from the Lowlands to North America or as impoverished Highlanders emigrated across the Atlantic),[8] and owned James Adair's *History of the American Indians* (1775).[9] In this, he participated in the general enthusiasm of his contemporaries for the customs of those they perceived as 'savages', recast as living evidence of the early stages of human history. These views were developed a generation before Scott by the Scottish Enlightenment, and most specifically by Adam Ferguson who delineates this conception in the clearest terms in *An Essay on the History of the Civil Society* (1767). According to him, humanity went through four stages and evolved from hunters to shepherds, farmers, and ultimately merchants. This stadialist view was taken up by several of his contemporaries, including John Millar in *The Origin of the Distinction of Ranks in Society* (1779) and Adam Smith, who saw Native Americans and Highlanders alike as living representatives of the early stages.[10] Scott, by repeatedly aligning his Highlanders with American Indians, drew directly from his predecessors: in *Rob Roy*, but also in the preface of *Ivanhoe* (1819), in 'The Two Drovers' (*Chronicles of the Canongate*, 1827), or in *The Pirate* (1822), Scott made extensive use of such comparisons. But it is in *A Legend of the Wars of Montrose* (1819), where the Highland clan is recurrently depicted as a 'wild tribe', that this association was most extensively used:

> Now, sir, you know the nature of our Highlanders. I will not deny them to be a people stout in body and valiant in heart, and

courageous enough in their own wild way of fighting, which is as
remote from the usages and discipline of war as ever was that of the
ancient Scythians, or of the savage Indians of America that now is.[11]

With such images, Scott directly echoed the view his contemporaries shared of Native Americans in the aftermath of the Seven Years' War (1756–63). By bringing Scottish soldiers face to face with Native American warriors, the conflict led to a revision of the earlier images of the Noble Savage conveyed by French philosophers Rousseau and Montesquieu. 'Indians' from the North American continent came to be seen not only as noble specimens, but rather as an 'irresolvable mixture of nobility and ignobility, heroism and brutality, dignity and savagery'.[12] Scott's Highlanders seemed patterned on this motif, while also integrating more contemporary fictional representations, like Wordsworth's portraits of 'Indian' characters or Thomas Campbell's elegiac scenes from his then popular *Gertrude of Wyoming* (1809).[13] Therefore, the recurrent references to Native Americans, as they appear in the early Waverley Novels, may first be read as the expression of shared representations, common to the literary sphere of the time, and an easy way for the author to bring to his readers' minds a whole set of images associated with savagery, ancient customs, and primitivism.

They are also evidence, however, of a thriving transatlantic circulation of texts, thoughts, and writers, precisely when, in the aftermath of American Independence, the two continents were being approached as two separate entities. The early nineteenth century and the Jacksonian presidency (1829–37) were times of patriotic expression, sanctioned by the Monroe Doctrine as it came to be known by 1850. If the circulation of the Waverley Novels has been studied and the influence of Scott in the United States widely documented,[14] one should also focus on the reverse journey and on how Scott's creative imagination may have been partly shaped by widely read American texts. Indeed, if American writers were themselves indebted to the Scottish Enlightenment and the works of the British romantics[15] and saw their own Native Americans in the light of stadialist history, Scott's later representations of Highlanders and his increasing use of comparisons with North American Indians seem to call for a further exploration of this transatlantic circulation beyond a one-way process of dissemination.

If *Rob Roy* already featured Indian wigwams, the late Waverley Novels seem to explore further this transatlantic connection: not only is Scott tapping into the now hackneyed association between Highlanders and Native Americans, he is using it to enhance similarities between Scotland and North America, thereby giving his construction of Scottish history a new turn. As Scott comes back to Scottish ground towards the end of his career with *The Fair Maid of Perth; Or, St Valentine's Day* (1828) and *Castle Dangerous* (1832), his last novel, he chooses to concentrate on the medieval wars between England and what he describes as an 'independent' kingdom of Scotland. Closing his Waverley Novels series, Scott focuses back on Scotland, but places its history within a more explicit transatlantic frame, blending representations of Scottishness and Scottish history with features borrowed from contemporary American writers.

American presence in *The Fair Maid of Perth*

The Fair Maid of Perth; Or, St Valentine's Day, published in 1828, towards the close of Scott's career, formed the second instalment of *The Chronicles of the Canongate* in which Scott returned to Scottish history, after having moved the plot of his Waverley Novels to England and Europe at large. With *The Fair Maid of Perth*, Scott revisited the Scottish background of his first Waverley Novels, but moved further back in time, towards what he referred to as 'the wildernesses of Scottish history'.[16] Moving away from the eighteenth century and the Jacobite context of the early Waverley Novels, the story takes place in the late fourteenth century around the historical event of the Battle of the Clans, or Battle of the North Inch, that took place in Perth in 1396 between two Scottish clans in front of Robert III and his court. Featuring prominently this historic trial by combat between the Clan Chattan confederacy and Clan Kay or 'Quhele', Scott shifted his interest back to Scotland and returned to his earlier focus on Highlanders portrayed as engaged in a twofold conflict – not only against Lowlanders and/or England, as in the early Waverley Novels, but also among themselves.

Against this background, these medieval Highlanders bear a strong resemblance to Native Americans, as they are portrayed in the romantic literature of the time, but mostly as Scott had come to witness their contemporary counterparts directly, involved as he was in the tour of Scotland of John Dunn Hunter, a 'white Indian', in 1823-24.[17] The late Waverley Novels seem to incorporate, to a fuller extent than the earlier *Rob Roy*, an imagery brought through the success of contemporary American historical novels in America and, further, in Europe. The fame of James Fenimore Cooper (1789-1851), then known as 'the American Scott',[18] gave him prominence amongst the other American novelists of the period. His personal close connection with Scott, as they had met in Paris in 1826 while the latter was working on his *Life of Napoleon* (1827), appears to have weighed on the writing of the Author of *Waverley* when he set to work on *The Fair Maid of Perth*. Indeed, quite early in the story, in a digression about William Wallace, Scott mentions the latter's encounter with Thomas de Longueville, more famously known as the 'Red Rover' (*FMP*, p. 71). The very mention of this name may well have been a hint at James Fenimore Cooper, who had recently published *The Red Rover* (1827). This early connection, which at first sight seems only a passing nod to the latest production of a fellow writer, is however much furthered in the rest of the novel.

This time, not only do wigwams emerge from the Scottish ground, but the vocabulary used by Scott seems to owe a great deal to the scenes presented by Cooper in his previously published *Leatherstocking Tales – The Pioneers; Or, The Sources of the Susquehanna* (1823), *The Last of the Mohicans: A Narrative of 1757* (1826), and *The Prairie* (1827).[19] If 'Indian wigwams' are mentioned (*FMP*, p. 285), the novel also features a 'settlement' (p. 279), and even a canoe, as a character handling someone else's stormy temper is compared to 'an Indian boy [...] who will launch his light canoe, secure from its very fragility, upon a broken surf, in which the boat of an argosy would be assuredly dashed to pieces' (p. 237).

The comparison goes beyond a simple ready association, when the Highlanders are time and again designated as a 'tribe', and even more so when Scott takes time to describe the 'wild war cry' (pp. 52, 54) that characterises the Highlanders going into battle. Even though the Highland war cry was a well-known historical phenomenon, such scenes and such terms would probably echo, for the readers of the time, some of the pages of Cooper's *Leatherstocking Tales*, or other American novels then widely read, in which the Indian 'war-whoop', revealing the imminence of battle, was a recurring staple: in *The Last of the Mohicans*, for example, Cooper writes 'the third was the well-known and terrific war-whoop, which burst from the lips of the young warrior, like a combination of all the frightful sounds of battle'.[20] More than just a passing reference as in *Rob Roy*, the repeated parallelisms eventually enable an imbrication of the Scottish medieval Highlands with the North American wilderness.

Against this background, the character of the Highlander Conachar – central to the plot and to the love quadrangle around the eponymous Catharine Glover – bears many similarities with Cooper's Indian heroes, most famously exemplified by Uncas in *The Last of the Mohicans*. One may hear in the name Conachar the very echoes of this transatlantic influence, as his name recalls that of a Native American leader, the Narragansett Canonchet, that Cooper takes up as Conanchet for a fictional character in his next novel *The Wept of Wish-ton-Wish*, written in 1828 and published in 1829, the year after *The Fair Maid of Perth*. Beyond the choice of name, the whole appearance of the Highlander chief closely recalls that of Cooper's Indian characters. Thus, the return of Conachar to Catharine, after he has come back as the long-awaited head of the clan Quhele, resonates with Cooper's descriptions of Uncas:

> [T]he handsome, stately, and almost splendidly dressed youth, who, springing like a roebuck, from a cliff of considerable height, lighted just in front of her. His dress was of the same tartan worn by those who had first made their appearance, but closed at the throat and elbows with a necklace and armlets of gold. [...] His arms were profusely ornamented, and his bonnet, besides the eagle's feather marking the quality of chief, was adorned with a chain of gold. [...] He bore no weapon in his hand, excepting a small sapling stick with a hooked head. His whole appearance and gait [...] was now bold, forward, and haughty. (*FMP*, pp. 153–54).

Placed side by side with Cooper's portrait of the Mohican leader, Scott's depiction seems to owe a great deal to his contemporary's style:

> At a little distance in advance stood Uncas, his whole person thrown powerfully into view. The travelers anxiously regarded the upright, flexible figure of the young Mohican, graceful and unrestrained in the attitudes and movements of nature. Though his person was more than usually screened by a green and fringed hunting-shirt [...] there was no concealment to his dark, glancing, fearless eye, alike terrible and calm; the bold outline of his high, haughty features, pure in their native red; or to the dignified elevation of his receding forehead, together with all the finest proportions of a noble head, [...] the proud and determined, though wild expression of the features of the young warrior forced itself on their notice. [...] The ingenuous Alice gazed at his free air and proud carriage, as she would have looked upon some precious relic of the Grecian chisel, to which life had been imparted by the intervention of a miracle. (*LM*, pp. 528-29)

If the Highlander is straightaway described as 'handsome', the Mohican leader is similarly introduced as 'graceful', bringing to both portraits a highly pictural dimension: if Uncas seems to have been carved by 'a Grecian chisel' and recalls classic statuary, Scott's depiction of his Highlander chief against a 'cliff of considerable height' calls to mind more contemporary romantic paintings of the Scottish Highlands. Both are distinguished by their majestic outlook and regal attributes, while their gear marks their affiliation – '[a] tartan [...] closed at the throat and elbows with a necklace and armlets of gold' or 'a green and fringed hunting-shirt [disclosing] the proud and determined, though wild expression of the features of the young warrior'. Scott's Conachar, 'bold, forward, and haughty', closely echoes Cooper's portrait of the 'dark, glancing, fearless eye, alike terrible and calm; the bold outline of [the] high, haughty features' of his Indian hero. Both framed through the admiring eyes of a young woman (Catharine Glover for one, Alice Munro for the other), whom they have taken upon themselves to protect, they eventually stand as embodiments of the Noble Savage, inherited from the eighteenth century. Besides, even their plots show similarities: if Conachar is part of the web of love interests surrounding the fair maid of Perth, his plea is soon set aside, as deemed unfit by Catharine's father, just as the romantic relationship between the Indian Uncas and the daughter of the Scottish Colonel Munro is discarded by Cooper.

Beyond parallelisms, Scott's novel seems to bear even more heavily the mark of Cooper's *Last of the Mohicans* in one of the other subplots of the general story, that connected with the historical event of the Battle of the Clans. Indeed, the intricate love quadrangle between Henry Smith, the citizen of Perth, Conachar the Highlander, and the duke of Rothesay, the son of Robert III, vying for the hand of the fair maid of Perth, plays out against the general backdrop of a feud between Conachar's clan Quhele and their long-time enemy clan Chattan, that will end in the bloody Battle of the North Inch. This feud between clans – or 'tribes' as they are repeatedly called – reminds the reader of the war between the Hurons and the Mohicans that forms the background of *The Last of the Mohicans*. There, Cooper similarly brings the Seven Years' War between the French and the British together with a long-standing feud between the Hurons and the Mohicans, two Native American peoples – or 'Indian tribes' as they are called in the text. The layout, and also the very terms used by Scott, recall Cooper's novel as the face-off between the two Highland clans, described as two 'primitive nations' (*FMP*, 296) fighting against one another closely echoes Cooper's own 'war of the nation[s]' (*LM*, 842) placed within the larger context of the Seven Years' War.

Scott's story thus introduces us to a world of chaos and violence that departs quite a lot from the earlier Waverley Novels set in Jacobite Scotland. If the Battle of Prestonpans, for instance, as featured in *Waverley; Or, 'Tis Sixty Years Since* (1814), is only described from the remote position of the eponymous character, *The Fair Maid of Perth* gives ample room to the dark and violent events it contains. The bloodbath of the final battle is now described in detail:

> For an instant or two the front lines, hewing at each other with their long swords, seemed engaged in a succession of single combats; but

the second and third ranks soon came up on either side, actuated alike by the eagerness of hatred and the thirst of honour, pressed through the intervals, and rendered the scene a tumultuous chaos, over which the huge swords rose and sunk, some still glittering, others streaming with blood, appearing, from the wild rapidity with which they were swayed, rather to be put in motion by some complicated machinery than to be wielded by human hands. [...] [B]lood flowed fast, and the groans of those who fell began to mingle with the cries of those who fought. (*FMP*, p. 369)

This grisly scene is actually prepared by a gradual expansion of the violence through a story full of severed limbs, deep and bloody wounds, street fights, skirmishes, and overall chaos. As such, it seems further from the early Waverley Novels, with their tamed-down, or averted moments of violence, and closer to the bloodier, gorier scenes to be found in Cooper, who features intensive hand-to-hand combat and bloody massacres with wrenched out hearts, or babies dashed against rocks. As Scott makes Robert III say: 'In Scotland, the first words stammered by an infant, and the last uttered by a dying grey-beard, are "combat—blood—revenge"' (*FMP*, 230). With such outbursts of graphic brutality, Scott seems to bring to Scottish ground what his British contemporaries described in tales of violence and bloodshed taking place exclusively on the North American Frontier.[21]

More than a simple passing reference to Native Americans in portrayals of Highlanders, the later Waverley Novels seem to make an extensive use of images and representations drawn from stories of the Frontier. Scott integrates elements developed by contemporary novelists, whose spearhead is James Fenimore Cooper, as the most popular of them all and the more generally sold, read, and commented on by British readers at the time.[22] By using plot elements, narrative devices, and recurrent echoes and motifs, Scott goes beyond merely tapping into a shared imagination inherited from the Scottish Enlightenment and early romantic poetry to bring elements of Frontier stories into his depictions of the Highlands. Thereby, he fosters a genuine parallelism between the Scottish medieval Highlands and the North American stage, which in the post-Independence context departs from the earlier view of Scottish history as developed in the Waverley Novels and asks for a repositioning of the perception of Scottish, and therefore British, history, towards the end of the series.

Re-evaluating British history in the late Waverley Novels

The region around Perth thus emerges as a world of violence and sometimes chaos, where the 'wildernesses of Scottish history', as announced in the introduction, echo another transatlantic wilderness and the wars that North America harboured before it became independent. The feud between the two Highland clans is set against two other, more long-standing conflicts – on the one hand, the hostility between Highlanders and Lowlanders, represented through the citizens of Perth, and epitomised in the dispute between Henry Smith and Conachar, and on the other, the looming war between England and an independent Scotland. *The Fair Maid of Perth* is thus built upon a threefold conflict that shapes the general atmosphere of the novel and makes the happy conclusion of the love subplot recede into the background. If the novel's end is built on the same pattern as the previous Waverley Novels, with an opening towards the future and a bridge towards the time of writing, the peaceful evocation of the descendants of the now married Henry Smith and Catharine Glover has a false ring to it. The bloody atmosphere of the novel places conflict, much more than love, at the heart of the text and violence looms beyond the conclusive lines.

If *Waverley* and the subsequent Waverley Novels set in Scotland seem to advocate the Union of the Crowns and the integration of Scotland within Britain, as symbolised in the marriage of Lowlander Rose Bradwardine with English Edward Waverley, *The Fair Maid of Perth* seems to tell a different story. The links woven between medieval Scotland and the setting of North American warfare, as narrated by James Fenimore Cooper, call for a revisiting of British history as initially told by Scott. Far from a history of aborted rebellions against what is presented as the natural path of progress and history, *The Fair Maid of Perth* goes further back in time to picture a kingdom of Scotland at loggerheads with England.

This view is even further explored in Scott's next – and last – Scottish Waverley Novel, *Castle Dangerous*. Published in 1832, as part of the fourth instalment of the *Tales of My Landlord* series, it comes alongside *Count Robert of Paris* (1832), and after *Anne of Geierstein; or The Maiden of the Mist* (1829). These two follow up on Scott's choice of exploring further the European medieval scene with eleventh-century Constantinople in *Count Robert of Paris* and fifteenth-century Switzerland in *Anne of Geierstein*. But for his last novel, Scott eventually returns one more time to medieval Scotland, with a plot that this time centres on Castle Douglas in Lanarkshire, at a period when it was contested within the larger context of the First War of Scottish Independence in the early fourteenth century. First alluded to as a distant backdrop in *The Fair Maid of Perth*, and then forming the direct historical frame of Scott's last novel, the Wars of Independence against English invasion are Scott's last setting for the concluding volumes of the Waverley Novels series, a choice that echoes even louder the themes of Cooper's American historical novels. Scott was himself familiar with American history and Fiona Robertson counts about two hundred works relating to North America in his library at Abbotsford.[23]

Not only are the Borders repeatedly referred to as 'the English frontier',[24] where the name 'Frontier' would have had a particular ring to nineteenth-century ears, but the two novels feature prominently the notion of independence. Although completely off the historical span of the plot, William Wallace appears recurrently in *The Fair Maid of Perth*. Described as 'the celebrated patriot [who] had for a time expelled the English invaders from his native country' (*FMP*, pp. 70–71), he becomes, alongside Robert Bruce, also mentioned in the text, a paragon for the fighting spirit of the medieval Scots, be they Highlanders or Lowlanders. *Castle Dangerous*, situated in 1307 Lanarkshire, features even more prominently Wallace and Bruce, now more aptly belonging to the historical frame of the plot. Although they do not appear as characters in the story, leaving the historical peg to the Earl of Pembroke, defeated by Bruce himself in a plot ellipsis, they are still brought up many times in the novel. The importance of Robert Bruce is announced from the first lines of the preface, as Scott acknowledges Barbour's *The Brus* (c. 1375) as the basis of the novel to come, and Wallace is repeatedly called for through the text as the emblem of the Scottish fight and 'the Champion of Scotland' (*CD*, p. 132). Thus recast as 'the patriot Wallace' (p. 110), and pitted against 'the tyrant Edward' (p. 149), he becomes the embodiment of a Scotland fighting for its liberties and its independence.

Indeed, this time, contrary to *The Fair Maid of Perth*, the opposition at the core of the novel is not between Highland clans, but between England and Scotland, and is re-envisioned not in the terms of a struggle between conflicted kingdoms, but as a war between nations. If the 'Scottish war of independence' is named as early as the introduction, it becomes, later in the novel, 'a bloody settlement of a national quarrel' (*CD*, p. 15), and is eventually reframed simply as 'the national quarrel' (*CD*, p. 151). If, as in *The Fair Maid of Perth*, *Castle Dangerous* places war and battles at the forefront of the plot, it repositions this time the love subplots very far at the back of a novel that now revolves almost entirely around the build-up to the conflict. Thus given centre stage, the contest for Castle Douglas is represented as a step towards the Battle of Bannockburn, itself eventually mentioned towards the conclusion of the novel. When *The Fair Maid of Perth* still opened on the future and the nineteenth-century descendants of Henry Smith and Catharine Glover, *Castle Dangerous* concludes on the (re)unions of the two main couples, but refrains from bridging the gap towards the time of writing. Rather than prolonging the novel towards reconciliation and a symbolic Union of the Crowns, *Castle Dangerous* provides an open ending, but one that foregrounds conflict and radical opposition between England and Scotland:

> This surrender of Douglas Castle upon the Palm Sunday of 19th March, 1306–7, was the beginning of a career of conquest which was uninterrupted, in which the greater part of the strengths and fortresses of Scotland were yielded to those who asserted the liberty of their country, until the crowning mercy was gained on the celebrated field of Bannockburn, where the English sustained a defeat more disastrous than is mentioned upon any other occasion in their annals. (p. 186)

The conflict, here reimagined as a war of independence between two nations, and the words chosen by Scott to describe it, must have echoed for the readers of the time the more recent war of American Independence, and the way it came to be part of collective memory through the surge of historical novels taking it as their central focus in the 1820s and in the wake of James Fenimore Cooper's *The Spy; A Tale of the Neutral Ground* (1821). Describing the fighting Scots as 'the obstinate rebels of this country' (*CD*, 98), or even as 'gentlemen of Scotland, who are now in arms, as they say, for the defence of their liberties' (*CD*, 135), Scott applies an anachronistic frame onto the war and establishes a parallelism, through a shared rhetoric, between the medieval battle and the American war of independence.

Here again, the influence of Cooper's first historical novel, *The Spy*, may be perceptible in the images used by Scott but also in the structure of the novel. Telling the story of the American Revolution through the adventures of a family living in a house on the 'neutral ground' between the two armies, the novel bears striking similarities with Scott's *Castle Dangerous*, itself revolving around a stronghold to be reclaimed as part of a conflict set in 'a country laid waste by war' (*CD*, 11). Inhabited both by English soldiers and Scottish sympathisers, Castle Douglas becomes itself a neutral ground, peacefully surrendered by the English, as the battle itself is displaced to the outskirts. The aligning of the two places is rendered possible by similarities in the plots of the two novels and of their openings, in particular.

Therefore, it looks as though Scott, returning to Scottish history towards the end of his career, brings into his narration scenes and vocabulary imported from Cooper's widely read historical novels, with their focus on life and violence on the Frontier, the fight for Independence, and confrontation with Native Americans. The role of Scott as the writer who managed to give back to Scotland its 'distinctive nationality' has to be questioned. One needs to get out of the national frame commonly associated with studies of the historical novels that has prevailed ever since the nineteenth century, when considering that Scott resorted to tropes and scenes imported from contemporary American novelists. If Scott has long been constructed as this champion of a distinct Scottishness who built a representation of Scottish history and traditions that were meant to endure, the comparative study of historical novels on both sides of the Atlantic belies the very notion of a *distinct* Scottishness about Walter Scott's work. The way 'the great chiefs and warriors of ancient Scotland [...] appear in his pages'[25] bears the imprint of American historical novels which had initially borrowed from Scott's fame but were in time borrowed back transnationally. The ways of apprehending the past on both sides of the Atlantic therefore appear to result from a crossbreeding of vivid circulations on the transatlantic stage.

On reading Walter Scott's novels within the wider literary culture of the time, his influence as a historical novelist over his contemporaries is certainly unmistakeable. However, when considering his later work, a counter effect can be perceived. We are certain that Cooper had read Scott. We know through the writings of his daughter, Susan, that he avidly devoured Scott's Waverley Novels as they came out:

> It is quite needless to declare that Mr. Cooper took great delight in the Waverley novels; when the secret of their authorship was still a subject for discussion, he was among those who never doubted that they were written by Walter Scott, the poet.[26]

Scott, meanwhile, even if he did not read his contemporary's novels themselves, would have known of their plots and characters, as they were widely circulated across the United Kingdom. If Scott helped the American novelists to shape their versions of American history, novelistic representations of North American history in turn enriched Scott's versions of Scottish history and its characters. Such readings call even further for a repositioning of romantic nationalism beyond the borders of nations onto a more transnational scale and for a re-evaluating of the role of Walter Scott as the champion of Scottish nationality when apprehended through this transnational lens.

Endnotes

1. Moncure D. Conway, 'The Scott Centenary at Edinburgh', *Harper's New Monthly Magazine* 44.261 (1872), pp. 321–49 (p. 340).
2. On this subject, see Joseph Rezek, *London and the Making of Provincial Literature: Aesthetics and the Transatlantic Book Trade, 1800–1850* (Philadelphia: University of Pennsylvania Press, 2015) and Emily Bishop Todd, 'Establishing Routes for Fiction in the United States: Walter Scott's Novels and the Early Nineteenth-Century American Publishing Industry', *Book History* 12 (2009), pp. 100–28.
3. Elise K. Kirk, '"Hail to the Chief": The Origins and Legacies of an American Ceremonial Tune', *American Music* 15.2 (1997), pp. 123–36.
4. Rufus Choate, 'The Importance of Illustrating New England History by a Series of Romances like the Waverley Novels', in *Addresses and Orations of Rufus Choate* (Boston: Little, Brown, and Company, 1878), p. 6.
5. Anonymous, 'Were All "The Waverley Novels" Written by Sir Walter Scott?', *The Living Age* 48.616 (1856), pp. 664–70.
6. This term is borrowed from Stuart Kelly's title: *Scott-Land: The Man Who Invented a Nation* (Edinburgh: Polygon, 2011).
7. Walter Scott, *Rob Roy* [1817] (Edinburgh: Edinburgh University Press, 2008), p. 293.
8. See Kenneth McNeil, *Scotland, Britain, Empire: Writing the Highlands, 1760–1860* (Columbus: Ohio State University Press, 2007).
9. Tim Fulford, *Romantic Indians: Native Americans, British Literature, and Transatlantic Culture 1756–1830* (Oxford: Oxford University Press, 2006), p. 8.
10. For further development on the stadialist conception of history and the perception of both Native Americans and Highlanders as tenants of the early stages of society, see Troy O. Bickham, *Savages within the Empire: Representations of American Indians in Eighteenth-Century Britain* (Oxford: Oxford University Press, 2005) and Colin G. Calloway, *White People, Indians, and Highlanders: Tribal People and Colonial Encounters in Scotland and America* (Oxford: Oxford University Press, 2008). See also Andrew Hook, *Scotland and America: A Study of Cultural Relations, 1750–1835* (Glasgow: Blackie, 1975).
11. Walter Scott, *A Legend of the Wars of Montrose* [1819] (Edinburgh: Edinburgh University Press, 1995), p. 22–23.
12. Fulford, p. 41.
13. Kate Flint analyses extensively the elegiac topos of the dying Indian in British poetry and in American literature. Appearing in the mid-eighteenth century in British literature, the topos develops into the nineteenth century, with variations in the elegiac tonality on both sides of the Atlantic: *The Transatlantic Indian, 1775–1930* (Princeton: Princeton University Press, 2009). See also, Masahiro Nakamura, 'Versions of *Yamoyden*: Native Americans in Early Nineteenth-Century Narratives', *Arizona Quarterly: A Journal of American Literature, Culture, and Theory* 70.3 (2014), pp. 129–56.
14. On this subject, see among others, Eve Tavor Bannet and Susan Manning, *Transatlantic Literary Studies, 1660–1830* (Cambridge: Cambridge University Press, 2012); Emily Miller Budick, *Fiction and Historical Consciousness: The American Romance Tradition* (New Haven: Yale University Press, 1989); Raoul Granqvist, *Imitation as Resistance: Appropriations of English Literature in Nineteenth-Century America* (Madison: Fairleigh Dickinson University Press, 1995); Andrew Hook, 'Scotland, the USA, and National

Literatures in the Nineteenth Century', in Gerard Carruthers, David Goldie and Alastair Renfrew (eds), *Scotland and the 19th-Century World* (New York: Rodopi, 2012); Linden Peach, *British Influence on the Birth of American Literature* (London: Macmillan, 1982); Harry E. Shaw, *The Forms of Historical Fiction: Sir Walter Scott and his Successors* (Ithaca: Cornell University Press, 1983); Ann Rigney, *The Afterlives of Walter Scott: Memory on the Move* (New York: Oxford University Press, 2012); Fiona Robertson, 'Walter Scott and the American Historical Novel', in J. Gerald Kennedy and Leland S. Person (eds), *The Oxford History of the Novel in English, Vol. 5: The American Novel to 1870* (Oxford: Oxford University Press, 2014).

15 On this subject, see Calloway, p. 78 and Robertson, p. 108. Fulford shows that Cooper's very own Indians are actually indebted to the work of British romantics and are influenced by Thomas Campbell and Scott's poetry ('The Lay of the Last Minstrel' [1805] and 'The Lady of the Lake [1810]), p. 196.

16 Walter Scott, *The Fair Maid of Perth* [1828] (Edinburgh: Edinburgh University Press, 1999), p. 10. Further references to this novel are given after quotations in the text (*FMP*).

17 Calloway, p. 84.

18 For an extensive study of Cooper as 'the American Scott' see George Dekker, *James Fenimore Cooper: The American Scott* (New York: Barnes & Noble, 1967). Although many of his contemporaries used the nickname, Cooper, himself, seemingly resented the phrase 'American Scott'. He only made it clear once, in a letter to Samuel Carter Hall, the editor of the *New Monthly*, from 21 May 1831: 'In a note you call me the "rival" of Sir Walter Scott—Now the idea of rivalry with him never crossed my brain. [...] If there is a term that gives me more disgust than any other, it is to be called, as some on the continent *advertise* me, the "American Walter Scott"': *Correspondence of James Fenimore Cooper* (New York: Haskell House Publishers, Ltd., 1971), pp. 226–27.

19 Two later *Leatherstocking Tales* came out to complete the series: *The Pathfinder; Or the Inland Sea* (1840) and *The Deerslayer; Or the First Warpath* (1841).

20 James Fenimore Cooper; *The Last of the Mohicans, The Leatherstocking Tales, Vol, I* [1826] (New York: The Library of America, 1985), p. 842. Further references to this novel are given after quotations in the text (*LM*).

21 For a study of the enthusiasm of British writers for the Western and the American Frontier, see Ray Allen Billington, *Land of Savagery, Land of Promise: The European Image of the American Frontier in the Nineteenth Century* (New York: Norton, 1981), pp. 29–47.

22 Willard Thorp, 'Cooper beyond America', *New York History* 35. 4 (1954), pp. 524–26.

23 Robertson, p. 110.

24 Walter Scott, *FMP*, p. 100 and p. 226; Walter Scott, *Castle Dangerous* [1832] (Edinburgh: Edinburgh University Press, 2006), p. 136. Further references to this novel are given after quotations in the text (*CD*).

25 Conway, p. 340.

26 Susan Fenimore Cooper, *Pages and Pictures from the Writings of James Fenimore Cooper* (New York: W. A Townsend and Company, 1861), p. 17.

8. Questions of Identity on the Stevenson Trail in Scotland

LESLEY GRAHAM

This chapter sets out to explore questions of identity present in the travel accounts of a number of writers who, since the late nineteenth century, have visited Scotland on the trail of Robert Louis Stevenson. They include John Buchan, Clayton Hamilton, Nicholas Rankin, Gavin Bell, Hunter Davies, Michel Le Bris, and Ian Nimmo. These footsteps-travellers are generally eager to (re)visit the townscapes and landscapes familiar to Stevenson; to see for themselves any traces left behind by the author in the homes and museums with which his name is associated and to get to know first-hand places familiar from works such as *Kidnapped*, *St Ives* and *Edinburgh: Picturesque Notes*, gathering 'clues toward a proper understanding of the man and a judicious estimation of his work'.[1] The main motivation underlying those objectives is, often quite explicitly, to establish a unique and personal connection with what W. E. Henley called Stevenson's 'spirit intense and rare',[2] a description reprised by at least one of the followers.

Footsteps travel writing in general demonstrates a heightened awareness of the ways in which places and the character of their inhabitants change over the years, or, on the contrary, the ways in which landscapes and cultures have survived, bringing, as Christopher Keirstead points out, 'an awareness of the layering of heritage and memory into sharp focus'.[3]

The accounts of these 'travels in the footsteps of' journeys often combine biographical, autobiographical and fictional experience, their narratives shuttling between present-day reality, Stevenson's life story from childhood to adulthood, and his fiction. Time is often further layered in such a way that the authors interact with their multiple past selves, those selves that read Stevenson as children, or those selves that may have followed in Stevenson's footsteps more than once, as is the case notably of Nimmo who followed in Stevenson's footsteps first as an eighteen-year-old and later as an older adult.⁴ The accounts reveal the shifting identities – national and otherwise – not only of Robert Louis Stevenson and the writer following him, but also that of people encountered on the journey and of the fictional characters Stevenson created.

The 'endemic, obsessive re-enactment of previous quests', as Steve Clark points out, epitomises much of what we now consider to be 'postmodern' travel writing.⁵ Similarly, the cultural sites and heritage trails that have been created to support these quests are, as Maria Lindgren Leavenworth remarks in her study of what she calls 'second journeys', 'all features of postmodern culture in which distinctions between separate fields and between the modernist binary opposites (such as the distinction between past and present, between past reality and contemporary experience) have, to an extent, collapsed'.⁶ The accounts of these second journeys interact on many levels with Stevenson's own texts which are often woven into the travelogue; with biographies of Stevenson, and with the texts left by each author's travelling predecessors, often through quite extensive quotations. As Keirstead argues, 'the need to remap this traveling doppelgänger through the authorial self invites a particularly close, intimate form of intertextuality long understood to be one of travel writing's defining attributes'.⁷ The most obvious intertextual encounter is the collision between biography and autobiography, the foliation or interleaving (sometimes materially in alternating chapters) of biographical and autobiographical observations, of the present journey and a past journey or journeys, and of fact and fiction. These encounters also demonstrate an awareness on the part of the traveller-followers of the ways in which their texts and their journeys open up opportunities for an ongoing interaction between these different layers of experience. Stevenson's Scottish places had been thoroughly mapped in a number of senses – culturally, historically, and cartographically – and his followers frequently highlight their awareness of those who have preceded them on the trail and acknowledge the ways in which previous subjectivities have depicted the reality of the terrain, although often simply in order to claim the originality of their own approach in comparison to any forerunners. They also often explicitly anticipate the use of their accounts as guidebooks by future footsteps-travellers.

The earliest followers were able to connect and converse with living memory; with people who had known Stevenson, cultivating the acquaintance of characters who had featured in his life such as his nurse Alison Cunningham,[8] his schoolmaster Mr Henderson,[9] his close contemporary at Edinburgh University Lord Guthrie, as well as his friend and mentor Sidney Colvin. Later travellers added a supplementary layer of surrogate intimacy with Stevenson through contact with the successors of the original characters in his life, notably seeking out Lord and Lady Dunpark (formerly Kathleen MacFie), the modern-day owners of the Stevenson family home at 17 Heriot Row in place of Thomas and Margaret Stevenson, and looking for the present-day shepherd in Swanston in lieu of the John Todd the shepherd that Stevenson wrote about.

The official and unofficial heritage trails[10] followed by the travellers in Stevenson's footsteps include visits to the three houses in which he lived in in Edinburgh – 8 Howard Place (now part of Inverleith Row), 1 (now 9) Inverleith Terrace, and 17 Heriot Row. The status of the house on Heriot Row changes over time. From a simple address at the beginning of the twentieth century, it becomes a 'prime pilgrimage spot', to use Davies's expression;[11] a locus invested with the footstep-travellers' theories about the character and history of Edinburgh, at the end. When Hamilton visited Edinburgh in 1910, the house was for sale, and it was still unoccupied when Watt visited in 1912.[12] Findlay describes the Stevenson home as 'a substantial house of that drab-hued masonry which reflects the prevailing climatic conditions and even the grave conventionalities of Edinburgh'.[13] Rankin, like Davies, was entrusted with the keys to the house and invited to 'stay the night, to get the real atmosphere'.[14] Ian Bell reads it as a statement in stone, symbolic of the spatial segregation of the classes, 'with its ornamental balconies, its astragals, high ceilings, fine staircase and protective gardens, [it] was part of the argument – a matter of class, culture and anglicisation – that was rupturing the life of Scotland's capital'.[15] Various rooms in the house can be read and recognised through a knowledge of Stevenson's texts, thus Rankin realises that one of the rooms is familiar through 'The Misadventures of John Nicholson'.[16] In Stevenson's study Davies consults a photostat of a letter in which Stevenson describes new bookshelves but is frustrated in his attempt to find how they must have been positioned.[17] In this way, the present reality of the rooms is somehow augmented by the superposition of descriptions of them and the followers' visualisations of their past significance.

Gavin Bell was put off by the brass plaque that eventually appeared on the façade of 17 Heriot Row, declaring 'This is a private house. Not a museum'.[18] The urban fittings outside the house are modified over time to reflect the interest in what was now the starting point of a Heritage Trail, and this in turn shaped future accounts of what was to become an officially sanctioned site of literary pilgrimage. Hamilton notes the presence of the lamppost outside the house because of which little children all over the world sing 'for we are very lucky, with a lamp before the door'.[19] Watt later notes that there is still a lamppost in front of number 17, but that 'no one uses a ladder to light street lamps nowadays; doubtless some up-to-date Leerie does it by a touch of his wand'.[20] Eventually the importance of the lamppost for Stevenson lovers was endorsed by the addition of a plaque confirming its literary and cultural significance.

When there are no plaques at other places associated with Stevenson, the followers anticipate their creation. In the late 1980s, Rankin, lamenting that there is 'no statue, street or monument in the city to honour him',[21] quotes from a letter from Stevenson to his friend Charles Baxter in which he evokes the 'dreary thoroughfare' beside Rutherford's bar and jokingly but specifically proposes the creation of a brass plate *in situ*. Rankin regrets that 'there is no brass plate, high or low, at the end of Drummond Street'.[22] Today, there is a plaque on the very site identified by Stevenson, but Rutherford's bar is no more.

So the stream of footsteps writers systematically wrings out all of the biographical matter from places associated with Stevenson, an itinerary which by the 1980s had been branded as the Robert Louis Stevenson Heritage Trail. Some on the trail ask what Stevenson himself would make of the route dedicated to him: 'Would he, I wondered, be puzzled by a life explained, and a carefully delineated Stevenson route?'[23] Others, even as they visit all of the places on the heritage trail, are at pains to tell their readers that they do not count themselves among the tourists for whom it has been created. Rankin, while acknowledging that a sign on the railings of Queen Street

Gardens announcing that this is the first stop on the Robert Louis Stevenson Heritage Trail is proof of perpetual interest in the author, says he 'had a vision of blue-rinsed ladies and querulous men in stetsons following it. Like The Shakespeare Country, it was a tourist package.'[24]

Before there was any museum collection in the city associated with Stevenson, Hamilton gained access to the Speculative Society to see the Union Jack from the *Casco* used to cover Stevenson's body that Baxter brought back to Scotland. Later, the expression of disappointment with the vestiges of Stevenson's life on display at Lady Stair's House (later the Writers' Museum) became another common trope. Gavin Bell declares,

> As museums go, it is fairly unimpressive [...] I had fondly imagined being ushered into the quiet sanctum of an RLS Society, and browsing through rare editions of Stevenson's works in a book-lined study. Instead, I found myself peering at an extract of a birth certificate, old photographs, and a sparse collection of oddments in glass cases such as a pipe, a fishing rod, and riding boots. [...] This was all dead stuff, with no attempt to breathe life into them.[25]

For Rankin, it is not just the museum that is full of dead stuff, but the city itself: 'Edinburgh is a city of the dead where the freight of the past lies heavy. The living seem oppressed by a sense of the deceased and their illustrious works.'[26] The colour grey, like the haar and the rain, impregnates these accounts of Scotland in general and of Edinburgh in particular. Hamilton, citing Stevenson himself, calls Edinburgh 'the gray metropolis of the winds' while Queensferry is 'utterly gray in colour', and Colinton Manse is 'constructed staunchly of gray stone'.[27] For Gavin Bell, Stevenson 'emerged from the grey half-light of a Scottish winter'.[28] Rankin writes that in the rain, 17 Heriot Row 'takes on the hue of lead'. Later, the reader is introduced to 'The slate-gray town of Ballachulish'.[29] Le Bris's description of his visit to Edinburgh is similarly steeped in misty greyness. He describes a mysterious, mythical Edinburgh, a maze of vennels and dead ends, permanently soaked in torrential rain; a city that corresponds not so much to any objective reality as to his French readership's idea of the ghost-infested

Scottish capital. The tourist pubs where he is served hot toddies made following ancestral recipes are conveniently peopled with stereotypical seamen. He writes,

> c'est ici, ce soir, dans le vieil Edimbourg «battu par les vents qui soufflent de partout, détrempé par les pluies, enfoui sous le brouillard glacial venu de la mer, saupoudré par toute la neige qui arrive en trombe des Highlands» qu'il me semble enfin le retrouver, et quelques-uns de ses fantômes.
>
> *it is here, this evening, in the old town of Edinburgh 'beaten by winds blowing all around, soaked by rain, buried under freezing fog coming in from the sea, sprinkled with the snow driven down from the Highlands' that I feel I have found him at last, along with some of his ghosts.*[30]

The details of his account are correspondingly shrouded in blurriness. Places and people are consistently given erroneous names when he enumerates the usual haunts associated with Stevenson: Inverleigh (*sic*) Terrace, 17 Herriott (*sic*) Row, Swanson (*sic*) Cottage, Duncan (*sic*) Brodie's pub. This disregard for accuracy in the transcription of the details of present reality is coupled with a correspondingly acute interest in the unnameable and indefinable atmosphere associated with the city and with Stevenson's past presence there, just as the all-pervasive fog and greyness reflect the elusiveness of the footsteps-travellers' quest to recover something of Stevenson's spirit in Scotland.

To track down the child Stevenson, many footsteps-travellers venture out of Edinburgh to the village of Colinton. Jefferson A. Singer, visiting Colinton Manse in preparation for writing his psychological biography of Stevenson, perceives there not a trace of his subject's past physical presence but rather a reflection of Stevenson's boyhood identity:

> To visit the manse at Colinton is to see in a relatively confined space a great passion play of interior life that possessed Stevenson as a boy.

[...] On the one side of the garden is the church, symbol of convention and constraint, a bounded vision of omnipresent sin and repentance. Beyond the hedge and stone boundaries is the wild current of river, leading to the city, and beyond that, to the sea and lands of foreign peoples and practices. To find the way through the hedge was to unlock the constricted geography of Calvinism, to step out of the shadow of the steepled church above and find freedom from convention and debilitating shame.[31]

The descriptions of Colinton manse and its garden where Stevenson played as a young boy are similar in their reliance on Stevenson's texts which condition the follower-travellers' reactions to the site and structure their accounts of it. Hamilton, for example, recommends reading Stevenson's essay 'The Manse' as one surveys the garden, in order to better understand 'the process of his art. He has selected very few details; but those few are precisely those which produce the most vivid impression.'[32] He also calls on his familiarity with *A Child's Garden of Verses* as he describes leaping down from the wall into the garden, 'that sacred province' where the traveller 'may identify the very trees and bushes that are commemorated in many of these poems'.[33] Rankin also quotes extensively from *A Child's Garden*. He recounts his realisation that searching out tangible proof of Stevenson's past presence in the garden is futile thus confirming Stevenson's message in the poem 'To Any Reader': past iterations of ourselves and others are irretrievable.

> As from the house your mother sees
> You playing round the garden trees,
> So you may see, if you will look
> Through the windows of this book,
> Another child, far, far away,
> And in another garden, play.
> But do not think you can at all,
> By knocking on the window, call
> That child to hear you. He intent

> Is all on his play-business bent.
> He does not hear; he will not look,
> Nor yet be lured out of this book.
> For, long ago, the truth to say,
> He has grown up and gone away,
> And it is but a child of air
> That lingers in the garden there.³⁴

This frustration inherent in the quest to recover something of Stevenson's boyhood is acknowledged by his followers who nevertheless appear to derive some pleasure from repeatedly coming up against the impossibility, as if the difficulty of the enterprise somehow validated the worthwhileness of undertaking it. Jacinta Matos observes that Rankin 'is aware that there is no direct access to the past, nor an empirically restorable "reality", but only [...] encoded configurations of it'.³⁵ Rankin is convinced, nonetheless, that the ghosts of Stevenson's lost childhood make Colinton different and his coming across the tomb of a young Balfour killed in action in the Falklands in Colinton cemetery takes on a particular significance,³⁶ given Stevenson's own awareness of heredity both familial and affinitive.

The next station on the heritage trail is often Swanston Cottage, the Stevenson family's summer residence just outside Edinburgh. Hamilton suggests that one should walk from Edinburgh to Swanston to get the full Stevenson experience, 'although it is at first somewhat difficult for the foot-farer to find, because it is folded so aloofly into a little lap of the hills'.³⁷ He also highlights the connection between *St Ives* and Swanston cottage, claiming that chapter seven can still serve as a guide to the modern traveller, as can the 'intimately personal' Scots poem 'Ille Terrarum', or the essays 'An Old Scotch Gardener' and 'Pastoral'. In this way, Stevenson's original texts again map the space in question which when visited can in turn enhance the reader's understanding of the texts. Hamilton informs future visitors that:

> A legend on the gate to the grounds of Swanston Cottage warns of unauthorised intruders that the place is private property; but an

accredited student of Stevenson has only to send in his card in order
to enjoy the generous hospitality of Lord Guthrie.[38]

A few years later, in 1917, while convalescing at Craiglockhart, Wilfred Owen took advantage of that hospitality and accompanied a group of pupils from Tynecastle school who had been reading *St Ives* to Swanston Cottage, 'to get nearer the romantic heart of Stevenson'. Guthrie showed them some Stevenson memorabilia and offered tea.[39]

Guthrie anticipated the development that would later take place around Swanston. He writes:

> The extended town of Edinburgh will some day creep out to the foot of Allermuir and Caerketton, and perhaps surround the Cottage and its grounds. Long before that happens I hope that the eastern end of the Pentland Hills, embraced in the farms of Swanston and Hillend, will be acquired by Edinburgh and made into a people's playground. One thing is certain: the day will never come when Swanston Cottage will lose its interest for the lovers of Robert Louis Stevenson all the world over.[40]

Frustration is evident when the followers come up against a site that has been built over; when the map does not match the terrain and the key word used in this situation is often 'overgrown'. Hamilton, for example, claims that North Berwick is 'now somewhat overgrown with seaside hotels' but suggests that with some effort the literary pilgrim may still identify landmarks familiar from the beginning of 'The Lantern Bearers'. Similarly, Kingussie, where Stevenson spent the summer of 1882, 'is now overgrown with many monstrous villas of recent erection', but the follower with knowledge of Stevenson's texts 'can still catch some of the echo of the music that Stevenson heard there from the burn'.[41] Similarly, on the trail of *Kidnapped*, Nimmo is dismayed to find that the spot where Colin Campbell was shot has been covered over by planting by the Forestry Commission. On Mull, Nimmo notes that the very landscape of the 'Kidnapped Trail' has changed forever, due to the changes brought about by the dam at Loch Uisge.[42] The present inaccessibility of certain sites and landscapes familiar to Stevenson is generally experienced by the footsteps-travellers as so many obstacles to be overcome in order to truly connect with the life of the author and the fictional lives of his characters. John Buchan, in an article based on a walking holiday in the Highlands in 1898, short-circuits any attempts to find the precise locations described in *Kidnapped*, claiming that Stevenson 'romanced with his landscapes', although they were 'always subtly correct in atmosphere'.[43]

Following the Kidnapped Trail on foot is not for the faint-hearted.[44] Hamilton claims that to follow the adventures recounted in *Kidnapped*, the traveller 'would have to circumnavigate the whole of the peninsula of Scotland', and of the route through Appin that 'only a very hardy adventurer would attempt to follow [it] on foot today' since 'the whole locality is unutterably lonely'.[45] This is exactly what Ian Nimmo did in 1960, before returning to the *Kidnapped* route forty years later on the trail of Stevenson, David Balfour and Alan Breck, the Appin murderer and his former self.

To get to the tiny island of Erraid from Edinburgh, Hamilton suggests a somewhat fanciful itinerary that involves travelling to Glasgow through the Trossachs, then taking the Crinan Canal to Oban ('the common track of tourists') then an excursion steamer around Mull 'from which you will see Erraid form with a few hundred yards'.[46] Again, followers generally revel in the unchanged nature of the appearance of certain places associated with Stevenson. This is the case when Nimmo visits Erraid, and claims that it is no different to when the twenty-year-old Stevenson landed in the summer of 1870.[47] Rankin, disagrees and relays Stevenson's own surprise at how much the island has changed on his second visit.[48] And again, it is suggested that the experience of being on the island is best decoded through one of Stevenson's texts: *Kidnapped*, 'Memoirs of an Islet' and *The Merry Men* are cited. In what is presented as a remarkable *acte manqué*, the young Nimmo, just like David Balfour, becomes stranded on the island and trapped on the island and selects Paul Johnson's cottage as a shelter for the night just as Stevenson did.

Mull presents new difficulties for the modern footsteps-follower. 'If David Balfour tried to tramp across Mull today, the chances are he would be mowed down by a tour bus within half-an-hour', according to Nimmo.

The same author in 1960 had been frustrated by the vagueness of David Balfour's route across Mull and had difficulty finding it. He later admits, however, that he did not know about the existence of a *Kidnapped* map drawn by David A. Stevenson in the Northern Lighthouse Board's offices. In this case, quite clearly, Stevenson's text was an inadequate map for the terrain.[49]

These travel accounts frequently feature performances of national identities as Scots or non-Scots or quasi-Scots, as well as observations on the performances of others. These notions of national identity – Stevenson's, the travellers', as well as those of the people met on the journey in Scotland – are almost always bound up with another common trope in this sub-genre: expressions of nostalgia and notions of an irretrievably lost Scottish heritage. Nimmo's account of Mull, for instance, is framed in a lament for the disappearance of the island ways of the past. Similarly, Davies writes of Leith, 'You should see that area today, with tarted up pubs, nicely painted old boats and twee shops. Edinburgh's Old Town has also been poshed up for the tourists.' He adds that 'Pilton now [in 1994] has the worst stats for crime and Aids'.[50]

This nostalgia expressed by the followers for a bygone Scotland they believe to have existed in the days when Stevenson frequented the Scottish sites they are (re)visiting, and the even more distant Scotland represented in his historical novels, is often mirrored by their intertextual flagging of Stevenson's own nostalgia for Scotland towards the end of his life when he was resident in Samoa. Le Bris and Ian Bell both evoke a passage in *The Silverado Squatters* in which Stevenson describes typical cleavages in Scottish culture, but also his yearning for Scotland and the joy of meeting another Scot when far from home:

> Scotland is indefinable; it has no unity except upon the map. Two languages, many dialects, innumerable forms of piety, and countless local patriotisms and prejudices, part us among ourselves more widely than the extreme east and west of that great continent of America. When I am at home, I feel a man from Glasgow to be something like a rival, a man from Barra to be more than half

a foreigner. Yet let us meet in some far country, and, whether we hail from the braes of Manor or the braes of Mar, some ready-made affection joins us on the instant. It is not race. Look at us. One is Norse, one Celtic, and another Saxon. It is not community of tongue. We have it not among ourselves; and we have it, almost to perfection, with English, or Irish, or American. It is no tie of faith, for we detest each other's errors. And yet somewhere, deep down in the heart of each one of us, something yearns for the old land and the old kindly people.[51]

Several authors jump forward in time in this way, anticipating a later period when Stevenson had left Scotland for the Pacific Islands in order to establish this link between his final years in Samoa and his hankering for Scotland. Both Hamilton and Rankin quote from the letter Stevenson wrote to S. R. Crockett from Vailima on 17 May 1893. In the letter, which anticipates the quest of his followers to find him post-mortem in the more out-of-the-way parts of Scotland with which he is associated, Stevenson asks Crockett:

Do you know where the road crosses the burn under Glencorse Church? Go there and say a prayer for me: *moriturus salutat*. See that it's a sunny day; I would like it to be a Sunday, but that's not possible in the premises; and stand on the right-hand bank just where the road goes down into the water, and shut your eyes, and if I don't appear to you! Well, it can't be helped, and will be extremely funny.[52]

With this flippant conclusion (omitted by Rankin), Stevenson anticipates and subverts the impossible quest undertaken by generations of footsteps-travellers to recapture his spirit at the Scottish sites with which he is associated.

Tom Hubbard and Duncan Glen explain the paradox of Stevenson's growing nostalgia for Scotland in these terms: 'Stevenson's love of his native land is understood mainly by means of his absence from it. He is perhaps the most celebrated "Scot abroad".[53] Edwin Morgan in a review of a Russian book on Stevenson noted that 'both the author and the blurb-writer [...]

refer to Stevenson as an "English writer", which will really not do. Few authors have been more conscious of being Scottish, and not English, than Stevenson.[54] For Le Bris: 'l'amour sincère, intense, de cette histoire, de cette terre, toujours se doublait d'une égale urgence à chercher un ailleurs' ('*His sincere and intense love for this history, this land, was always coupled with an equally urgent need to seek out an elsewhere*'). This he claims, paraphrasing David Daiches, is due to 'une "objection morale" à l'Ecosse de son temps, sournoise, et pudibonde – rétrécie' ('*a "moral objection" to the devious, prudish, shrunken Scotland of his time*').[55] From afar, in Samoa, Stevenson's view of Scotland, as his followers note, is less judgemental, less complicated than when he resided in the country. Guthrie quotes a passage from Stevenson's final, unfinished novel, *Weir of Hermiston*, in which he underlines what he sees as an essential element of Scottish identity this time in clear opposition to English identity: a radically different attitude to heredity:

> For that is the mark of the Scot of all classes: that he stands in an attitude towards the past unthinkable to Englishmen and remembers and cherishes the memory of his forebears, good or bad; and there burns alive in him a sense of identity with the dead even to the twentieth generation.[56]

It is primarily Stevenson's Scottishness that is being explored by the footsteps-travellers, but following his traces in Scotland, while combining autobiography and biography, can make these writers more aware not only of the deep-rootedness and importance of that identity to the author they are pursuing as evidenced by their interactions with his later writing, but the journey frequently also incites an examination and questioning of the followers' own Scottishness, or non-Scottishness, or partial Scottishness. As Keirstead observes, 'following so closely in the paths of others invites critical questioning of oneself'.[57] The Scottish footstep-travellers make a point of claiming their Scottishness as an important point of convergence between their own lives and that of Stevenson, perhaps even an explanation for their identification with the writer. Others claim that their non-Scottishness is more complicated than it might seem. Rankin, for example, is at pains to invoke the legitimacy of his own Scottish heritage when he describes an interaction with a friend whose Edinburgh flat he borrowed:

> 'Scotland is a nation, but not a state'. Jim had said when I picked up the keys from him in London. I had an uncertain relationship to the country. My father was born in Glasgow and I had a Scottish name and mien, but I had never lived there, although I had inherited some sentimental pride in the place.[58]

Rankin's consciousness of his heredity is heightened aptly enough on this heritage trail. He considers himself a child of the Scots diaspora whose face fits but who suffers from the 'yearning of the deracinated' – another focal point of identification with the deracinated Stevenson yearning for Scotland from Samoa.

Stevenson refers in the passage cited earlier to an immaterial 'community of tongue' among Scots. The continuity of that 'community of tongue' allows Ian Bell to claim that Stevenson can still be heard 'in the speech of the Edinburgh streets'.[59] Scottish identity is indeed often perceived and conceived of through auditory rather than visual observation, especially among the often-recurrent array of minor characters that play supporting roles in the travelogues. This is the case when the working-class Scottishness of the language used by a museum attendant in Edinburgh is flagged by Gavin Bell when he recounts attempting to buy a poster in his own less marked speech patterns: '"Ah havana sold wan o' these posters for years. Naebody's interested." "Well, I am, how much are they?"'[60]

On Mull, Nimmo regrets in particular the erosion of that particular facet of Scottish identity associated with Gaelic speaking. After citing Stevenson on the extreme kindness of the gentleman who hosted David Balfour near Erraid, he adds that in 1960, when he made his first journey on the Kidnapped Trail:

> The people I met along the way were also the epitome of good manners, hospitable, tolerant, shy – and full of pride in their island.

It seemed to me at the time many spoke Gaelic or had a grasp of it, in spite of the language being under pressure in what had been a bastion of Gaeldom. But that was before the great people movement came to Mull, hand-in-hand with a culture change so that the accents of Birmingham, Sheffield, Manchester, the Home Counties, Glasgow and Edinburgh have muted the Gaelic voices to relative silence.[61]

Alasdair MacKechnie, a local historian, tells Nimmo, 'Many of the changes are for the good. But some are maybe not the Mull way. We're not a pushy people and sometimes our voices go unheard.'[62] In Nimmo's account of the recent history of the Scottish Highlands and islands, the outward sign of the effacement of national character is the impression that native accents have been replaced by those of people he does not hesitate to label 'white settlers'.[63] He goes as far as to draw a parallel between the present replacement of local people and Stevenson's description in *Kidnapped* of the cries from the emigrant ship.

Davies, who left Scotland as a young boy, also displays a hyper-sensitive awareness of questions of belonging (or not) in Scotland as betrayed by voice. In the National Library of Scotland where he is consulting a Stevenson manuscript, his attention is attracted by an impatient man whose books have not been delivered. A librarian tells him that he has not filled in the form correctly.

'It must be my accent,' the bearded man said sarcastically, in clear and educated Edinburgh tones. 'That's why you can't understand me. So sorry about that.' Then he sat down and waited, very huffily. Looking around, and listening to the voices, it did seem to me that most people were foreign, or at least non-Scottish.[64]

In his study of footsteps travel, Keirstead argues that this sub-genre of travel writing 'rather than typifying the form's past or its postmodern exhaustion, can actually propel author and reader alike to a deeper awareness and critical understanding of the politics of travel, especially in post-colonial contexts'.[65] Without going as far as to characterise Scotland as a post-colonial context, we can see a clear political subtext to these travel accounts and observe that those who follow in the footsteps of Stevenson in Scotland are often either willing to reassess their own national identities or experience an intensification of that identity, and may come to question the nature of the national identities of the people that currently inhabit the townscapes and landscapes associated with Stevenson. What they do not however question in their intersubjective, polyphonic footsteps accounts is the reality of Stevenson's attachment to and identification with Scotland, nor indeed Scotland's current embracing of Stevenson in such a way that his past existence and his writing are mapped onto the land in plaques, place names and settled heritage trails, and that land can be apprehended through reference to his texts. Scotland shaped Stevenson and he in turn has defined the cultural identity of parts of his native city and great tracts of his native country chosen to be projected and sold to tourists, literary and otherwise, from within and outwith Scotland.

Endnotes

1 Clayton Hamilton, *On the Trail of Stevenson* (New York: Doubleday, 1915), p. 5.
2 W. E. Henley, 'Apparition', in *Poems* (London: David Nutt, 1889), p. 39. Quoted by, for example, Gavin Bell, *In Search of Tusitala: Travels in the Pacific After Robert Louis Stevenson* (London, Picador, 1995), p. 49.
3 Christopher M. Keirstead, 'Mapping Genre in Contemporary Footsteps Travel Writing', *Genre* 46.3 (Fall 2013), pp. 285–314 (p. 294).
4 Ian Nimmo, *Walking with Murder: On the Kidnapped Trail* (Edinburgh: Birlinn, 2005).
5 Steve Clark, '"Bang at Its Moral Centre": Ideologies of Genre in Butor, Fussell, and Raban', *Studies in Travel Writing* 4.1 (2000), pp. 106–25 (p. 106), cited by Keirstead, 'Mapping Genre', p. 215.
6 Maria Lindgren Leavenworth, *The Second Journey: Travelling in Literary Footsteps* (Umea: Institutionen för språkstudier, 2010), p. 42.
7 Keirstead, p. 286.
8 In 1911, when Jessie Findlay published *In the Footsteps of R. L. S.*, Cummy was still alive and holding court in the south side of Edinburgh where 'her rooms are filled with many interesting mementos of R. L. S': Jessie P. Findlay and John Patrick, *In the Footsteps of R. L. S.* (Edinburgh: W. P. Nimmo, Hay, & Mitchell, 1911), p. 11. At around the same time, Clayton Hamilton was also, by his own account, a frequent visitor to Cummy's house. He writes: 'Until a year or two ago, it was possible for privileged visitors to Edinburgh to be taken nearer to the heart of R. L. S. than any one can ever reach henceforward by making a pilgrimage upon his trail. The death of Alison Cunningham in the summer of 1913 severed the last link that connected the childhood of Louis Stevenson with the living world' (Hamilton, p. 19).
9 Watt writes, 'Mr. Henderson was always reported a careful and accurate teacher. I had some slight acquaintance with him ; he struck me as pedantic, but after all that is the way of his calling, especially in its lower walks, and he had no pretension to scholarship, which except in an elementary form cannot count for an advantage in such work. If he did not make very much of R. L. S., no one will blame him.' Francis Watt, *R.L.S.* (London: Methuen, 1918), p. 30.
10 See Edinburgh World Heritage, 'Walk in the Footsteps of Robert Louis Stevenson' ewh.org.uk/trails/walk-in-the-footsteps-of-robert-louis-stevenson/ and www.rlstevenson-europe.org/en/. See also The European Network, *In the footsteps of Robert Louis Stevenson* (accredited in May 2015 as a Cultural Route of the Council of Europe) [accessed 6 May 2022], www.rlstevenson-europe.org/en/le-reseau/les-temps-forts-du-reseau/ [accessed 6 May 2022].
11 Hunter Davies, *The Teller of Tales: In Search of Robert Louis Stevenson* (London: Sinclair Stevenson, 1994), p. 15.
12 Watt, p. 39.
13 Findlay, p. 15.
14 Davies, p. 44.
15 Ian Bell, *Dreams of Exile – Robert Louis Stevenson: A Biography* (Edinburgh: Mainstream, 2014), p. 25
16 Nicholas Rankin, *Dead Man's Chest: Travels After Robert Louis Stevenson* (London: Faber and Faber, 1988), p. 15.

17 Davies, p. 44.
18 Rankin, p. 15.
19 Hamilton, p. 13.
20 Watt, pp. 29–30.
21 Rankin, p. 10.
22 Ibid., p. 57.
23 Alastair Learmont, 'A Walk through Craiglochart and Colinton Dell', alastairlearmont. wordpress.com/tag/craiglochart/ [accessed 6 May 2022].
24 Rankin, p. 14.
25 Gavin Bell, *In Search of Tusitala: Travels in the Pacific After Robert Louis Stevenson* (London: Picador, 1995), p. 16.
26 Rankin, p. 16.
27 Hamilton, pp. 9, 36 and p. x.
28 Gavin Bell, p. 10.
29 Rankin, pp. 15, 41.
30 Michel Le Bris, *A Travers L'Écosse* (Bruxelles: Éditions complexe, 1992) pp. 8–9 [my translation]. It is unclear who and what is being quoted.
31 Jefferson A. Singer, *The Proper Pirate, Robert Louis Stevenson's quest for identity* (New York: Oxford University Press, 2017), p. 598.
32 Hamilton, p. 28.
33 Ibid., pp. 28–29.
34 Robert Louis Stevenson, 'To Any Reader', in *A Child's Garden of Verses*, The Works of Robert Louis Stevenson, Swanston edn, 25 vols (London: Chatto and Windus, 1911), XIV, p. 59.
35 Jacinta Matos, 'Old journeys revisited: aspects of postwar English travel writing', in Michael Kowalewski (ed.), *Temperamental Journeys: Essays on the Modern Literature of Travel* (Athens: University of Georgia Press, 1992), p. 225.
36 Rankin, p. 35.
37 Hamilton, p. 31.
38 Ibid., p. 32.
39 Rankin, p. 41.
40 Lord Charles John Guthrie, *Robert Louis Stevenson: Some Personal Recollections* (Edinburgh, W. Green, 1924), p. 72.
41 Hamilton, pp. 37, 44. Occasionally, the overgrowth may be cut back to uncover a putative touchstone. Findlay describes the discovery in the Quarry Garden of Swanston Cottage, when a mountain ash shed its bark, of Stevenson and his father's initials with the date 1877. They had, he suggests, been cut into the bark in a spirit of 'freakish humour' since between the two sets of initials he had 'carved the bold outline of the rising sun – evidently a pun on his relationship to his father'. Jessie P. Findlay, p. 45.
42 Nimmo, p. 81.
43 John Buchan, 'The Country of Kidnapped', *Academy*, May 1898.
44 See The Stevenson Way: www.stevensonway.org.uk [accessed 6 May 2022].
45 Hamilton, pp. 38, 41.
46 Ibid., p. 39.
47 Nimmo, p. 48.

48 Rankin, p. 49.
49 Nimmo, pp. 57, 58, 60, 64, 76.
50 Davies, p. 25.
51 Robert Louis Stevenson, *The Silverado Squatters*, The Works of Robert Louis Stevenson, Swanston edn, 25 vols (London: Chatto and Windus, 1911), II, quoted by Le Bris, p. 13, and John Cairney, *The Quest for Robert Louis Stevenson* (Edinburgh: Luath Press, 2004), p. xi.
52 *The Letters of Robert Louis Stevenson*, ed. B. A. Booth and E. Mehew, 8 vols (New Haven: Yale University Press, 1995), VIII, p. 75. Quoted by Hamilton, p. 28, and Rankin, p. 39.
53 Tom Hubbard, and Duncan Glen (eds), *Stevenson's Scotland* (Edinburgh: Mercat Press, 2003), p. xiv.
54 Edwin Morgan, '[Review] N, Ya. Dyakonova, Stivenson i angliyskaya literatura XIX veka', *Scottish Slavonic Review* 8 (Spring 1987), pp. 132-33.
55 Michel Le Bris, pp. 13, 14 [my translations].
56 Robert Louis Stevenson, *Weir of Hermiston* (London: Chatto and Windus, 1896), pp. 113-14.
57 Keirstead, p. 312.
58 Rankin, p. 10.
59 Ian Bell, , p. 282.
60 Gavin Bell, p. 16.
61 Nimmo, p. 58.
62 Ibid., p. 79, 70.
63 Nimmo, pp. 69, 79.
64 Davies, p. 59.
65 Keirstead, p. 286.

9. The Safe Nationalisms of Hugh MacDiarmid and Compton Mackenzie

BÉATRICE DUCHATEAU

In 2005, under the Freedom of Information Act, the MI5 personal files on the poet Hugh MacDiarmid (Christopher Murray Grieve, 1892–1978)[1] and the novelist Compton Mackenzie (1883–1972)[2] were released by the National Archives in Kew. The MI5 and Special Branch monitored MacDiarmid from 1931 to 1943, mostly because of his communist and nationalist activities according to Scott Lyall's detailed account of MacDiarmid's MI5 file.[3] As for Mackenzie, a former intelligence officer during the First World War in Greece, he was kept under surveillance from 1931 to the early 1950s. The reports on him focus mostly on the publication of his book *Greek Memories* (1932). From about 1918 to the late 1950s, it was common practice for the Security Services to watch British writers, MacDiarmid and Mackenzie making two interesting study cases as they were involved in political and literary Scottish nationalism between the two wars. Thanks to the exploration of their personal files, this chapter will endeavour to disclose the intricate relationship between British intelligence and Scottish nationalism during the inter-war period. While the surveillance of communists and fascists has been heavily documented, a history of the Security Services in relation to the issue of Scottish nationalism remains to be done.

When studying intelligence archives, one is faced with irreducible 'epistemological issues'.[4] Indeed, what is disclosed is rather slight: MI5, the British domestic counterintelligence and security agency, has released only a tiny fraction of its records while Special Branch, Britain's counter-terrorist police force, originally founded within the Metropolitan Police in 1883 to investigate Irish nationalist activities, has destroyed much of its. The specific files under study seem complete though: no information has been withheld and all the documents listed in the minute sheets are available (eighty-two items for MacDiarmid, one hundred and twenty-five items for Mackenzie). But while the surveillance of MacDiarmid looks uninterrupted, Mackenzie's is not documented in 1946 and 1948. Despite the partial nature of intelligence archives, these documents still represent a valuable avenue of research to understand political movements and how they were perceived at the time, especially by governments that were guided by their Security Services to identify potential ideological threats.

With regards to the history of Scottish nationalism, the inter-war period is crucial as it witnessed the birth of an organised and unified political movement, a process which culminated in the creation of the Scottish National Party in 1934 and the blossoming of Scottish art, especially literature, with the Scottish Renaissance Movement. Building on previous measures like the establishment of the Scottish Office in 1885, this period also corresponded to the implementation of greater measures of administrative devolution identified by Christopher Harvie, such as the upgrading of the Scottish Secretary to Secretary of State for Scotland in 1926 or the transfer of the Scottish government departments to Edinburgh in 1939.[5] The pragmatic reasons behind such decisions have already been described by historians like Harvie and Richard Finlay: successive British governments implemented measures of administrative devolution to appease national grievances, safeguard existing state and economic structures, and oppose the rise of a national sentiment.[6] Paradoxically, the National Party was a rather insignificant political force at the time and, according to the aforementioned scholars, its impact on furthering devolution was very limited. Tom Devine, for example, described Robert McIntyre's famous Motherwell by-election victory in 1945 as 'a false dawn'.[7] Yet, he rightly argues that the conversation about the reality of the nationalist threat and its role in such decisions should continue.[8]

Requesting an expansion of the powers of the Scottish Office in November 1932 during a debate in the House of Commons, John Buchan, the writer and MP for the Combined Scottish Universities, suggested that the most important feature of the nationalist movement was its cultural dimension: 'The main force clearly in the movement is what might be called the cultural force, the desire that Scotland shall not lose her historic personality.'[9]

Could such an argument have played a part in furthering administrative devolution? Could cultural nationalism have been instrumental in convincing legislators and leaders to give more powers to the Scottish Office?

Historians and critics are also still coming to terms with the issue of the legacy of the Scottish Renaissance, of MacDiarmid's work in particular, and its influence on the rise of the nationalist movement. As a generalisation it can be argued that literary critics recognise the important role played by cultural nationalism, Alan Riach being a leading example when he says: 'Partly as a result of the re-imagining of Scotland by MacDiarmid and other writers, artists, composers, critics and historians, the 20th century saw the irreversible development and reestablishment of cultural and political self-consciousness and ideals of self-determination in Scotland.'[10] Meantime, some historians tend to undervalue its political and social influence, as demonstrated by the political scientist Jack Brand's dismissive comments in 1978. Then, he explains he does 'not believe that one can explain the rise of support for the SNP as a result of the thinking of these intellectuals', while paradoxically conceding that 'one may look at modern Scottish literature both as a symptom of an awakened Scotland and also as a force that encouraged some Scotsmen to work in the political field'.[11] More recent work, however, on the Scottish question by Ben Jackson has acknowledged the role played by cultural nationalism without, however, being able to provide further analysis of the 'elusive role of culture in Scottish nationalist ideology'[12] and the rise of political nationalism. Meanwhile, James Mitchell has observed that the 'Scottish literary renaissance is normally dated from the 1920s to around the middle of the century but its impact would be felt well beyond that period'.[13]

However partial, the opinion of the Secret Services on MacDiarmid and Mackenzie is a good place to start investigating the issue again. How threatening was political and literary nationalism for these government agencies? What perception did they have of these two staunch defenders of Scottishness and of these two representatives of the Scottish Renaissance Movement? This chapter will explore first how the political nationalism of the two writers was looked at by the Security Services and, secondly, how their writings about Scottish political identity and its potential translation into subversive nationalism were perceived.

Two nationalist extremists

Both Mackenzie and MacDiarmid had been heavily involved in the creation of the National Party of Scotland in 1928. Along with other writers like R. B. Cunninghame Graham, they helped with the formation of the party, ran for elections, spoke on platforms and published many articles related to the nationalist movement in Scotland. However, the poet and the novelist then both got caught in the ideological debates that led to the merging with the more moderate right-wing Scottish Party and the birth of the Scottish National Party in 1934. They came to be labelled as Celticists and identified as 'extremists' (an expression used by Mackenzie himself in his 1933 article 'Quo Vadis' published in the *Free Man*)[14] in the party because, amongst other things, they advocated complete independence which was not to the taste of the party's moderates who favoured devolutionary measures. Furthermore, the two writers considered the use of non-parliamentary means to reach this goal.

They both became involved in a secret organisation called 'Clann Albainn' ('Scotland's children'): this short-lived society was created by MacDiarmid himself in 1929 and the point was to 'raise the consciousness of the Scots voters by undertaking politically sensitive and illegal acts'.[15] In an article published in May 1930 in the *Daily Record* newspaper, MacDiarmid defined it as a 'Scottish Sinn Féin movement' and also conferred on Mackenzie the title of 'Chief of Clann Albainn'.[16] There were ensuing rumours that Edinburgh Castle would be occupied and the Stone of Scone stolen, which infuriated the more moderate leaders of the NPS[17] like R. E. Muirhead, who declared that same month:

> The goal of Celtic dictatorship is not in my opinion one that many Scots have sympathy with [...], we are getting in more and more members and doubtless if Grieve and Mackenzie do not frighten them away we may gain a number of young men and women holding normal Scottish nationalist ideals.[18]

This dispute piqued the interest of Special Branch, which investigated the issue over summer 1930 and interviewed Mackenzie, who denied all involvement.[19] No mention of it is made in Mackenzie's file while three allusions to the issue can be found in MacDiarmid's MI5 file from 1932 and 1933:[20] they all appear in reports drawn by Special Branch informants and the matter is raised nowhere else in the file, possibly because there was not much evidence this organisation had really existed. MI5 was also probably not really interested in 'Clann Albainn' since it had been set up just before 1931, before the Metropolitan Police Special Branch's responsibility of countering civil subversion was transferred to MI5 who 'became Britain's primary domestic and imperial security intelligence service',[21] thus explaining why the two personal files under study start in 1931.

The creation of 'Clann Albainn' and the friendship between the two writers were sealed by a common desire for the revival of Scottish cultural identity and interest in the idea of a Celtic revival. Recalling his meeting with MacDiarmid in 1928 in his 1967 autobiography, Mackenzie says: 'we discussed the possibility of forming a society [...] the members of which would be pledged to foster the Celtic idea with a vision [...] of rescuing the British Isles from being dominated by London'.[22] However, they disagreed on what a new independent state would be like: MacDiarmid sponsored the idea of a Scottish Republic when Mackenzie, a Jacobite and royalist at heart, held tight to the Union of the Crowns he wanted to preserve. As he later put it, 'I was strongly against any idea of republicanism and felt that the Union of Crowns should at all costs be maintained'.[23] All these theories were not endorsed by the NPS leadership at the time; they wanted the party to be taken seriously and appear as moderate, and they additionally warned against the negative influence the two writers might have on public opinion.[24] MacDiarmid was such an unruly character that he was expelled from the NPS in 1933.[25] Despite his lack of Scottish ancestry, Mackenzie, a native of West Hartlepool in England, was never expelled from the party but, after MacDiarmid's eviction, he gradually lost interest in the movement. The NPS, then the SNP, were, as Christopher Harvie asserts, 'left with the enduring stigma of being hostile to the intellectuals'.[26]

Overall, the nationalist movement was not considered a real threat by MI5. In his seminal history of MI5, Christopher Andrew does not mention the issue[27] and, when searching the website of the National Archives, one cannot find any other MI5 personal file dedicated to nationalists or Scottish literary figures between the wars. Scottish communists and fascists were the main focus of such investigations since fascism and communism were in fact seen as the main causes for worry in the 1930s and 1940s. It can be contended that one of the rare mentions of Mackenzie's nationalism in his MI5 records was not really due to this ideology. He did give a talk on Scottish nationalism at the January Club in July 1934 and, indeed, his suggestion that 'the Scottish people should be allowed to manage their own affairs' was transcribed by an informant. However, the report was in fact triggered by the 'friendly conversation' he had the same evening with the founder of the club and leader of the British Union of Fascists, Sir Oswald Mosley.[28] This account dates to July 1934, right after MI5 had acknowledged the urgent need to gather information on the British fascist movement, and immediately after the infamous Olympia meeting of June 1934.[29] The report on Mackenzie is in fact a cross-reference from Mosley's own file, proving that the topic of the night was not initially of real concern.

Mackenzie was not sympathetic to communism and its ideology, but a letter to Harry Pollitt, the General Secretary of the CPGB, was intercepted in November 1936[30] and his friendship with the communist and former Russian spy Wilfred Macartney occasioned the writing of several reports showing concern between 1935 and 1950.[31] MacDiarmid's file is, unsurprisingly in the international political context of the time, also filled with more reports related to communism than nationalism, bearing out the extent to which MI5 was then targeting that particular threat. Most of the material relates to the poet's 'twists and turns in relation to the CPGB' after he first became a member in 1934.[32] His surveillance started before that of other more prominent British writers including Cecil Day-Lewis (first mentioned 1933), W. H. Auden and Stephen Spender (both 1934),[33] possibly because he was a Scot. Despite the fact that communism was no real electoral threat in the UK, people were a little more sympathetic to it[34] in Scotland and the Red Clydeside activities that took place soon after the First World War had truly frightened the government.

Despite a few isolated extreme comments from some of its members, the main nationalist party – the NPS, then the SNP – already promoted nonviolent separatism in the 1930s.[35] Finlay records, for instance, a comment made by Lewis Spence in 1927: 'We do not yet advocate taking up the rifle, because that is a course I feel that would hardly appeal to the majority of our fellow countrymen – although it is the method I would prefer.[36] So, that is why when Special Branch transferred some of its files to MI5 in 1931, William Phillips, the head of A Branch (MI5 administration division), could disagree 'with keeping files on Scottish nationalists who, in his view, were currently "a perfectly sound constitutional movement, aiming at strictly limited autonomy, similar to Northern Ireland"'.[37] It appears that Special Branch was indeed defining 'extremism' and 'subversion' more broadly than MI5 at the time and, prior to 1931, they had been very much interested in nationalist movements. As James Smith observes,

> Special Branch conducted surveillance on a wide variety of political groups under the catch-all category of 'extremist', such as international anarchism, communism, nationalist movements, and the suffragettes. [...] Its reports made up a significant portion of many MI5 files. [...] Within this close relationship, however, certain tensions and rivalries emerged. For one, intelligence and policing officers had often divergent views of what constituted political extremism or subversion.[38]

As a result, Special Branch continued keeping a sustained surveillance of the more extreme or eccentric elements in the nationalist movement, especially when there was still some form of misunderstanding regarding Hitler before the war.[39] (While there is no Security Service personal file on Arthur Donaldson to be found in the National Archives, one can access a 1941 Home Office record dealing with his participation in the formation of the Scottish Neutrality League, and his detention under Defence Regulation 18B.[40]) One intercepted letter of 12 July 1941 shows that the issue of MacDiarmid's interest in Nazism was worrying the Secret Services during the war since the poet gives his thanks to Oliver Brown, a former member of the SNP (then Labour), for sending his new book *Hitlerism in the Highlands*.[41]

MI5 also investigated the anti-conscription advocates within the ranks of the SNP, like MacDiarmid himself, since they were seen as potential Nazi sympathisers. In a letter to SNP member Florence MacNeill, which was intercepted by the Inverness branch of MI12 in December 1940, MacDiarmid praises Arthur Donaldson's and Douglas Young's works and admires those who 'have taken on Scottish Nationalist grounds against the ill conscription'.[42] MI5 also intercepted letters in which the poet argues against the war by referring to Scots law and the need to safeguard the clauses of the Union Treaty.[43] Consequently, towards the end of his surveillance, between 1940 and 1943, he was more actively spied on, which was also linked to his living in Shetland, a Protected Area: Shetland was a very important location during the Second World War as it was a war base hosting thousands of servicemen, and also had to be secured due to its close proximity to Norway, invaded by Germany in 1940. Had MacDiarmid lived elsewhere, his case might have been treated differently.

As a result, a debate took place between the various London and Scottish officers as to the need to add his name to the so-called Invasion List. Undeniably, MI5 had real trouble categorising MacDiarmid; they could not determine if this 'rabid Scottish Nationalist', as he was described in several reports, was really dangerous or not. The conversation starts on 16 March 1941 with a letter from Lieutenant-Colonel Richard Brooman-White to Major Peter Perfect, asking 'Is this fellow on the invasion list?'.[44] If, at first, the former argues that 'it is probably unnecessary', he then changes his mind a month later and describes MacDiarmid on 21 April 1941 as 'a fanatic only too ready to give his allegiance to any extremist cause'.[45] When reconsidering MacDiarmid for the Invasion list in 1942, a London MI5 officer, R. Retallack, sent the following report to Major Perfect in Edinburgh:

I do not think it is necessary to add his name to the Suspect list. The Scottish extremists have turned out to be much less formidable than they were considered to be last year, and I think Grieve is genuinely anti-Nazi. [...] I think Grieve's Communist convictions go pretty deep.[46]

A month later, Major Perfect got a different second opinion from T. M. Shelford, another London MI5 officer:

It would be as well, however, to keep an eye on him, for I think that if he shows any indication that he is opposed to the war effort, it would prove that his Nationalism, which also goes pretty deep, is the dominant side of his political outlook. In such event, he would appear to me to be a suitable candidate for the Suspect List.[47]

MI5 officers were thus still wondering in 1942 whether he was more of a communist or a nationalist, a very unproductive question since MacDiarmid promoted John Maclean's earlier theory of a Scottish Workers' Republic and never dissociated communism from nationalism.

The Security Services also took the nationalist movement seriously when its members took part in physical action. For example, the Scottish Patriots, an independent nationalist group funded by Wendy Wood, were more prone to advocating violence and were consequently closely monitored, especially its leader who, presumably after listening to an inspiring speech by Mackenzie at a commemoration of the Battle of Bannockburn, went on to remove Stirling Castle's Union Jack in 1932.[48] The Security Services also took an interest in all the people involved in the actual theft of the Stone of Destiny in December 1950, a major propaganda coup for the nationalist movement, orchestrated by four students who were, ironically, supporters of the more consensual Scottish Convention of John MacCormick.[49] The Home Office was regularly kept up to date with those 'Scottish disturbances' between 1933 and 1954.[50] MacDiarmid had attempted and failed to steal the Stone in 1934 when he travelled to London hoping to steal it from Westminster

Abbey, which he visited several times, and carry it all the way to the Borders where he intended to throw it in a river.[51] This plot, however, does not appear in the MI5 records.

One may assume that the Secret Services did not even notice it in the first place because the project came to a very quick end when the poet spent all the money needed to buy the car in a London pub. As Alan Bold explains,

> According to Willa [Muir], MacDiarmid made several visits to Westminster Abbey but spent more time in his favourite pub, the Plough, in Bloomsbury, where he generously stood drinks all round. When his two fellow-conspirators, both rugby forwards, arrived by train from Edinburgh the poet told them there was an insurmountable problem. He had spent the money and could not now secure a Fast Car.[52]

The absence of mention may be also due to disorganisation and lack of communication between MI5 and Special Branch. As Kevin Quinlan puts it,

> Bureaucratic tussling clearly hampered the work of the intelligence services between the World Wars, but it alone was not to blame for shortcomings. [There were] problems of 'coordination, control, incentives, the sharing of information, and intelligence decision making' across agencies.[53]

This unrecorded failure demonstrates that MacDiarmid's attempted coups were not seen as posing a real threat to the British state, contrary to the actions of other nationalists like Wendy Wood or Arthur Donaldson. The conspicuous absence of nationalist references in Mackenzie's file also confirms that, after 1931, the two writers' political stance, however extreme at times, was irrelevant for the Security Services. It was only when the anti-conscription issue was raised during the Second World War that the dangerous potential of MacDiarmid's nationalism was re-assessed.

The 'Bonnie Broukit' Scottish Renaissance Movement[54]

In spite of the failed 'Clann Albainn' initiative, MacDiarmid and Mackenzie stood as inspiring role models for the next generation of nationalists who agreed with such energetic actions as the reclaiming of the Stone of Scone. After the actual removal of the stone in 1950, Mackenzie gave his support to the thieves in an article for the *Sunday Dispatch*. As a consequence, Special Branch 'questioned his neighbours about his movement at the time of the Stone's disappearance'.[55] Once again no mention is made of it in his MI5 file which, as suggested earlier, is maybe due to disorganisation between the two agencies. Special Branch investigated Mackenzie at the time because of the congratulatory comments he made in a press article but, conversely, they had not worried when similar views had been expressed in literary form.

The theft of the Stone of Destiny had been a major part of the plot of Mackenzie's 1944 novel *The North Wind of Love*. The nationalist John Ogilvie, the main character, encourages illegal action and plans the removal of the Stone but fails to do so in the end.[56] This form of political subversion – here embedded in fiction – might have been, but was not, investigated by the Secret Services.[57] Influential intellectuals and writers who were affiliated to the Communist Party were very closely monitored by the Secret Services for they thought that they 'were one of the most important avenues by which the Soviet Union garnered support in the West'.[58] However, they did not show much interest in the literary expression of radical nationalism or in the Scottish Renaissance movement as a whole.

Even though he was more famous at the time than the Scottish poet, Compton Mackenzie is today loosely associated with the Scottish Renaissance as such. Despite his friendship with MacDiarmid, his renowned burlesque Scottish novels like *Whisky Galore* (1947) have been seen by some commentators, in the words of Douglas Gifford, Sarah Dunnigan, and Alan MacGillivray, as displaying a 'condescending and manipulative view of Scottish people and culture'.[59] Others, however, reflect Ian Brown's less negative view when he suggests that in the novel and subsequent film, Mackenzie 'shows "natives" outfoxing the forces of central authority [... as] they subversively achieve their own forms of Highlandist island liberation'.[60] Certainly, Mackenzie championed the cultural movement and some of his works were trying to come to terms, often ironically, with Scottishness and nationalism. In one of his most famous novels, *The Monarch of the Glen* (1941), two young nationalists are members of a secret society called the Scottish Brotherhood of Action and plan a campaign to kidnap lairds (local hereditary landowners, or their nouveau-riche successors as owners, who often had quasi-feudal powers over tenants even into the twentieth century) to achieve independence.[61] Even if the novel is a comedy, this element of the plot might have worried MI5. However, they were more interested in the publication and re-publication of the third volume of his memoirs, *Greek Memories* (1932).

During the First World War, Mackenzie served as a secret service agent in Athens where he was known as 'Z' and became the head of counter-espionage under the leadership of the head of MI6 Mansfield Cummings. In 1929, he settled on writing an account of that time but, in 1932, he was prosecuted for violation of the 1911 UK Official Secrets Act: he was revealing in *Greek Memories* that the head of MI6 was known as 'C', allowing readers to identify Cummings.[62] In 1938, MI5 also paid close attention to the serialised publication in the *Sunday Dispatch* of his book *The Windsor Tapestry*, as shown by a large amount of filed press cuttings that are devoted to it and to the resulting scandal. The point of the book was to explain the reasons behind the Duke of Windsor's abdication, supposedly plotted by Conservative PM Stanley Baldwin and the Archbishop of Canterbury.[63]

The surveillance of Mackenzie was thus principally centred on his non-fictional and non-nationalist works while his imaginary narratives were being conspicuously left out. There was still an unnamed MI5 officer who chose to quote an extract from an article entitled 'Nationalism in the Scottish Arts' found in the *Manchester Guardian Weekly* of August 1933:

> It is not without significance that, with hardly any exceptions, those actively engaged in literature or music or painting in Scotland today are in some sorts Nationalists. [...] The election of Mr. Compton Mackenzie as their Lord Rector by the undergraduates of Glasgow University was a good deal more than a slightly comic accident.[64]

The report makes, therefore, an obvious link between political nationalism and the arts, revealing that, somehow, MI5 had identified the movement. But this is given without any form of analysis and the movement is never discussed again in their records. This is despite the fact that the writer's victory as the Rector of Glasgow University was a symbolic triumph for the NPS that had attracted much media attention in 1932.[65]

As for Hugh MacDiarmid's poetic output, it is only referred to briefly in the file devoted to him, despite its seminal role in fostering the Scottish Renaissance movement. One intelligence officer gives a positive literary assessment of his work when he says that 'this man writes rather good revolutionary poetry' on 21 December 1931[66] and MacDiarmid's 'First Hymn to Lenin' appears in the poet's letter of application for membership to the CPGB in 1934.[67] So, once again, it is his communist stance that aroused interest. Yet, in March 1941, when forwarding MacDiarmid's letters to the London officer Richard Brooman-White, the Scottish MI5 officer John Mair quotes MacDiarmid praising the works of Sorley MacLean, George Campbell Hay and Douglas Young,[68] proving that the Scottish Renaissance (here the second generation) had been identified by the agency as worthy of the security force's notice. In fact, as early as August 1933, MacDiarmid's experimental Scots work is reported as being not fully appreciated by the Scots. At first sight, this can prove that the movement had been acknowledged. However, the author of the account is quoting in fact an extract from the same article 'Nationalism in the Scottish Arts' of the *Manchester Guardian Weekly* mentioned in Mackenzie's MI5 records:

> If the bold, too frequently rebellious experimentalism of Hugh MacDiarmid has ruffled a few dovecotes outside Scotland it is probable that the astonishing bulk of more than competent verse in Scots produced during the last 15 years or so is scantily appreciated by those on whom dialect is apt to act emetically.[69]

These two reports, the only ones in which the Scottish Renaissance is alluded to directly, were probably typed by the same officer in the Press Section of the MI5, where they focused their attention on the literary columns of several English newspapers including the *Manchester Guardian* and *The Times Literary Supplement*.[70] There is no evidence that they knew of the literary periodicals and works of art that were produced at the time in Scotland and, so, they could only have a very limited knowledge of the Scottish Renaissance. Another record held by the National Archives – a Home Office folder released in 2000, the content of which spans the years between 1933 and 1954 and concentrates on 'DISTURBANCES: Scottish nationalism: activities of Democratic Scottish Self-Government Organisation, Scottish Defence Force and Scottish National Party'[71] – gives credence to that argument.

Amongst Special Branch reports on bomb scares and nationalist demonstrations, on the Scottish Patriots and Wendy Wood, and on failed and successful attempts at stealing the Stone of Destiny, one suddenly comes across an advertising flyer for the re-publication of MacDiarmid's *A Drunk Man Looks at the Thistle* by the Caledonian Press in April 1953. Comprising several tributes to the poet or his poem, including one by Compton Mackenzie praising 'MacDiarmid's fertilising force', this document was certainly discovered in the April issue of the *National Weekly* that advertises the event in its pages and that can be found alongside the flyer.[72] The *Drunk Man*, a seminal book of the Renaissance, is only referred to here by chance. The poet is the most significant figure in this movement but his presence in this Home Office file is clearly fortuitous. It was probably kept by chance inside the paper and shows no real interest in the movement. Now, even if the intelligence officer who had come across the flyer had willingly chosen to retain it, no one decided to investigate the issue further. Once again, it demonstrates that, apart from a few individuals trying to shed a semblance of light on the matter (but not even reading the literature in question), the agency was not really aware of the Scottish Renaissance and was even less aware of its subversive power. As such, they could not take the movement seriously.

In the case of MacDiarmid, this stance was possibly also adopted because the surveillance job was partly done by someone else. In the same intercepted letter to Florence MacNeill cited earlier, MacDiarmid is quoted complaining about how the publishing house Macmillan cut down the introduction of his anthology *The Golden Treasury* by leaving out 'the anti-English and anti-Imperialist elements'.[73] A month later, on 29 January 1941, the Criminal Investigation Department of the Glasgow Police was sending a report to MI5 Brigadier O. A. Harker in which they declared: 'Grieve's Scottish Nationalist and Communist views permeate all his writings but many of the most bitter sections have to be eliminated by the publishers before the books are accepted.'[74] MI5 had no power to censor a book[75] but most publishing firms were conservative enough to prevent the publication of sensitive material anyway. Not being able to find an outlet for voicing his most angry and extreme ideas, MacDiarmid could not represent a substantial political threat.

Several possible reasons for the lack of interest in literary nationalism emerge from the reading of the writers' files. First, in the case of MacDiarmid, the Secret Services were probably aware that, thanks to censorship by established publishers, the circulation of his works was rather limited and to peruse his work was unnecessary. Second, communism and fascism being seen as more worrying, MI5 and Special Branch may also have willingly chosen to leave out some subversive elements, in spite of their awareness that literature 'might be used as an ideological weapon'.[76] Finally, as the sources of the Secret Services did not include literary productions from Scotland, the Scottish Renaissance could not have appeared more prominently in the records of both MacDiarmid and Mackenzie; it was doomed to remain a historical blind spot.

Conclusion

If we are to exclude real physical threats to the state and the anti-conscription period from the history of the Scottish nationalist movement, the study of Compton Mackenzie's and Hugh MacDiarmid's files reveals that nationalist ideology, whether expressed on a political platform or in a book, was not perceived as a threat by the Secret Services after 1931. Nonetheless, and as it has already been argued by scholars such as Gavin Bowd,[77] nationalism in the inter-war period could be of various hues, which means that nationalism might be considered a brand of fascism.

Mackenzie's file stops in 1951, a year before he was offered a knighthood by Winston Churchill, attesting to his stepping back into the good graces of the establishment. The surveillance of MacDiarmid was suspended earlier, in 1943, when the Communist International was dissolved and when he was back to mainland Scotland, from Shetland. This premature end shows that the potential subversive power of their speeches and books on Scotland, Scottishness and Scottish politics was overlooked by the Secret Services, and that their political power was considered insignificant. In the sake of national security, the Secret Services were right to do so; there was nothing actually dangerous there. As a result, the information about them was probably not passed on to successive governments, whether the Scottish Office or the Home Office. Leaders had to find other information channels, making it hard to see how the productions of the Renaissance could have had a direct impact on state politics and devolutionary measures.[78] The release of Mackenzie's and MacDiarmid's files in 2005 certainly proves that the two men are still seen today, by the state, as harmless game pieces in the political arena of that period.

If other state records on Scottish nationalists ever come to be made public, such an analysis would have to be revaluated. However, at present, one can surely argue that Special Branch, MI5, and the governments they were advising, could not have foreseen the delayed subversive impact that both cultural and political nationalism would have on the nation's consciousness. Even if their definition of what was subversive was not restricted to violence or illegal actions, they only focused on a small selection of facts. They could not see that, as Alan Riach claims, 'all arts [...] represent things, actions, relations of purpose and power. We learn from them and act.'[79] In the long term, the ideas expressed in poetry or novels can have the power to challenge fixed systems, undermine political loyalties, and even re-shape political identities.

Endnotes

1. The National Archives (TNA), KV 2/2010.
2. TNA, KV 2/1271-72.
3. Scott Lyall, '"The Man is a Menace": Macdiarmid and Military Intelligence', *Scottish Studies Review* 8.1 (Spring 2007), pp. 37-52.
4. Len Scott, Peter Jackson, 'Journeys in Shadows', in Len Scott and Peter Jackson (Eds), *Understanding Intelligence in the Twenty-First Century: Journeys in Shadows* (London: Routledge, 2004), pp. 1-28 (p. 6).
5. Christopher Harvie, *Scotland and Nationalism: Scottish Society and Politics, 1707-1977* (London: George Allen & Unwin, 1977), p. 51.
6. See, for example, Richard Finlay, *Modern Scotland: 1914-2000* (London: Profile Books, 2004), pp. 166-67.
7. Thomas M. Devine, *The Scottish Nation: 1700-2000*, 2nd edn (Harmondsworth: Penguin, 2000), p. 565.
8. Ibid., p. 552.
9. House of Commons Debate, 24 November 1932, vol. 272, c. 263 hansard.parliament.uk/Commons/1932-11-24/debates/cff73358-ad73-4032-8f94-53b5ab582ba4/OrdersOfTheDay [accessed 23 May 2022].
10. Alan Riach, 'Exploring MacDiarmid's Legacy. Part Two', *National*, 8 September 2017. Author's final PDF version: eprints.gla.ac.uk/161622/.
11. Jack Brand, *The National Movement in Scotland* (London: Routledge, 1978), p. 91.
12. Ben Jackson, *The Case for Scottish Independence: A History of Nationalist Political Thought in Modern Scotland* (Cambridge: Cambridge University Press, 2020), p. 9. See also pp. 8-10.
13. James Mitchell, *The Scottish Question* (Oxford: Oxford University Press, 2014), p. 110.
14. The full article can be found in *Modernism and Nationalism: Literature and Society in Scotland 1918-1939*, ed. Margery Palmer McCulloch (Glasgow: Association for Scottish Literary Studies, 2004), p. 353.
15. See Andro Linklater, *Compton MacKenzie: A Life* (London: Chatto & Windus, 1987), p. 234.
16. Alan Bold, *MacDiarmid: A Biography*, 2nd edn (London: Paladin, 1990), p. 282.
17. Linklater, p. 234.
18. In a letter to Tom H. Gibson quoted in Richard Finlay, *Independent and Free: Scottish Politics and the Origins of the Scottish National Party, 1918-1945* (Edinburgh: John Donald Publishers, 1994), p. 87.
19. Bold, p. 283.
20. The different references are the following: 'Grieve, who, about 2 years ago was leader of "Clan na Nalba" a rebel organisation in Scotland' (TNA, Special Branch report, August 1932, KV 2/2010, f 4a); 'the Scottish Nationalist Party [sic] is supplying the money to keep the "Inner Circle" (Croileagan na h Alba) operative' (TNA, Special Branch report, 17 October 1932, KV 2/2010, f 5a); 'In September 1930, she [Margaret Grieve] was the secretary of 'Clann Albainn, an auxiliary of the National Party of Scotland' (TNA, Special Branch report, 21 October 1933, KV 2/2010, f 7a).
21. Kevin Quinlan, *The Secret War between the Wars: MI5 in the 1920s and 1930s* (Woodbridge: The Boydell Press, 2014) p. 14.

22 Compton Mackenzie, *My Life and Times: Octave 6* (London: Chatto & Windus, 1967), p. 174.
23 Ibid., p. 189.
24 See Finlay, *Independent and Free*, pp. 87, 92.
25 See the account by Bob Purdie: *Hugh MacDiarmid: Black, Green, Red and Tartan* (Cardiff: Welsh Academic Press, 2012), pp. 55–56.
26 Harvie, p. 156.
27 Christopher Andrew, *Defend the Realm: The Authorized History of MI5* (New York: Vintage Books, 2010).
28 TNA, KV 2/1271, f 31a.
29 See Martin Pugh, *'Hurrah for the Blackshirts!': Fascists and Fascism in Britain between the War* (London: Jonathan Cape, 2005), p. 154, and John Stevenson, *Britain in the Depression: Society and Politics 1929–1939*, (London: Longman, 1994), p. 226.
30 TNA, KV 2/1271, f 33a.
31 See TNA, KV 2/1271, ff 32a–34a and TNA, KV 2/1272, ff 91a, 98a, 99a, 100a, 101a, 102, 114b, and 123a. Maccartney's MI5 personal file is referenced and available on the National Archives website (KV 2/648).
32 Lyall, p. 47.
33 James Smith, *British Writers and MI5 Surveillance, 1930–1960* (Cambridge: Cambridge University Press, 2013), p. 34.
34 See Stevenson, p. 145.
35 See John E. Schwarz, 'The Scottish National Party: Nonviolent Separatism and Theories of Violence', *World Politics* 22.4 (July 1970), pp. 496–517.
36 Finlay, *Independent and Free*, p.75.
37 Quoted in Andrew, *Defend the Realm*, p. 129.
38 Smith, p. 10.
39 See Finlay, *Independent and Free*, p. 165.
40 TNA, HO 45/23801.
41 TNA, KV 2/2010, f 65a. For a more detailed account of MacDiarmid's supposed fascism in his MI5 file, see Lyall, 'The Man is a Menace', 2007.
42 TNA, KV 2/2010, f 45a.
43 TNA, KV 2/2010, f 48a.
44 TNA, Letter from 16 March 1941, KV 2/2010, f 51a.
45 TNA, Letter from 21 April 1941, KV 2/2010, f 56a.
46 TNA, Letter from 24 February 1942, KV 2/2010, f 68a.
47 TNA, Letter from 10 March 1942, KV 2/2010, f 69a.
48 Linklater, p. 247.
49 For accounts of the event, see Peter Lynch, *The History of the Scottish National Party* (Cardiff: Welsh Academic Press, 2013) p. 84, and Devine, p. 567.
50 HO 45/25472, TNA.
51 See Bold, pp. 366–67.
52 Bold, p. 367.
53 Quinlan, p. 14, quoting Richard A. Posner, *Preventing Surprise Attacks: Intelligence Reform in the Wake of 9/11* (New York, Oxford: Rowman & Littlefield, 2005), p. 133.
54 Reference to MacDiarmid's poem 'The Bonnie Broukit Bairn' (Beautiful neglected child).
55 Linklater, p. 312.

56 See Compton Mackenzie, *The North Wind of Love* (London: Chatto & Windus, 1944).
57 See Andrew, p. 140.
58 Smith, p. xii.
59 *Scottish Literature*, ed. Douglas Gifford, Sarah Dunnigan and Alan MacGillivray (Edinburgh: Edinburgh University Press, 2002), p. 713.
60 Ian Brown, *Performing Scottishness: Enactment and National Identities* (London: Palgrave Macmillan, 2020), p. 212.
61 See Compton Mackenzie, *The Monarch of the Glen* (London: Vintage Books, 2009), p. 40.
62 For more information about that episode, see: Kenneth Young, *Compton Mackenzie* (London: Longmans, 1968), p.7; Linklater, pp. 147–72; Mark David Kaufman, 'Spyography: Compton Mackenzie, Modernism, and the Intelligence Memoir', *The Space Between: Literature and Culture 1914–1945* 13 (2017), scalar.usc.edu/works/the-space-between-literature-and-culture-1914-1945/vol13_2017_kaufman; Roger Faligot, Rémi Kauffer, *Histoire mondiale du renseignement, Tome 1: 1870–1939* (Paris: Robert Laffont, 1993), p. 127.
63 See Paul Gueguen, *Compton Mackenzie, romancier* (Lille: Atelier National de reproduction des thèses, 1982), p. 54.
64 TNA, KV 2/1271, f 29b.
65 See Linklater, pp. 237–38.
66 TNA, KV 2/2010, f 3a.
67 TNA, 11 August 1934, KV 2 2010, f 9a.
68 TNA, KV 2/2010, f 48a. The same names were also listed in an intercepted letter of 27 December 1940 (TNA, KV 2/2010, f 45a).
69 TNA, KV 2010, f 6a.
70 See Smith, p. 18.
71 TNA, HO 45/25472.
72 *National Weekly*, 18 April 1953.
73 TNA, KV 2/2010, f 45a.
74 TNA, KV 2/2010, f 47b.
75 See Smith, pp. 155–56.
76 Ibid., p. 17.
77 Gavin Bowd, *Fascist Scotland: Caledonia and the Far Right* (Edinburgh: Birlinn, 2013).
78 For further reading on the first and second Renaissance and political representation, see Scott Hames, *The Literary Politics of Scottish Devolution. Voice, Class, Nation* (Edinburgh: Edinburgh University Press, 2019).
79 Alan Riach and Alexander Moffat, *Arts of Independence: The Cultural Argument and Why it Matters Most* (Edinburgh: Luath Press, 2014), p. 7.

10. Situating the Gael in Scottish Landscapes: Self-Identity and Change in Twentieth-Century Gaelic Poetry

EMMA DYMOCK

For centuries, the Gaelic poet's role was as 'voice of the people', celebrating and remembering the exploits of chief and clan, and later beyond clanship and into crofting, the moments of community life. But, within a twentieth-century context, who is the poet representing? Even for modern Gaelic poets, the emphasis may be as much on the communal as the individual. However, the Gaelic community, whether real or imagined, is constantly shifting and the work of the poet undoubtedly reflects this altering state of identity, what it means to be both Scottish and Gaelic, and whether a synthesis of these two identities is even possible. The effect of the Highland–Lowland divide in Scottish history and literature is a lingering influence, and centuries of linguistic and cultural injustice, including the Statutes of Iona (1609), the aftermath of Culloden (1746–), the eighteenth- and nineteenth-century Highland Clearances and Education Acts (e.g. 1872 and 1918), have played their part in how the Gaels perceive and situate themselves within their own country. It could be argued that it is often easier for the Gael to bypass 'Scottishness' altogether in favour of exploring identity within a wider pan-Celtic and European context.

This chapter seeks to explore the ways in which Gaelic poets of the twentieth century and beyond have continued to define and redefine their identity as Gaels within Scotland at a time when the geographic position of Gaelic is rapidly changing. While the twentieth century was certainly not the first period in which, from a literary perspective, the Gael crossed the 'Highland Line',[1] it is the century which has revealed the greatest extent of change and variation in the style and content of poetry on this subject. Against the backdrop of the Gaelic Literary Renaissance, the establishment of Gaelic as a minority language and culture within a European and global context, the advent of learners and 'new speakers' of the language, and the effect of migration into and out of the Gàidhealtachd, the way in which Gaels situate themselves through their writing can be seen to reflect the ambiguity of their position. This chapter will focus on how the urban and rural identities meet and merge in the poetry of the Gael. Cultural and political nationalism, non-linear experience of time, memory and identity, and the attachment to multiple imagined communities will be examined through the lens of the poetry of Sorley MacLean (1911–1996), Derick Thomson (1921–2012), Iain Crichton Smith (1928–1998), Mary Montgomery (b. 1955), Meg Bateman (b. 1959), and others. This chapter will take a thematic rather than chronological approach, in order to best reflect the ways in which the different traditions of poetry in Gaelic existed simultaneously.

The influence of the Scottish literary renaissance: redefining and strengthening Gaelic tradition in the poetry of Sorley MacLean and Aonghas MacNeacail

As a Gaelic poet, operating within the context of the mid-twentieth century, Sorley MacLean exhibits a clear conviction and confidence in his own identity. While MacLean conducts much soul searching in relation to his role as political poet of conscience, there is never a question mark over his self-identity as a Gael. He knows who he is, from the perspective of his family, clan, and ancestral links, and his role as a spokesperson and poet for the imagined community; he views himself as part of a direct line which includes Màiri Mhòr nan Òran/Mary MacPherson (1821–1898) and Alexander MacDonald/Alasdair mac Mhaighstir Alasdair (1698–1770). In 'An Cuilithionn', he wonders 'An robh mi air beireachd air MacDhòmhnaill, / a dh'aindeoin beithir-teine a ghlòir-san?' ('Would I have caught up with MacDonald / for all the lightning fire of his glory?') and he is 'Sgitheanach ro taobh Màiri Mòire' ('a Skyeman by the side of the great Mary').[2] While he may be implying that he is unworthy in their presence, the very act of placing himself in their company is indicative of his sense of self within a wider Gaelic literary framework and tradition. His self-confidence may be traced not only to his own understanding of his Gaelic roots, but also from the context of the wider Scottish Literary Renaissance from which he was emerging in the 1930s. Hugh MacDiarmid's (1892–1978) respect and belief in the importance of the Gaelic world to the whole of Scotland[3] should not be underestimated for the conviction that it bestowed on MacLean himself. In a letter dated 23 January 1977, MacDiarmid wrote to MacLean that

> There is, I think, no doubt about you and I being the two best poets in Scotland [...]. By definition, every good poet has something that is sui generis – something that is his alone and couldn't be done by anyone else.[4]

His words hint at the idea that there are two 'Scotlands' – one Gaelic-speaking and the other Scots/English-speaking.

While MacLean never veered from his linguistic trajectory as a Gaelic-language poet, he was nevertheless at home within the two worlds; he operated in the traditional Gaelic world as a tradition-bearer and supporter of Gaelic causes, and, while living in Edinburgh, firstly at the University of Edinburgh as a student of English Language and Literature and then in his profession as a teacher, he mingled with political and cultural circles of friends, which included MacDiarmid, Douglas Young (1913–1973), the Muirs – Willa (1890–1970) and Edwin (1887–1959) – George Davie (1912–2007) and James Caird (1919–1989).[5] It could be argued that it was precisely his identity as a Gaelic poet that served him so well within the Scottish literati. His political poetry from this period, particularly 'An Cuilithionn' ('The Cuillin') has, at its centre, his Gaelic identity – in Part VI of the poem, he acknowledges Skye, Lewis, Harris and Mull, before moving outwards to encompass the Hebrides in general, the rest of Scotland, Europe, and the world.

> 'S mise Clio Innse Gall:
> chunnaic mi allaban is call,
> chuala mi ceòl mòr MhicCruimein
> agus a' chaora mhaol a' criomadh.

(I am Clio of the Hebrides: / I have seen suffering and loss; / I have heard the great music of MacCrimmon, / and the hornless sheep cropping)[6]

However, MacLean's vision of Scotland in his poetry goes beyond a regional Gaelic-centredness. He deftly ties Lowland Scotland into his imagined community – a 'Celtic communism' flavoured with crofting and the Land Wars – by concentrating on the socialism of the Lowland cities. He does this in two ways. Firstly, in the case of Glasgow, through his admiration for Red Clydeside and, in particular, his deep respect for John Maclean (1879–1923), the Scottish socialist, who had been appointed Bolshevik consul in Scotland in 1918 and was imprisoned on charges of sedition, and whose commitment to Marxism-Leninism and the cause of Scottish independence alienated him from the British Communist Party.[7] MacLean effectively 'adopts' John Maclean as one of his own due to his surname (and John Maclean was the grandson of a Mull crofter), thereby bringing Glasgow left-wing politics into the fold of his own imagined community. Sorley MacLean wrote to Douglas Young that 'I occasionally heard hints from two of my uncles that they had come into contact with a saint and a hero – John Maclean'.[8] John Maclean is mentioned numerous times in MacLean's poetry, particularly in 'Clann Ghill-Eain' ('The Clan MacLean')[9] and in 'An Cuilithionn':

> ach chunnaic mi ròs dearg Chluaidh a' sgaoileadh
> 'na bhrat cumhachdach mòr feirge
> is MacGill-Eain a' togail meirghe.

(but I saw the red rose of Clyde spreading / to a great mighty mantle of anger / when Maclean raised a banner.)[10]

Secondly, in the case of Edinburgh, he focuses on the Irish figure of James Connolly, who grew up in the Irish slums of the Cowgate before he returned to Ireland and took part in the 1916 Easter Rising. In 'Àrd-Mhusaeum na h-Èireann' ('The National Museum of Ireland'), MacLean's love for Connolly and all that he stood for is also given a Gaelic rendering, albeit one from the perspective of Gaelic Ireland.

> Anns na làithean dona seo
> is seann leòn Uladh 'na ghaoid
> lionnrachaidh 'n cridhe na h-Eòrpa
> agus an cridhe gach Gàidheal
> dhan aithne gur h-e th' ann an Gàidheal

> (In these evil days / when the old wound of Ulster is a disease / suppurating in the heart of Europe / and in the heart of every Gael / who knows that he is a Gael)[11]

MacLean surveys Connolly's bloodstained shirt in the museum, and just as John Maclean is described as a 'saint', Connolly's shirt is treated as akin to a holy relic. In the poem, MacLean blurs the edges of time, and Irish and Scottish Gaelic history and politics appear to exist in a continuous present.

> Tha an curaidh mòr fhathast
> 'na shuidhe air an t-sèithear,
> a' cur a' chatha sa Phost-Oifis
> 's a' glanadh shràidean an Dùn Èideann.

> (The great hero is still / sitting on the chair, / fighting the battle in the Post Office / and cleaning streets in Edinburgh.)[12]

The 'Irishness' of Connolly is not an issue for MacLean; Gaelic Ireland and Scotland have historical connection and this pan-Gaelic/Celtic identity is a natural fit for a Gaelic poet like MacLean who had knowledge of the shared tradition of Bardic poetry. What is interesting here is MacLean's ease in interpreting modern political history in Scotland through his own Gaelic lens. There is not the embarrassment or unease of some postmodern Gaelic writers regarding their place, and by extension, the place of Gaelic, in Scotland. On the contrary, MacLean's sense of 'Scottishness' is one branch of a tree which has its roots in a much older linguistic and cultural tradition, much in line with the ethno-symbolic approach to nationalism held by Anthony D. Smith.

MacLean is not the only Gaelic poet whose sense of place and history is both personal and very much in the eternal present in his poetry. Aonghas MacNeacail (b. 1942), from Uig, Skye, grew up in a Gaelic-speaking household but lost much of his Gaelic once he entered English medium education,[13] before returning to Gaelic later in life, effectively reclaiming his birthright. Perhaps due to his own personal experiences of language loss and reclamation, in 'oideachadh ceart' ('a proper schooling'), events such as the Highland Clearances, emigration, and the Land Wars, are very close to the surface – 'cha b' eachdraidh ach cuimhne' ('it wasn't history but memory').[14] What was taught in schools pales into insignificance next to what was passed on through the oral tradition for MacNeacail. The older Gaelic poets such as Màiri Mhòr, Uilleam Ros (1762–1791) and Donnachadh Bàn (1724–1812) are his way-markers and signposts of cultural identity and, thus, it can be seen that in the Gaidhealtachd, there is more than one line of history. Like MacLean, MacNeacail's sense of identity is firmly connected to that which links land, culture and people together.

The poetic dilemma of 'Gaelic Nationalism' in late twentieth-century Scotland

Mary Montgomery's 'Soraidh Leibh' ('Farewell') succinctly captures the feelings of embarrassment relating to Scottish Gaelic linguistic identity coupled with national identity and goes some way to showing the predicament which Scottish Gaels in the late twentieth century found themselves in when faced with their more self-confident Irish cousins. Montgomery focuses on the setting of a Gaelic poet's tour of Ireland in 1990:

> Soraidh leibh
> nuair a thig oirbh
> a dhol a Cheann Trá a sheasamh
> ris an tAmhrán Náisiúnta

's adh'aideachadh
gun do dh'fhàg sibh a'Bhànrigh aig an taigh.

(Farewell / when your day comes / to go to Ventry and stand / for the National Anthem / and admit / you've left the Queen at home.)[15]

While the Irish poets are able to stand for their own National Anthem, sung entirely in the Irish language, the Scottish Gaelic poets have a number of issues to contend with. Not only do they feel obliged to reject 'God Save the Queen', which is not a 'Scottish' anthem and would undoubtedly sit strangely in the context of a Gaelic poetry tour, it then becomes apparent that they have no appropriate Scottish Gaelic equivalent.

'Flower of Scotland'
O chan e
Nach e?
Dé eile?
'Soraidh Leibh
is Oidhche Mhath Leibh'
is mise còmh' ribh
le beag nàire
'na mo laige leis a' ghàire

('Flower of Scotland' / Oh no / No use? / what else? / 'Soraidh Leibh / is Oidhche Mhath Leibh' / and me along with you / embarrassed / and quaking with laughter)[16]

While 'Flower of Scotland' is a Scottish anthem, which no song other than perhaps Dougie MacLean's 'Caledonia' has ever come close to replacing, the fact that it is an English-language song again renders it unsuitable in a Gaelic context. The song 'Soraidh Leibh is Oidhche Mhath Leibh' ('Farewell and Goodnight be with you') by John MacFadyen, which was composed in 1907 and which they end up choosing, is best described as a Gaelic 'parting song' and lacks the strength of the Irish anthem, with Montgomery acknowledging that

> Is iadsan 'Laochra Fáil
> Atá faoi gheall ag Éirinn'
> Is sinne sluagh na dàil
> A thar o mhall ag éirigh

(*They're* 'The mighty warriors of Fate / Who're under oath to Ireland' / While *we're* the people who procrastinate / And are too slow in rising)[17]

This deceptively simple poem shows that the Scottish Gaelic experience of nationhood is both confused and ambivalent; by the end of the poem and by the time the poets' tour had reached Tallaght, the Scottish Gaels had reassembled and sung a Gaelic-language translation of 'Flower of Scotland', 'agus leag sinn an taigh' ('and brought the house down').[18]

The poem, nevertheless, finishes on a slightly dissatisfied note. The Scottish Gaelic 'nation' had had to settle for a translation to achieve the same effect as the Irish. Montgomery's poem shows that the Scottish Gaelic sense of nationhood exists in a 'between place'; her use of the word 'refugee' in line twenty-eight[19] goes some way to revealing the true extent to which Gaels may feel at odds with the idea of 'Scottishness' in their own physical and imagined landscapes. The close identification with Irish Gaels likewise creates a sense of dislocation. When modern political Irish nationalism is invoked in lines twenty-nine to thirty[20] it begs the question of who exactly the Scottish Gaels have been too slow to rise up against? While English and/or British imperialism is undoubtedly the force against which Irish literary and cultural figures measure their rebel status, is Montgomery referring to the same imperialist power or a more complicated amalgamation of influences against the minority language and culture of Gaelic in Scotland? After all, the history of Gaelic linguistic and cultural injustice was largely due to a Scottish-based education and religious system.

The 'slowness to rise' is an acknowledgement of the tendency of Scottish Gaels in the past almost willingly to relinquish their language and culture; the erosion took place from within. Alexander Carmichael (1832–1912) highlights the impact of Evangelical Protestantism in the introduction to the first volume of *Carmina Gadelica* (1900) and shows a discourse which influenced the perceptions of Gaels and their own self-identity well into the twentieth century.

> 'And have you no music, no singing, no dancing now at your marriages?' 'May the Possessor keep you! I see that you are a stranger in Lewis, or you would not ask such a question,' the woman exclaimed with grief and surprise in her tone. 'It is long since we abandoned those foolish ways in Ness, and, indeed, throughout Lewis. In my young days there was hardly a house in Ness in which there was not one or two or three who could play the pipe, or the fiddle, or the trump. And I have heard it said that there were men, and women too, who could play things they called harps, and lyres, and bellow-pipes, but I do not know what those things were.' 'And why were those discontinued?' 'A blessed change came over the place and the people,' the woman replied in earnestness, 'and the good men and the good ministers who arose did away with the songs and the stories, the music and the dancing, the sports and the games, that were perverting the minds and ruining the souls of the people, leading them to folly and stumbling.' 'But how did the people themselves come to discard their sports and pastimes?' 'Oh, the good ministers and the good elders preached against them and went among the people, and besought them to forsake their follies and to return to wisdom. They made the people break and burn their pipes and fiddles.'[21]

It is interesting that a more suitable contender for most stirring Gaelic anthem on the Gaelic Poets Tour described by Montgomery, could have been 'Cànan nan Gàidheal' ('The Language of the Gael') by Murdo MacFarlane (1901–1982), 'the Melbost Bard'.[22] In this song the sense of pride in geographical and cultural location returns again to linguistic difference within Scotland. This is the most important signifier of Gaeldom in the twentieth century. The poem is traditional in both metre and content, perhaps deliberately so. The poet is using the symbols and images familiar to the Gaels to recall a Gaelic past, redolent of Jacobite heroes, bards and great halls.

> Fair a-nuas dhuinn na coinnlearan òir
> 'S annt càiribh na coinnlean geal cèir,
> Lasaibh suas iad an seòmar a' bhròin
> 'N taigh-fhaire seann chànan a' Ghaidheil
> 'S e siud o chionn fhad' thuirt a nàmh
> Ach fhathast tha beò cànan nan treun

> (Fetch down the golden chandeliers / And set the white wax candles in them / Light them up in the chamber of sorrow, / The wake house of the old Gaelic language / That's what the enemy said a long time ago / But the Gaelic language still lives.)[23]

Despite the song's traditionalism, 'Cànan nan Gàidheal' shares a common theme with Montgomery's more stylistically postmodern 'Soraidh Leibh'; the inherent sense of shame and failure in 'rising up' – 'O Ghaidheil O, càite 'n deach d' uaill/ A dualchas, cànan is tìr?' ('O, Gaels, O, what's happened to your pride / In your heritage, language and land?').[24] Throughout MacFarlane's song, the focus is on 'the West' and the fact that Gaelic is even being displaced in its traditional heartland:

> Uair chite fear-fèilidh sa ghleann
> Bu chinnteach gur Gàidhlig a chainnt,
> Ach chaochlaidh i dùthaich nam beann,
> 'N àite Gàidhlig cluinn cànan a' Ghoill –
> Chan e 'n dùthaich a bh' ann a th' ann,
> 'N-diugh 's dùthaich nan 'Colonels' a th' innt'.

(Once when a kilted man was seen in the glen, /There's no doubt that Gaelic was his tongue, / But the land of the glens has been changed / And instead of Gaelic the Lowlander's tongue is heard, / It's not the same country it once was, / Today it's the land of the 'Colonels'.).[25]

Even in this song, steeped in romanticism and nostalgia, however, a dichotomy exists. While on the surface, MacFarlane appears to celebrate and call for a return to an idealised Gaelic in the 'West' – perhaps a modern 'Lordship of the Isles' with its cultural flowering – there is an undercurrent which seems to hint at a more inclusive Scottish identity. Despite the accusation in the first stanza that the disease which has blanched the blossom, foliage, stem and roots of the Gaelic language has come from the south of the country, later in the song, MacFarlane widens the lens to include the whole country, rather than a specifically rural and regional focus: 'Albainn gad easbhaidh 's gad dhith / 'S clàrsach-aon-teud is cuislean gun fhuil' ('Scotland is wanting and needing you / Like a one-stringed harp or a vein without blood').[26] This is certainly not the only instance in which this lack of clarity in relation to nationality and self-identity is played out. The final stanza in which the Gael is urged to create 'Gàidhealtachd nuadh' ('a new Highlands')[27] could perhaps be said to be happening in the present day, with, for example, governmental support of Gaelic through the Gaelic Language Act, increase in Gaelic Medium Education and increased visibility of Gaelic in the media.

Location and dislocation: Gaelic poets and the urban Scottish experience

By the late twentieth century and early twenty-first century, a 'new Highlands' can be seen with the upsurge of 'new speakers', learners of Gaelic and so-called 'urban Gaels', who have managed to create a Gàidhealtachd of the mind, even in cities such as Edinburgh and Glasgow, by surrounding themselves with Gaelic language and culture on a daily basis. These Gaels have no qualms about exploring their identity through literary expression, proudly exhibiting their urban experiences of Gaeldom while knowingly retaining the distinguishing features of their Gaelic language and culture. The ease with which writers now inhabit different facets of their Scottish identities was not always so easily navigated. Gaelic writers have been exploring the sense of dislocation and bewilderment that exists alongside the Gaelic migration from the Highlands to the towns and cities of the Scottish Lowlands almost as long as migration has been taking place: the trope of the 'Gael in the big city' is not uncommon in Gaelic poetry and prose from the nineteenth century and beyond. It is interesting to view the ways in which Gaels successfully transplanted their rural experience into a city setting. The poem 'Bùth Dhòmhnaill 'IcLeòid' ('Donald MacLeod's Pub')[28] by Donald MacIntyre (1889–1964) is a traditional poem in the 'bard-baile' style, celebrating individuals and events within the community with the crucial difference that the pub in the title is situated near Paisley Road Toll in Glasgow. In the case of this poem, the geographic location is irrelevant; it is the people who create and place this pub in a Gaelic context within Lowland and urban Scotland.

Other poets explore the Gaelic city experience through their psychological responses: it is the landscape of their mind which is the 'between place' and the images and symbols relating to their memories of Gaelic childhood in their native places intermingle with the sights and sounds of city life in strange ways. Both Derick Thomson and Iain Crichton Smith touch on existentialism and absurdity in their 'city poems'. If the definition of absurdity can be described as the notion of contrast between two things, in the case of Thomson and Smith it is a perceived sense of what it means to be 'Gaelic' in contrast to the experience of their present/current life in Scotland. Camus explains in *The Myth of Sisyphus* that the absurd is born out of this confrontation between the human need and the unreasonable silence of the world.[29] For these Gaelic poets, it seems to be that the human need here is the need of their Gaelic identity which cries out for recognition in the silence of the city. All of this plays out against a Scottish backdrop: no other country is involved. Yet, it becomes increasingly obvious that even in a small country such as Scotland (and, interestingly, for poets such as

Thomson who are Scottish Nationalists), the issue goes beyond simple definitions of nationality: deeper concepts of identity, culture and history endure. Linear time collapses and these poems prove that more than one mindset can exist.

> 'Bheil cuimhn' agad...'
> – seo air bus ann a Sauchiehall Street –
> ars esan, 'an là bha sinn anns a' mhòine ...?'
> Tha. 'Na mo chuis-bhùirt ann am meadhon Ghlaschu,
> Ann am meadhon mo bheatha,
> Ann am meadhon Alba

> ('Do you remember ...' / – this on a bus in Sauchiehall Street – / said he, 'the day we spent at the peats ...?' / Yes. Making an ass of myself in the middle of Glasgow, / in the middle of my life, / in the midst of Scotland)[30]

There can be found the tinge of guilt in Thomson's work with lines such as 'Eil fada bho nach d'fhuair sibh bhon taigh?' ('Is it long since you heard from home?')[31] and 'Na canadh duine gun do chuir mi cùl riut / ged a thionndaidh mi air falbh' ('Let no one say I turned my back on you / although I turned away').[32]

It is worth noting that the regret pertaining to Thomson's relocation to the Lowlands, and even his perceived betrayal of his homeland of Lewis in his poetry, does not necessarily align with his other work outside of his poetic career. Thomson did more for the furtherment of Gaelic language in the twentieth century than any other writer; as the 'father of modern Gaelic publishing', he co-founded the quarterly *Gairm* in 1952, inaugurated the Historical Dictionary of Scottish Gaelic in 1966, and founded the Gaelic Books Council in 1968.[33] It could be argued that he could not have achieved all he did in his lifetime if he had not been living in Glasgow. Thus, the poetic writing of place serves a different function for the individual than the sense of place in economic and professional terms. The two strands can co-exist, particularly for a Gael who is operating in a modern setting.

This experience and reaction to the shift of perception is also explored in Iain Crichton Smith's 'Innsidh mi dhut mar a thachair' ('I'll tell you how it happened'), albeit in a more symbolic way.

> Innsidh mi dhut mar a thachair.
> Bha mi air cabhsair an Glaschu
> nuair a chunnaic mi
> a' deàlradh air balla
> 'Gealach abachaidh an eòrna –
> bheir i sinne Leódhas dhachaigh.'

(I'll tell you how it happened. / I was on a pavement in Glasgow / when I saw / shining on a wall / 'The moon that ripens the barley – / she will take us home to Lewis.')[34]

Significantly, it is Gaelic songs which more often seem to cause this shift in perception:

> 'S aon oidhche cuideachd
> 's mi 'nam laighe 'nam leabaidh
> chunna mi an Caióra a' seòladh

(And one night too / as I lay in my bed / I saw the Kai-Ora sailing)[35]

'An Caióra' is a Lewis song by Murdo Morrison (1840–1930), which Crichton Smith would have known well. In the same poem he recounts his experience of seeing Dòmhnall Ruadh Chorùna's (1887–1967) song 'An Eala Bhàn' ('The White Swan') written on his desk in his office.[36] Crichton Smith knows these experiences are not signs of insanity:

> Ach tha e àraidh
> a bhith fuireach ann am baile
> 's a' coiseachd troimh shràidean
> cho buidhe 's cho falamh
> 's a' coimhead òrain dhathte

(But it's odd / to be living in a city / and walking through streets / so yellow and so empty / and seeing coloured songs).[37]

Crichton Smith's experience is not unusual. For many Gaels living in cities in the mid- to late twentieth century, the 'colour' in their minds – the very make-up of their identity and concept of Gaelic Scotland – would be an amalgamation of childhood memories of songs and family lore, learned through a process of osmosis within the context of the ceilidh-house. Crichton Smith, due to his work in both Gaelic and English, is often viewed as a Gaelic-language writer by those reading his Gaelic output, which includes plays, and an English-language writer by those more familiar with his poetry and prose in English. It is clear that Smith is knowing of his position when he writes in his essay 'A Poet in Scotland',

> Writing here in this room in Oban, what do I think of being 'a Scottish poet'? I don't think of being a Scottish poet at all, I think of the act of writing poetry [...]. When I have finished the poem I do not ask myself, 'Is this a good Scottish poem?' I only ask myself, 'Is this a good poem?' I am aware of other poets, some Scottish, some not. I am aware of the past – of so much history and fable, and some of it again is Scottish and some is not – but in the end I ask myself, 'Is this a good poem?' I do not ask whether my Scottishness will save it. I know that in the end it will be in some sense Scottish because it was written by me and I live in Scotland.[38]

There can be no better description of the process of writing within Scotland as this one given by Crichton Smith and yet he knows that the process of self-identity within writing is never simple. He is well aware of the difficulties of 'hybridity' and of the dangers of the outsider discourse, which so often also becomes the discourse of the insider. While Crichton Smith's 'Innsidh mi dhut mar a thachair' describes one line of experience of the Gael in the city, he is wary of romanticising this experience:

> To grow up on an island is to grow up in a special world. Many of the books I have read on the Hebrides, however, make this world appear Edenic and unreal: others suggest that the islander is a child who appears lost in the 'real world'.[39]

Crichton Smith's main aim is rather to be a 'real person in a real place'. For the Gael, writing in Scotland in the twentieth century, it may be that a choice has to be made. There can be no doubt that 'place' is about more than simple physical geography, particularly when it is taken into consideration that many Gaelic poets were living their lives in urban environments in Scotland, which were quite removed from their childhoods in the Highlands and Islands, and yet their language of choice in their poetry was Gaelic.

Some poets, such as Sorley MacLean, made the choice from an almost political standpoint, taking into consideration the need for the survival of his native language – a minority language within its own country – as well as a more personal belief that he would always write with more truth and ease when using Gaelic.[40] He destroyed all of the English-language poetry he had written and never composed in English again. His choice was final and he was, from that point onwards, a 'Gaelic poet' whether he was living in Edinburgh or Plockton. Smith's words in 'Poetic Energy, Language and Nationhood' are pertinent here. He writes that poetry demands the truth and cannot come from a divided person.

> Poetry is not made of words alone: the matter goes much deeper than that. The source, the ultimate energy, is in a place where language and nationhood meet, in the garden of psychic freedom, where play, gravity, obscenity, are all permitted in the rhythms which are the guarantees of freedom.[41]

Perhaps for the Gaelic poet, the very admission of being within a 'between place', physically, culturally, and linguistically, is sufficient. By the mid- to late twentieth century there was no going back to a monoglot experience of Gaelic within Scotland.

EMMA DYMOCK

Knowing their place: writing new identities in the work of Meg Bateman and Christopher Whyte

The predicament of the Gaelic poet, writing in a 'between place' in Scotland can be taken a stage further when the issue of Gaelic-learner poets are considered. Their situation differs in that they do not have the loss of the traditional cultural signifiers to mourn within the context of a changing landscape. Their decision to write poetry in a minority language such as Gaelic is an important statement of intent and yet there can be evidenced a sense of discomfort and perhaps a need for acceptance from the Gaelic-speaking community. Meg Bateman, who grew up in Edinburgh, and learned Gaelic as a student at Aberdeen University and while living on South Uist,[42] has fully embraced the more traditional markers of Gaelic Scotland. She teaches and is now a professor at Sabhal Mor Ostaig, the Gaelic college on Skye, and, while she also writes poetry in English, much of the poetry which is based within the Gàidhealtachd or, perhaps even more significantly, which she composed while living in the Gàidhealtachd has a Gaelic sensibility. She has actively embraced the land and the culture. In 'Do Alastair MacIlleMhìcheil' ('To Alexander Carmichael'), she addresses the folk collector of the *Carmina Gadelica*:

> Chuir na leabhraichean agad tnùth orm
> mar nach do chuir càil eile,
> oir ghlac mi annta saoghal seunta,
> ortha aig an tuath an cois gach gnìomha,
> pàirt an urra riutha de rian dìomhair.

> (Your books have filled me with envy / as nothing else has, / for in them I glimpsed a charmed age, / everything done prayerfully / as part of a greater whole.)[43]

This longing for a different way of life and the juxtaposition of modern lifestyle with a more traditional culture can be evidenced with Bateman's mention of 'smooring the TV',[44] but by the conclusion of the poem, she finds solace in a common humanity which transcends the centuries:

SELF-IDENTITY AND CHANGE IN TWENTIETH-CENTURY GAELIC POETRY

> Thug thu dhuinn an ortha bha san àbhaist
> a chluinneas mi nist an srann nam wipers,
> mi a' feitheamh aig na solais
>
> (You showed us the prayer in the mundane / that I hear now in the whine of the wipers / as I wait at the lights)⁴⁵

On the other hand, Christopher Whyte (b. 1952), who is also a learner of Gaelic and who writes poetry in the Gaelic language, feels no such compunction to embrace a culture of which he does not feel completely a part. In 'Bho Leabhar-Latha Maria Malibran' ('From The Diary of Maria Malibran') he goes as far as to address an imagined Gaelic readership who he feels does not appreciate his work or who have perhaps rejected him because of his perceived lack of 'Gaelicness':

> Mura bheil mi comasach
> air dàintean fìor-Ghàidhealach a sgrìobhadh,
>
> tha sin a chionns nach eil mi 'nam fhìor-Ghàidheal,
> a-rèir coltais.
>
> (Possibly my power / to give my Gaelic poetry full flower // is limited because I'm not a Gael / if that's what you suggest.)⁴⁶

He feels that he is expected to write in a certain way about certain subjects but he refuses to be positioned in that place.

> B' fheàrr leibh a bhith leughadh,
> math dh'fhaodt', mun chianalas 's mun chiont a bhios
> mi faireachdainn aig deasg na h-oifis àird,
> faram na trafaige san t-sràid gam bòdhradh
>
> (By now you're waiting to be told of how / homesickness and guilt shadow my brow / as I sit at a desk, stuck in a job / above the city traffic and hubbub)⁴⁷

While this approach may be confrontational, it nevertheless raises a pertinent question in relation to issues of identity and belonging in late twentieth-century Scotland. In the case of Whyte, it may be that the subject matter and content of his poetry coupled with his place as a Scottish writer operating within the Gaelic language means that, in the late twentieth century, there was not a readership which was ready for his work – a situation which has undoubtedly now been righted as the twenty-first century continues.

The place of Gaelic within modern Scotland may always be a contentious subject for both Gael and non-Gael alike, and it is perhaps that debatable place – the fluidity of cultural, linguistic and political boundaries – which also gives rise to twentieth-century Gaelic poets' exploration of their geographical location and situation. For the Gaelic poet, operating in multiple spheres of influence, including city and island, imagined and real communities, and Scottish and Celtic nationalisms, the very difficulty in locating their sense of identity within the literary landscape is also what gives the poetry its richness and strength of purpose. From the cultural confidence of the Gaelic modernists coupled with the postmodern ambivalence and vulnerability of hybridity, Gaelic poetry has navigated itself into new and interesting places within the writing of Scotland.

Endnotes

1. See for example, Christopher MacLachlan and Ronald W. Renton (eds), *Gael and Lowlander in Scottish Literature: Cross-currents in Scottish Writing in the Nineteenth Century* (Glasgow: Scottish Literature International, 2015).
2. Sorley MacLean, *Caoir Gheal Leumraich/White Leaping Flame: Collected Poems*, ed. Christopher Whyte and Emma Dymock (Edinburgh: Polygon, 2011), pp. 372-73.
3. Margery Palmer McCulloch and Kirsten Matthews, 'Transcending the Thistle in *A Drunk Man* and *Cencrastus*', in Scott Lyall and Margery Palmer McCulloch (eds), *The Edinburgh Companion to Hugh MacDiarmid* (Edinburgh: Edinburgh University Press, 2011), pp. 48-67 (p. 64).
4. Letter from MacDiarmid to MacLean, 23 January 1977. See www.thesorleymacleantrust. org.uk/english/harvest_genius.htm.
5. Joy Hendry, 'Sorley MacLean: the Man and his Work', in Raymond J. Ross and Joy Hendry (eds), *Sorley MacLean: Critical Essays* (Edinburgh: Scottish Academic Press, 1986) pp. 9-38 (pp. 12, 15, 25).
6. MacLean, *Caoir Gheal Leumraich*, pp. 394-95.
7. Sorley MacLean, *An Cuilithionn 1939 / The Cuillin 1939 and Unpublished Poems*, ed. Christopher Whyte (Glasgow: Association for Scottish Literary Studies, 2011) pp. 160-61.
8. Edinburgh, National Library of Scotland (NLS), Acc. 6419, Box 38b: Letter dated 7 September 1941.
9. MacLean, *Caoir Gheal Leumraich*, pp. 30-31.
10. Ibid., pp. 394-95
11. Ibid., pp, 270-71.
12. Ibid.
13. *An Tuil: Anthology of 20th Century Scottish Gaelic Verse*, ed. Ronald Black (Edinburgh: Polygon, 1999), p. 801.
14. Aonghas MacNeacail, *dèanamh gàire ris a' chloc/laughing at the clock: New and Selected Poems* (Edinburgh: Polygon, 2012), pp. 162-63.
15. Black, pp. 680-81.
16. Ibid.
17. Black, pp. 682-83.
18. Ibid.
19. Ibid.
20. Ibid.
21. Alexander Carmichael, *Carmina Gadelica, Vol. 1* (Edinburgh: T. & A. Constable, 1900) pp. xxxv-xxxvi.
22. Murchadh MacPhàrlain, *An Toinneamh Dìomhair: Na h-Orain le Murchadh MacPhàrlain* (Stornoway: Stornoway Gazette, 1973).
23. MacPhàrlain, p. 10.
24. Ibid.
25. Ibid., p. 12.
26. Ibid., p. 13.
27. Ibid.
28. Black, pp. 180-85.
29. Albert Camus, *Myth of Sisyphus* (London: Penguin, 2000).

30 Derick Thomson, *Creachadh na Clàrsaich / Plundering the Harp: Cruinneachadh de Bhardachd 1940–1980* (Edinburgh: Macdonald Publishers, 1982), pp. 156–57.
31 Ibid., pp. 154–55.
32 Ibid.
33 Black, p. 784.
34 Ibid., pp. 524–25.
35 Ibid.
36 Ibid., pp. 526–27.
37 Ibid.
38 Iain Crichton Smith, 'A Poet in Scotland', in *Towards the Human: Selected Essays by Iain Crichton Smith* (Edinburgh: MacDonald Publishers, 1986), pp. 84–86 (p. 84).
39 Iain Crichton Smith, 'Real People in a Real Place', in *Towards the Human*, pp. 13–70 (p. 14).
40 Hendry, p. 13.
41 Iain Crichton Smith, 'Poetic Energy, Language and Nationhood', in *Towards the Human*, pp. 87–93 (p. 93).
42 Black, p. 815.
43 *Modern Scottish Women Poets*, ed. Dorothy McMillan and Michel Byrne (Edinburgh: Canongate, 2003), pp. 215–17.
44 Ibid.
45 Ibid.
46 Christopher Whyte, *Bho Leabhar-latha Maria Malibran / From the Diary of Maria Malibran* (Stornoway: Acair, 2009) pp. 88–91.
47 Ibid., pp. 88–89.

11. Critiquing Scotland's Clever Clocks and Macgrundies: Willa Muir's Nationalist Feminism

EMILY L. PICKARD

In 2004, Margery Palmer McCulloch wrote that 'early studies' of the Scottish Renaissance movement were 'defined by its male contributors alone, and it is only in recent years that women poets and fiction writers have been given their place in assessments of the literary revival'.[1] The inherently patriarchal nature of the literary movement that sought to revitalise and renew Scottish culture meant that texts written by women have been difficult to retrieve, but in recent years, as Palmer McCulloch shows, a Second Renaissance has taken place. Since the 1980s, Scottish academics, writers, and publishing houses, as well as readers and critics, have aimed to reframe what is perceived as the 'canon'. During this time, the male definition of the Scottish Renaissance in the interwar period has been challenged, and women writers from the period have made a 'comeback' of sorts. Among the best known of these women writers whose work was revitalised is Willa Muir (1890–1970). Although her main contributions to the Renaissance lie outwith an analysis of and argument for 'Scotland as Nation', her texts 'Clock-a-doodle-doo' (1934), *Mrs Grundy in Scotland* (1936), and 'Women in Scotland' (1936) provide a nuanced perspective on the state of 'Woman' and 'Nation'. With classic wit, each piece takes on a satirical tone, narrating the history of the effect of the separate spheres on women, and the patriarchal hypocrisy that has coloured the liminal space held by women. Moreover, Muir's understanding of gender and oppression in *Mrs Grundy* offers up a singularly Scottish theory of internalised misogyny decades before the birth of that term. Muir offers insight into how women understood a contemporary version of internalised misogyny, and how unique their position was within a literary revival that saw Woman as Muse. When read together, these texts reveal her argument for 'Scotland as Nation', not as a cry for independence, but as a call for gender equity within an engrained patriarchy. Only by improving the status and treatment of women can Scotland improve itself, and therefore, one could argue, begin to consider itself as an autonomous nation with an individual, highly valuable culture.

Wilhelmina Anderson was born 13 March 1890 in Montrose to Shetlandic parents. Her early experiences of Calvinism in the North-East shaped her understanding of gender and nation, raised, as she was, in a trilingual household: Shetlandic at home, English at school, and the dialect of Montrose on the streets. She was treated as an outsider when speaking Shetlandic outside the home, and, as she outlines in her memoir *Belonging* (1968), these childhood experiences of being a linguistic outcast continued to influence her throughout adulthood. On the other hand, she writes, her trilingual childhood gave her a pronounced linguistic ability and contributed to her prowess as a translator, allowing her to introduce European writers like Franz Kafka, Hermann Broch, Lion Feuchtwanger, and Christa Winsloe to English-speaking readers. But her mother's lifelong valuing of men over women, and her insistence that women should be able to darn socks, cook for their families, and maintain a clean house, framed Willa's outlook on the origins of gendered restrictions for women (to avoid confusion I will, when appropriate, use first names for Willa and her husband Edwin). It was likely this upbringing that influenced Muir's understanding of Mrs (Mac)Grundy. Mrs Grundy, a well-known bogey of the nineteenth and early twentieth centuries, defined the attitudes and behaviours that good (Victorian) households and individuals should maintain. In *Mrs Grundy in Scotland*, Muir invents Mrs MacGrundy as that bogey's Scottish counterpart – the attitudinarian, Calvinist censor who brings the fear of the Kirk into Scottish homes in order to 'keep up appearances'. More than this, the Scottish 'Kirk, then, and Mrs MacGrundy had already established a code of sexual propriety more severe and denunciatory than Mrs Grundy's.'[2] Sexuality and gender, then, and the Kirk's control of both, are inherently linked to Muir's understanding of Mrs MacGrundy and of Scotland.

In *Belonging*, Muir writes of her mother's first impression of Willa's husband, Edwin:

I knew that she had been disappointed at my marrying a mere clerk instead of a minister of the Kirk or a university professor, but Edwin was an Orkney-man, a sound recommendation to her. In a day or two she was inclined to favour him rather than me, for she valued men more than women and would have been sorry for any man I married. He would never have a button on his shirts, she told him, or on his trousers, or a pair of whole socks to put on his feet, poor Edwin.[3]

From this we can infer Muir's understanding of the values of religious Highland and Island women, especially those born during Queen Victoria's reign. First, Edwin's status as an Islander reflects upon him. Mrs Anderson assumes that his origins attest to his values, personality, and respectability in a way that overshadows his (in her eyes) less desirable profession. Second, Mrs Anderson's religious values are shown – she is within the Church of Scotland and desires her daughter to be as well. Finally, the cleanliness and appearance of her daughter and her daughter's husband are of paramount importance to her, and she shrewdly observes that these are not important to Willa. These aspects of Elizabeth Anderson's value system are framed by the particularly North-East Scottish internalised misogyny that informs her religious, attitudinarian, but Highland/Island-preferring, outlook. This background evidently influenced the Highland/Island and Calvinist focus of *Mrs Grundy in Scotland*, informed the bias against separate spheres as shown in 'Women in Scotland', and coloured her perspective of Renaissance men's utilitarian relations with women as depicted in 'Clock-a-doodle-doo'.

Muir's two novels, *Imagined Corners* (1931) and *Mrs Ritchie* (1933), had been out of print since their original publication until Canongate took up the mantle of reprinting these texts in 1996 in a collection alongside her feminist essays, *Women: An Inquiry* (1925), *Mrs Grundy in Scotland*, and 'Women in Scotland'. Both novels focus on the impact that mothers have on the restriction of their daughters, with the title figure of Annie Rattray/ Ritchie becoming the authoritarian tyrant whom Muir later theorises in

Mrs Grundy. After their republication in 1996, Muir's writings have not gained mainstream readers' attention and it was only Aileen Christianson's monograph *Moving in Circles: Willa Muir's Writings* (2007),[4] which reprinted some of Muir's unpublished and out of print works including 'Clock-a-doodle-doo', that allowed for a brief spotlight before she once more fell out of interest. While Muir is given her dues in studies on the Scottish Renaissance and modernism in Scotland, an analysis of her relationship with national concerns is often brief. This is probably due to Muir's own professed desire to have nationalism remain quite separate from her works. In July 1931, she wrote to Florence Marian McNeill of her first novel, *Imagined Corners*, and the decision to leave Calderwick (Montrose) by one of its central characters, Elise: 'it was supposed to be 1913, when there was little Nationalism: also, I was thinking more of Elise, when I followed her, than of national sentiment'.[5] Muir's rebuke is clear – her concern was gender inequality and telling women's stories, not building upon a (male-dominated) 'national sentiment'. To drive the point home, she continues in reference to her next novel (*Mrs Ritchie*): 'you needn't look for Nationalism with a big N in it'.[6] She believed that 'Some people can talk and fight and work politically' but writing 'a great book' would mean she had 'served Scotland too'.[7]

Muir's comment could not have been more pointed. Though this letter was written five years prior to hers and her husband's falling out with Hugh MacDiarmid and F. G. Scott, her relationship with the Scottish Renaissance's great bard and his composer friend had never been perfectly smooth, and MacDiarmid's wife Valda was particularly critical of Willa. Of F. G. Scott, Willa writes that he was 'a bit of a tyrant, especially to his wife and daughters whom he expected to be conventionally respectable, more so than his sons'.[8] As this chapter will show, this is the type of treatment of women and girls of which *Mrs Grundy* is so critical. Her description of MacDiarmid, while respectful towards his skill as a poet, includes an embarrassing episode of overindulgence in whisky which deeply upset his wife.[9] MacDiarmid's 1938 publication in *Voice of Scotland* of Barbara Niven's 'visual version of [Wyndham] Lewis's 1930 assault on the Muir relationship' in his *Apes of God* shows 'Edwin as a small fawn at the side of a large headless Willa in a bathing costume'.[10] This caricature was, apparently, Valda's idea and based on a memory she had of Willa on a beach in St Andrews speaking about Freudian phallic symbolism: there is a common anecdote, passed around Muir scholarship, of Valda complaining about Willa 'holding forth' on St Andrews' beach on 'her favourite topic – phallic symbolism'.[11]

While these criticisms of Willa's 'influence' over Edwin fail to criticise his influence over her, Willa's later break from the main figures of the Renaissance was clearly in motion well before Edwin's and may have encouraged her distaste for some of their more radically political viewpoints. It is important, however, to note that her memories of this time in *Belonging* are not aggressive or argumentative toward the main actors in the Renaissance, and she acknowledges their ambition and cultural contributions, even if she makes clear they were not always in agreement. They could 'talk and fight and work politically' for the literary renaissance; she would write for it. 'Clock-a-doodle-doo', *Mrs Grundy*, and 'Women in Scotland' make evident Susanne Hagemann's statement that 'women and nation are constructs, and any interpretation of the relationship between them depends to a considerable extent on the political interest which motivates it'.[12] Muir's motivation was not nationalism but improving the representation of women in Scotland. While she did not fight for a free Scotland to the extent of Scott or MacDiarmid, her writings nonetheless help to lay the groundwork for a Scotland that – if and when it gained its independence – would be a freer and kinder place for those who reside within her borders. Because her construction of women is, although essentialist in *Women: An Inquiry*, altogether freer and more positive than that of MacDiarmid's or Scott's, her motivation is ground in 'Loving-Kindness' and in a desire to upset the separate spheres by making transparent the history of women in that nation, not unlike Virginia Woolf's similar goal in *A Room of One's Own* (1929).

Willa published 'her satire on Modernism and the maleness of Scottish Renaissance' 'Clock-a-doodle-doo' in 1934 in *The Modern Scot*, published by James Whyte in St Andrews.[13] This could be considered quite a bold move – Hugh MacDiarmid, after all, was a regular contributor to *The Modern Scot*, and as its name suggests, that publication was at the centre of the Scottish literary Renaissance and political discussion. Muir's open distaste for the framework of the literary movement in this short story is also surprising, given that, according to Christianson, she wrote 'Clock-a-doodle-doo' 'specifically for publication in volume 5 of *The Modern Scot*, apparently the only short story (as opposed to chapter from a novel) that she published'.[14] Christianson calls *The Modern Scot* the 'house journal of Scottish renaissancism in the nineteen thirties', and the men at whom Muir pokes fun (including, arguably but subtly, her own husband whose 1934 poem sequence was titled *Variations on a Time Theme*, and who may have played the role of the older clock) looked to that publication for evidence of Scotland's movement into cultural progress.[15] Moreover, that – of all the short stories she wrote – this was the only one to be published suggests that the story held some level of importance to her. Whether she thought the story too good to remain unpublished or whether this was because the topic was too important is unclear. What is evident, however, is that 'Clock-a-doodle-doo' acts as a counternarrative to the one which sprouted from *The Modern Scot* generally.

The story, which, as already noted, can be found in full in Christianson's monograph, critiques both the men in the Renaissance – grown-up children, who are similar to the adult weans Muir critiques in *Mrs Grundy* and *Imagined Corners* – and their fascination with grand, philosophical themes. In this case, she emphasises their fascination with Time and their desire to break with the past by using animated clocks to represent the major Renaissance actors. Pound's 'Make it new!' becomes 'Let us make a beginning – any beginning!'.[16] The story is set in a four-walled room, three of which are covered in a variety of clocks in various shapes, sizes, and personalities. The fourth wall is entirely of glass, a 'show-case', and Muir gives her readers the impression that these clocks yearn for 'the gaze' – they want space to boast and show off, such as, by implication, toddlers in front of new friends. Notably, they require this gaze to remind themselves of their intelligence, and rely on their own feelings of self-importance and confidence to remind themselves of their existence when not gazed upon. The clocks rely on the 'Woman' to wind them up every day. As Christianson points out, this is her sole duty within the story and according to the clocks, and she is otherwise 'indifferent' to them. This is distressing for the clocks, who 'resent her for this and for their fear, for if the mechanism of a clock fails in the night it is as if its reality is annihilated. An opposition between natural and clock time is established.[17] After all, the clocks 'were proud of their cog-wheels inside their heads, especially when daylight failed and they could not see each other', and so they were 'puzzled by her indifference'.[18]

The Clever Clock, 'who claimed to have twice as many cog-wheels as any of the others' decides he wants to break with the 'Author of their Being', who lights upon the room daily and dictates their regularity.[19] He decides that 'the Truth of things lay inside their own heads, and was to be discovered only by the study of their own cog-wheels' so 'a knowledge of the springs of their own conduct would enable each of them to detach himself from routine and become an independent moon'.[20] (Kirsten Stirling suggests this reference to the 'moon' may allude to MacDiarmid's *A Drunk Man Looks at the Thistle* (1926) in which the 'silken leddy' is 'closely associated with the fluid and unstable symbols of alcohol and the moon' and may also 'be a vision of the Drunk Man himself' as he contemplates nation, sexuality, home, and identity.)[21] The Clever Clock realises that he does not need the Woman to wind him up, as his cog-wheels run independently: 'Not one of you is capable of becoming a free agent, except myself. [...] I shall be famous when you are all on the scrap-heap'.[22] He believes the Woman would not dare to contradict him: 'Does she not handle our weights simply and solely to minister to the cog-wheels?'[23] His view of the Woman is merely as one to serve his needs, and here it is implied that those needs are both that of a child – basic nourishment, shelter, and affirmation of their intelligence ('minister to the cog-wheels') – and sexualised ('handle our weights'). Yet because he believes in his absolute unique talents and in the Woman's sole duty to care for him, even when there 'was a tiny screw loose in the Clever Clock, [...] he was too busy boasting and studying Pure Horological Thought to observe anything of the kind'.[24] His inability to self-reflect and consider the value of others and their work, especially women and their emotional labour, becomes his downfall. Muir's snide description of him having 'a tiny screw loose' makes clear her perspective on these self-serving intellectual pursuits and his declaration that each can 'detach himself' makes evident her understanding of these cultural centres as male-dominated. As a result of this, the Clock desires to become 'unintelligible' and 'unique among clocks' and, upon discovering that 'he shrugged himself so hard that his numbers fell into confusion', he decides to knock all of his screws loose.[25] His 'pendulum was clacking wildly' and, in his excitement, despite being breathless and exhausted, he clack-clack-clacks away until not one number or pendulum balance remains.[26]

Muir is critiquing MacDiarmid's 'desire to follow Pound and to "make it new"'.[27] This debate among the clocks, with the older, wiser clock encouraging respect for the natural order of Time, and receiving arguments (clacking) from the younger clocks, shows 'opposition between natural and the mechanical'.[28] Christianson provides an excellent overview of the way in which this story critiques modernism in Scotland, specifically Futurism and the desire for the split between Victorian and Edwardian Britain. She argues that MacDiarmid was 'something of an *enfant terrible* and a clever clogs (in the colloquial sense of showing off his own knowledge and cleverness), politically both Marxist and nationalist, and swinging wildly between the two at times'.[29] Muir's focus is insistently non-nationalist and her work is not to boast of her own cleverness. Instead, she provides an alternative perception – that the work of these clocks would be impossible without Woman – and, in the process, questions who is truly behind the Renaissance movement. But, though Muir and MacDiarmid were never the best of friends, it would be her husband's book *Scott and Scotland* in 1936 that would break their friendship permanently. While Christianson argues that this satire was simply taken as a light-hearted, necessary commentary on the maleness of the modernist movement in Scotland, Muir's own distaste for boastful politics, nationalism, and patriarchy lends a more serious and weighted analysis to this story.

Important is the role of Woman. She never speaks, but it is her indifference to the clocks which is most striking. She administers to their cog-wheels, as the Clever Clock believes, but this becomes a routine for her, an insignificant chore in her day to take care of those who cannot care for themselves, but for whom she does not much concern herself. When the Clever Clock decides to make a rowdy noise, he interprets her silence toward the matter as 'a mere servant of the cog-wheels'.[30] The narrator, however, swiftly reinterprets her silence: 'the Woman did not look at his face at all. He was a clock who could run for months at a time without her, and she disregarded him'.[31] She is more concerned with those in need of care. At the conclusion of the story, 'the Woman came in' and 'her foot struck against a little pile of discarded numbers and a pendulum balance. Also, she could hear the Clever Clock clack-clacking at furious speed.'[32] When the Woman takes him from the wall, blowing 'the dust off the little wooden figures', the Clever Clock declares: 'Now I move from the wall as I promised you. This Woman is the servant of my will.'[33] Yet, when the door shuts behind him, we are left in no doubt as to the fate of the Clever Clock, hinted at by Muir's choice of the word 'discarded' and her suggestion that the clock had been so often ignored and disregarded – an insignificant factor in the Woman's life – that he had gathered dust. As she carries him out in her arms, there is an overarching suggestion of a naughty child combined with the implication of a malfunctioning mechanism which, once it has failed at its single purpose, will be thrown away. Here, Muir 'compares the management skills of a housewife [and mother] with those necessary to run government', and indeed, to lop off those 'Clever Clocks' who would make 'the mother-figure of Scotland [...] suffer the actions of other people'.[34]

When read alongside *Mrs Grundy in Scotland* and 'Women in Scotland', it is evident that this short story is actively discouraging the type of 'Clever Clock' behaviour that Muir believed MacDiarmid to enact. The Woman's tossing out of the clock suggests what Muir believes can happen to those who act in the way of the 'Clever Clocks' of the Renaissance and modernist movements – they are not worth women's time. Moreover, the story allows her to express a certain amount of resentment towards MacDiarmid for his misogynistic handling of the Renaissance, and the writers (usually male poets) he chose to champion. In direct contrast with the men of the Renaissance, Muir removes the Woman from the status of 'Muse'. Unlike MacDiarmid, who 'identified [Helen] Cruickshank, in this domestic and supportive role, along with his wife Valda Trevlyn, as a manifestation of "the Scottish muse"', Muir shows how these women have their own work and aims, despite the needs of the men in their care.[35] Muir suggests that to make a great Scotland, these Clever Clocks with all their extra cogs rely on women for all their basic needs. Without women who attend their needs – 'winding their cog-wheels' with meals, emotional support, and clean houses – these clocks would simply stop ticking. In so doing, she makes evident that women are the true foundation of the country, and therefore, that Nation can never be a primary focus for women until they are no longer viewed as Servants of Men's Will. In other words, she grounds women's place within nation as in the physical realm, as Stirling suggests: 'Muir's use of nation-as-woman imagery differs from the male construction in that the mystical aspect of female existence is removed, and the emphasis is on women as individuals within the political economy and within the narrative.'[36] Though overtly the 'Woman' is without individual identity, her 'Everywoman' status is not mystical and ethereal. Muir grounds the Woman's position firmly within the physical world. She resists enacting the Muse and refuses to become the 'servant' to the will of the Clever Clock.

That Muir was highly critical of the male-dominated Renaissance movement was no secret. In 'Women in Scotland', published in 1936 in *Left Review*, she shows how the centuries-old relegation of women to the domestic sphere has meant that 'the ordinary women of Scotland, petty bourgeois and proletarian alike [...] are untrained in public life, almost unrepresented, relatively unorganized and largely inarticulate outside the home.'[37] Muir believes that this perpetuates the cycle – if they are unable to speak up for themselves in public or in government, women will therefore be unable to speak up for their independence. Her comparison of the status and rights of women to a pre-devolution, post-Union Scotland is subtle, but clear. Yet, this statement's critique of the Renaissance's underrepresentation of women is tangible as she criticises the journal in which she publishes: 'The ratio of men to women contributors in this Scottish number of the *Left Review* is a fair reflection of what happens in Scottish public life.'[38] Muir's implication is one of hypocrisy. The Left – harbingers of freedom and equity for all – has not 'made good' on its promise: it is neglecting to allow fair and equal representation of women.

Published two years after 'Clock-a-doodle-doo', *Mrs Grundy in Scotland* provides Scottish-specific insight into gender and class that is in line with

'Women in Scotland'. Commissioned by Lewis Grassic Gibbon as part of his series on Scotland, *Mrs Grundy*'s aims were more political than any of Muir's other works. While Muir does not lambast nationalism overtly, she draws attention to Renaissance men's use of women figureheads to represent 'nation'. In so doing, she 'reminds us that the female figure cannot be separated from the flesh and blood existence of actual women'.[39] She draws attention to internalised misogyny, and, perhaps most importantly, shows how women figureheads have been exploited as masks for the patriarchal institution functioning below the surface. Elphinstone notes that Muir attempts to 'embody in female form the repressive forces in Scottish society'[40] but consequently, according to Stirling, falls within the awkward position of depicting Woman-as-Nation. Her unsuccessful attempt at this is perhaps because her true purpose is to show how Woman in her bodily form *cannot* be Nation. Instead, Muir shows that the models created and yearned for by the male state – those same models who are oppressed and despised by that same state – are in fact the patriarchy hiding below a mask of 'Woman'. She shows how this disadvantages all women, and even the men-children whom it purports to benefit. Published the same year, 'Women in Scotland' proffers similar critiques of the separation between the domestic and public spheres. Woman, able to control only what is in the domestic sphere, ends up becoming a tyrant within that realm. She is blocked from bringing forth her skills and insight to aid and improve greater society, and so over-exerts in private. As a result, everyone suffers, but the patriarchy – specifically a Calvinist and capitalist patriarchy – is the initial and root culprit.

In this work, the distinction is not just England versus Scotland, but also Highland versus Lowland. She begins the chapter 'MacGrundy in the Highlands' by explaining that '[s]omething had happened to discredit Highland ways in the eyes of Lowland Scots', noting that those who wore tartan shawls in Glasgow were dubbed 'shawlies' and that, much to the dismay of Queen Victoria, lowland bands were unfamiliar with Highland reels.[41] This is a main distinction for Muir in Grundy versus MacGrundy: 'It could not have been Mrs Grundy who objected to Highland culture: she would not have ventured to disagree with her august sovereign, whose fondness for Highland music and Highland tartans was well known.'[42] It must, then, have been Mrs MacGrundy; unlike the Queen who went 'all girlish and Balmoral about the Highlands', 'Mrs MacGrundy from the Lowlands [...] disapproved of Highland ways'.[43] These were, she goes on to show, used to justify the Clearances.

In this discussion, she explains that adherence to MacGrundy's strict gender norms reveal how much 'these rural Scots repress each other' and 'how far they distrust themselves' – 'Behave yoursels before folk!'[44] She writes for pages on the strict rules for women. These are often, particularly for the minister's wife, in order to defend the honour of both herself and her male family members: 'The minister saves the face of the parish before God and Mrs MacGrundy; the minister's wife saves both his face and her own.'[45] After all, he cannot 'save face' unless his own virtues are clear and unquestioned. Throughout the chapter 'Mrs MacGrundy', Muir defines and analyses each strict rule, noting by the end that this is attitudinarian – it is, fundamentally, 'a negative social consciousness' that is based on appearances, not on ingrained morals and concern for the community's wellbeing.[46] As a result, everyone suffers, but women especially, whose lives (and sex lives) are dictated from birth until death. 'The women', after all, 'enveloped their men. They were environments for their families. The men had no occasion to remember that women too might be individuals.'[47]

Muir argues that prior to Mrs (Mac)Grundy's influence in the Highlands, communities there 'looked on marriage with a very different eye [...] a convention which, for all I know, may once have been a general in Europe and was certainly of respectable Norse antiquity'.[48] Without citing her research, Muir explains that 'young men and women only married if a child was born to them, or expected. Courting couples did not "walk out" together: they did their courting in bed' and, accordingly, '[n]o stigma was attached to illegitimate children, no monopoly value was attached to virginity'.[49] After Mrs (Mac)Grundy's influence, however, 'poor little Susannas [...] were probably scared stiff by the conflict between the tradition of country wooing and the tradition of the Kirk'.[50] She argues, with information from her Orcadian husband no doubt, that there in 'the Orkneys, which are

Norse islands, the convention persists openly even in these post-war years' but this did not prevent women from taking the punishment for the community when a pregnancy outside of wedlock occurred.[51] Within this system, in which 'Girls murdered their illegitimate children rather than face the ordeal of being pilloried', it was decided that either women could give in to the 'progress' which saw her every move dictated by the Kirk, or she could face the consequences.[52] In this system, women and girls, 'these lesser individuals, needed a man to direct them' and, contradictorily, these women are also expected to be men's 'conscience'.[53] In other words, they were allowed a certain level of 'power' within the household, but only insofar as that 'power' was used to direct (read: take responsibility for) their men's and children's actions: 'the men, like selfish children, tried rather hard the racial patience of the women who mothered them, but the women, so long as they remained at the centre of home life, had the recognized prestige of mothers'.[54] Scotland's systems, Muir argues, and the patriarchal Calvinism to which these adhere, limit the freedom of these men-children and dictate the lives of these women.

This introduction of Mrs MacGrundy to Scotland and its Highlands, particularly after the Clearances and Calvinism, has meant that what was once – as Muir frames it – a musical, artistic, communal culture has become a state of 'puir auld mithers': 'Scotland as a nation has been for so long a "puir auld mither" that Scottish mothers are likely to have a fellow-feeling for her.'[55] As Margaret Elphinstone notes, 'Mrs Grundy is not merely the symbol of tragedy; the tragedy is her own. It takes place in her inner world. [...] the tragedy of every Scottish woman [...] [who] outwardly enacts the repression of the unconscious self', while she lives within her own 'inner world' in which 'a microcosm of a massive struggle centred upon the meaning of self, gender and society' takes place.[56] Muir reveals how, until this changes, Scotland's culture – and its ability to be a nation-state – is lacking.

Muir's focus is not the nationalist agenda. Her experiences in Eastern Europe before and after the Second World War no doubt contributed to her scepticism towards nationalism. In a 'private, unofficial account' of the PEN Congress in Hungary in 1932, Muir stressed the atmosphere of tension, fear, conflict, and oppression connected to hyper-nationalist elites and government in Budapest.[57] In this letter, she writes about a book that was stripped of the honour of receiving the best Hungarian book award:

> The Government however intimated that this book was not to get the prize, since it was merely a study of peasant life and in no way furthered the Chauvinist aspirations of Hungary. The Government added that should the PEN persist in awarding the prize to this book it would not grant a single pengo for the International Congress.[58]

Here, she shows how class inequalities contribute to which works of literature are valued or otherwise. But what is also significant for this chapter is Muir's understanding of the gendered inequities within this atmosphere of 'oppression' and her connection of this atmosphere and sexism to the neglect of Scotland as Nation. At the 'official reception' in the Royal Palace:

> there was no separate provision made for Scotland: we were to be lumped together in one crowd with the English. Of course we protested [...] and although we stood beside the English we did so with a little gap between us, and Edwin, as the Head of the Delegation (wha !!!! that was a story!) was separately presented to Horthy. All this made Edwin so nervous that he forgot to present me, I might say: and I had the dubious distinction of being the only person in the room who did not grab Horthy's hand.[59]

Muir suggests a link between national oppression and gender, and in so doing, shows the hypocrisy of a male-dominated Scottish Literary Revival. She makes evident that she *does* see and requires a separation between Scotland and England – that to her, this distinction is tangible enough to necessitate acknowledgement of the two nations' different literary cultures at the PEN conference.

Union or not, 'the Scottish PEN is established as an independent centre' and the 'Congress invitation was given in the name of *Scotland*'.[60] She speaks up for an 'independent Scotland' and it is unclear if she limits this to Scottish

PEN or Scotland more broadly: 'a thoroughly Scottish Congress in 1934 would educate a vast mass of opinion throughout Europe'.[61] Once more, it is unclear if she means Scotland's PEN or Scotland generally when she acknowledges that 'as an independent Scotland we must rank with the smaller nations, and cannot have the prestige of England or France or Germany. But it will be our own prestige, and we must establish it.'[62] This letter to Helen Cruickshank makes evident that Muir did believe in an independent Scottish literary culture and she worked for it in her own way – Scottish PEN *did* host the twelfth annual International PEN Congress in 1934 and she and Edwin were founding members.[63] Her focus on gender in her literary pursuits was not to disregard entirely 'national sentiment' but to suggest other ways in which Scotland could be improved in order to gain freedom and improved lives for *all* of its population. 'Clock-a-doodle-doo', 'Women in Scotland', and *Mrs Grundy* can be read, then, as guidelines for recreating the Scottish landscape to benefit all, to lay the groundwork for an equal and fair Scotland, and for a literary culture that – while it struggles its way to independence and international acknowledgement, away from an overshadowing Empire – embraces all of its writers and does not continue oppressive practices over those who are marginalised. In this way, Willa Muir can be recognised as a crucial contributor to both the First and the Second Scottish Renaissances.

Endnotes

1. Margery Palmer McCulloch (ed.), *Modernism and Nationalism – Literature and Society in Scotland 1918–1939* (Glasgow: Association for Scottish Literary Studies, 2004), p. xvi.
2. Willa Muir, *Mrs Grundy in Scotland* (London: George Routledge and Sons, Ltd., 1936), p. 120.
3. Willa Muir, *Belonging* (London: Hogarth Press, 1968), p. 33.
4. Aileen Christianson, *Moving in Circles: Willa Muir's Writings* (Edinburgh: Word Power Books, 2007).
5. Muir, letter to F. Marian McNeill (1931), reproduced in *Modernism and Nationalism*, pp. 208–09 (p. 208).
6. Muir, *Modernism and Nationalism*, p. 209.
7. Ibid.
8. *Belonging*, p. 117.
9. Ibid., p. 116.
10. Christianson, p. 29.
11. Alan Bold, *MacDiarmid: Christopher Murray Grieve; A Critical Biography* (London: John Murray, 1988), p. 333, quoted in Christianson, p. 71.
12. Susanne Hagemann, 'Women and Nation', in Douglas Gifford and Dorothy McMillan (eds), *A History of Scottish Women's Writing* (Edinburgh: Edinburgh University Press, 1997), pp. 316–28 (p. 326).
13. Christianson, p. 46.
14. Ibid., p. 47.
15. Ibid. See also chapter five of Emily L. Pickard, 'The Other Muir: Willa Muir, Motherhood, and Writing' (unpublished doctoral thesis, University of Glasgow, 2022), for an in-depth analysis of the Muirs' relationship in the 1930s.
16. Muir, in Christianson, p. 203.
17. Christianson, p. 47.
18. Muir, 'Clock-a-doodle-doo', reproduced in Christianson, pp. 201–05 (p. 201).
19. Ibid., p. 202.
20. Ibid., pp. 202–03.
21. Kirsten Stirling, *Bella Caledonia: Woman, Nation, Text* (Brill, 2008), p. 41: ebookcentral.proquest.com/lib/gla/detail.action?docID=556358.
22. Muir, in Christianson, p. 203.
23. Ibid.
24. Ibid., p. 204.
25. Ibid.
26. Ibid.
27. Roderick Watson, *The Literature of Scotland: the twentieth century*, 2nd edn [1984] (Hampshire: Palgrave Macmillan, 2007), p. 35.
28. Christianson, p. 47.
29. Ibid., p. 50.
30. Muir, in Christianson, p. 203.
31. Ibid.
32. Ibid., p. 205.
33. Ibid.
34. Stirling, p. 62; 60.

35 Ibid., p. 54, quoting Hugh MacDiarmid, *Lucky Poet: A Self-Study in Literature and Political Ideas* [1943] (London: Cape, 1972), pp. 400–01.
36 Ibid., p. 63.
37 Willa Muir, 'Women in Scotland' (1936), reproduced in Kirsty Allen (ed.), *Willa Muir: Imagined Selves* (Edinburgh: Canongate Books Limited, 1996), pp. 1–4 (p. 1).
38 Ibid.
39 Stirling, p. 58.
40 Margaret Elphinstone, 'Willa Muir: Crossing the Genres', in Douglas Gifford and Dorothy McMillan (eds), *A History*, pp. 400–15 (p. 413).
41 *Mrs Grundy*, p. 147
42 Ibid.
43 Ibid., p. 148.
44 Ibid., p. 63.
45 Ibid., p. 62.
46 Ibid., p. 63.
47 Ibid., p. 98.
48 Ibid., p. 118.
49 Ibid.
50 Ibid., p. 119.
51 Ibid., p. 120.
52 Ibid., p. 125.
53 Ibid., pp. 125, 75.
54 Ibid., p. 99.
55 'Women in Scotland', p. 4.
56 Elphinstone, p. 414.
57 Willa Muir, letter to Helen Cruickshank (1932), reproduced in P. H. Butter (ed.), *Selected Letters of Edwin Muir* (London: The Hogarth Press, 1974), pp. 72–76 (p. 72).
58 Ibid., pp. 72–73.
59 Ibid., p. 75.
60 Ibid.
61 Ibid.
62 Ibid., pp. 75–76.
63 Scottish PEN, 'The urgent present: the 1930s': scottishpen.org/about/history/.

12. 'This is Scotland, by Christ!': Cultural Nationalism and National (Re)Branding in the Cinematic Adaptations of Irvine Welsh

ANNE-LISE MARIN-LAMELLET

In 1996, one year after the release of Mel Gibson's *Braveheart*, based on 'Blind' Hary's *The Wallace* (c. 1477), *Trainspotting* popularised a new image of Scotland on screen. Based on Irvine Welsh's debut novel, the film provocatively did away with a cultural tradition, dating at least from Walter Scott's stage-management of George IV's 1822 royal visit to Edinburgh, which identified Scotland with the Highlands. In its iconoclastic view, the film instead saw a contemporary disenfranchised, marginalised and drug-using Scottish youth in those Highlands where, cinematically speaking, the iconic scene undermined 'the filmic trope that sees Highland and rural areas as places of escape from capitalist exploitation and of self-reshaping'.[1] In terms of aesthetics and cultural politics, the 'Trainspotting effect'[2] came to counter the 'Braveheart effect'[3] and was interpreted as reflecting an anti-Thatcherite perspective which typically transpired in a confrontation between deindustrialised Leithers and Highland lovers. Because cinema is both art and industry, it deals with culture, politics but also economics. Some might say *Trainspotting* simply launched a new trend, judging by the spate of films that clearly drew their inspiration from it such as *Twin Town* (Kevin Allen, 1997) or *Human Traffic* (Justin Kerrigan, 1999), a niche genre more intent on depicting various subcultures in the form of coming-of-age films than Scottishness *per se*. It is true that most Irvine Welsh's film adaptations could potentially be taking place elsewhere than in Edinburgh. With their universal themes (youth, gender relations, anti-consumerism, etc.), youth film codes-inspired style and rather soft accents, the films are set in a 'Scottish anywhereland'[4] and it may therefore be difficult to approach them as typical expressions of cultural nationalism. Moreover, out of the five feature films adapted from Irvine Welsh's works to this day, only *The Acid House* (1999) and *Filth* (2013) were directed by Scots, respectively Paul McGuigan and Jon S. Baird. *Trainspotting* and *T2 Trainspotting* (2017) were directed by the Englishman Danny Boyle (although penned by Scottish screenwriter John Hodge), and *Ecstasy* (2012) by the Canadian Rob Heydon.

However, whatever their directors' nationalities or funding sources, these films – probably owing to their source material – show a consistent willingness to engage with Scottish identity, the evolution of Scotland and its future. As such, they are truly Scottish films since 'one major function of Scottish cinema is to engage domestic audiences in shared processes of socio-cultural debate and self-definition'.[5] They are also 'cultural ambassadors' to international audiences, part of their controversial critical and commercial success (or failure) being related to the fact that these Irvine Welsh adaptations replace 'heritage' with 'garbage'.[6] Because, in presenting their versions of Scottishness, these films make a point of going against a whole literary and cinematic tradition, the so-called Scotch myths,[7] they can be perceived as disturbing or even unpleasant especially since they often do so in an outrageous way. Engaging with Scottishness has also been a way for Irvine Welsh and his adapters to be quite critical about Scottish society, which might explain the difficulties some directors have faced in financing their films. In this context, referring to an earlier common perception of Scottish cinema, David Archibald has commented:

> If you associate Scottish cinema with monochrome tales featuring alcohol-sodden fathers, battered mothers and children in short trousers struggling stoically for a bite of a cold sausage roll, you are, I'm afraid, not alone. It's a perception inspired by films such as those in the *Bill Douglas Trilogy*, a 1970s sequence based on the director's upbringing in a mining village near Edinburgh. Magisterial but undeniably austere, it remains widely under-appreciated even in the director's country of birth. So too is an expansive body of work by other directors, including Ken Loach, Lynne Ramsay and Peter Mullan, focusing on the darker aspects of Scottish urban life. Of course, there is also a fine comedic strand to film-making in Scotland, running from Ealing Studios' *Whisky Galore!* to Bill

Forsyth's *Gregory's Girl* and Loach's last Scotland-set feature, *The Angels' Share*. But the notion endures that film-making north of the border remains dominated by dour, proletarian, if not presbyterian, miserabilism.[8]

Yet, far from wallowing in miserabilism or gratuitous childish provocation, these films based on Welsh's novels are evidence of an increasingly assertive, bold nation at ease with itself, and willing to show its dark and bright sides, and shed the lucrative clichés which are still widely used by American and Bollywood productions. The purpose of this transdisciplinary chapter (studying a society through its film production) is thus to show how Irvine Welsh adaptations both undermine and celebrate Scottishness, and how their ambivalence testifies to the complexity of contemporary Scottish society while also fitting in perfectly with the cultural history of that nation. As such, these films are a way to keep writing about Scottishness (semiotically speaking, a film is a text) since they contribute to the shaping of audiences' representation of Scottish national identities both domestically and internationally.

Writing off or rewriting Scottishness? Debunking the 'Scotch myths'

Versions of Scottishness on screen have evidently become increasingly varied, complex and sometimes darker since post-war films such as *Whisky Galore!* (Alexander Mackendrick, 1949). The unexpectedly massive success of *Trainspotting* as a film further reinforced the star status of Irvine Welsh whose name is now associated with a certain vision of Scottishness. He has become a sort of Scottish brand himself[9] as shown by his cameos in these adaptations, the promotional material and the film credits that all put forward their connection with the writer. Besides, catchphrases ('based on the novel/short stories by Irvine Welsh', 'from the creator of *Trainspotting*'), the orange colour of the original edition of the soundtrack album[10] and the book design[11] are now used as a code to establish the connection with what might be considered the *Trainspotting* franchise. The author's name is included in the film title 'Irvine Welsh's *Ecstasy*' to make sure that what might otherwise be taken as a standard youth rave film is calling on potential fans. Irvine Welsh usually leaves the adaptation process to other writers but has turned to production, presumably to facilitate the financing of these films in a nation that still struggles to have an industry of its own, let alone one that can or will produce Scottishness in what may be state-of-the-nation films catering both for local and international audiences. That is probably why Rob Heydon, director of *Ecstasy*, has expressed some regrets in not being able to secure the author's involvement in the production process that made later projects possible.[12] But despite the author's fame that may be seen as a guarantee for his adaptations' bankability, he and other directors have mentioned the difficulties they had to convince other producers and resist post-production pressures. The presence of a well-known actor in the lead role seems necessary. James McAvoy explains how he tried to 'protect' the director's vision while *Filth* was being edited.[13]

Knowing that one of the criteria to obtain funds from organisations such as Scottish Screen or Creative Scotland has been to emphasise the 'cultural relevance to Scotland' of the project,[14] could it be that the version of Scottishness presented in Irvine Welsh adaptations is somehow problematic to some decision-makers? The director of *Ecstasy* explains the difficulties he had to produce his film because it 'was quite apparent [from his conversations with representatives of regional and national agencies in the UK, 'especially Scotland'] that they just did not want films showing this part of Scotland to be made, they did not want another *Acid House* to be made in Scotland'.[15] For what it is worth, it would also be interesting to study the distribution and marketing of these films that reveal some tensions due to the version of Scottishness they present. For example, a website such as VisitScotland.com advertised the release of the *Trainspotting* sequel in 2017 in a way that shows it may still have a problem with that image of Scotland although it cannot ignore it.[16] Because it apparently refused to show stills from the film, it chose an angle that enabled it to dodge the issue by referring to the filmographies of the cast members since their scandalous debut, carefully selecting the works that most matched its traditional heritage illustrations.[17] The institution has nonetheless officially 'embraced' Irvine Welsh-inspired films as examples of 'cultural noir' and as the basis for an increasing interest in 'dark tourism'.[18]

Part of the resistance mentioned by the film-making crews could be related to the fact that Irvine Welsh's adaptations parody or debunk some 'Scotch myths'. International audiences, who may have a limited understanding of Scottishness, are deliberately not shown Highlanders in kilts. Both *Trainspotting* and *T2 Trainspotting* use the Highlands briefly to better thwart expectations based on cinematic tropes, not to say clichés. That willingness to expand the meaning of Scottishness explains the comedic effect produced in the first film when Renton rants against 'the great outdoors' because of its discrepancy with the 'Tartan exteriors'[19] of the scene. In the second film, the scene when Renton and Simon have to walk home naked is used to show that wind farms have come to dot the Scottish landscape and its moors. It is also meant to be an ironic twist of traditional Scottish imagery since the garb and wellies they steal from a farmer make them look like atypical clansmen, the evocation of the kilt being deprived of any show of force or manliness but rather a symbol of their cowardice and humiliation by the local gangster. Although it might be sociologically or culturally inaccurate, the opening of *T2 Trainspotting* seems to want to make a stand. When Renton arrives at the airport, his interactions with the welcoming ladies are there to insist on the fact that those who show ostentatious signs of Scottishness are migrants. The scene may be an echo of the American tourist in *Trainspotting*, who is beaten up by Renton's gang since his wearing of a kilt in their local pub paradoxically signals his foreignness. The decision to expand the meaning of Scottishness also explains Bruce covering his ears and wincing when he comes across a piper in town in the opening scene of *Filth*. Films inspired by Irvine Welsh have in common their provocative rejection of the 'Balmorisation of Scotland'[20] and cinematic traditions such as Tartanry.[21] The recurrent claims by characters such as Renton (*Trainspotting*) and Bruce (*Filth*) that they are 'a bad person/used to be a good person' may be interpreted as going against Highlandism, i.e. the traditional image of Scots, especially Highlanders or rural people, as noble savages[22] or sources of integrity,[23] since these films prove that Scots can be as ruthless as Thatcherite English people.

These films also indirectly address Kailyard, the literary/filmic convention which defined Scottishness in terms of rural sentimentality, through their use of space. *Ecstasy* and *T2 Trainspotting* emphasise youth subcultures, notably Edinburgh's club scene, and present the capital as a city full of franchised shops, trendy bars and fine restaurants, with hectic traffic, giant wheels and trailing lights. This depiction of Edinburgh may be seen as an attempt to show a more positive image of the country in a post-national and globalised context. By comparison, Toal's office (*Filth*), shot in Stirling's municipal buildings, looks like a Victorian interior reflecting the man's outdated character. In *T2 Trainspotting*, Renton is criticised for his nostalgia that can be interpreted both as individual and representative of a national sentiment, notably by Veronica, the Bulgarian migrant. Her reaction to Renton and Simon's enthusiastic logorrhoea about 1974, in a pre-Americanised Scotland where junk food and obesity were scarce, is sobering: 'you live in the past. Where I come from, the past is something to forget. But here, it's all you talk about.' Renton's nostalgia is symbolically cured by the use of an electro remix of *Trainspotting*'s iconic Iggy Pop soundtrack 'Lust for Life' at the end of the film. He had previously started listening to the original vinyl found in his old bedroom, kept like a shrine by his mother, but had immediately stopped the needle, thereby showing that no man ever steps in the same river twice.

However, despite their willingness to somehow expose any backward-looking cinematic clichés associated with Tartanry or Kailyard, these films are not nostophobic.[24] Rather, they mix old and new Scotland and present characters finally at peace with their roots (*Ecstasy*, *T2 Trainspotting*). One of the recurring phrases heard is that the world is changing and Renton's return to his hometown is there to prove it (*T2 Trainspotting*). The montage that shows him looking out of the tram window echoes that of London in *Trainspotting*, as if he were a tourist in his own city. The later films show a more fluid Scottish society in which people are not completely stuck in their derelict council schemes as was the case in *Trainspotting* or *The Acid House*.[25] The last tower blocks standing are soon to be taken down as confirmed by the animated end credits in *T2 Trainspotting*, and the Port Sunshine pub is a sort of time capsule standing alone in a half demolished street, its interior being covered with faded pictures and a life-size poster of Dean Martin. Gentrified Leith is being connected with the city centre by trams (*Ecstasy*,

T2 Trainspotting). That topographical fluidity goes along that of characters' identity. Lloyd (*Ecstasy*) walks from his beloved clubs through Calton Hill to his old father's flat. *Filth* and *T2 Trainspotting* combine shots of seedy back alleys or ungentrified wasteland with establishing heritage shots (Princes Street, Edinburgh Castle, Charlotte Square) and renovated areas such as Persevere Court or the Scottish Parliament Building/Holyrood. The effects of gentrification can take their toll on some working-class men as shown by the recurrent sepia flashbacks in *T2 Trainspotting* offering a sharp contrast between the lively atmosphere of the pub in Simon's childhood and its now gloomy and depressing aspect, or the recurrent shots of the scrapyard with cars getting crushed near his flat – an allusion to the stranded lives of male protagonists. These shots offer an illustration of Begbie's questions at the end of the film and Spud's comment as an attempt to show the fading of the Scottish working class. But, overall, the elegiac tone is compensated by Welsh's irony. The changes affecting Leith, as they were strongly encouraged by somewhat candid local authorities and supported by generous European funding (*T2 Trainspotting*), are testimony to the passing of time. As long as people write about the memories of that world, the spirit of the place does not really die. Spud is thus a sort of projection of Irvine Welsh himself in *T2 Trainspotting* since what he calls his stories are the chapters of *Trainspotting* (the book). Cranes are still visible on the docks and renovated buildings are decorated with murals depicting their industrial past (*T2 Trainspotting*). Montage sequences may show the new face of Edinburgh with its vibrant nightlife and pounding club scene; they also include more traditional imagery with old pipers and tartan-wearing Scots (*Ecstasy*). The bridges (Queensferry Crossing, Forth Road Bridge) emerging from the mist mix references to the sublime and contemporary architectural achievements (*Ecstasy*, *T2 Trainspotting*). The atmospheric shots showing characters sitting on top of Calton Hill (*Ecstasy*) or Arthur's Seat (*T2 Trainspotting*) at all times of day and night can be seen to express the bond they feel for their city.

Although Irvine Welsh adaptations are keen on showing their Scottishness, these films clearly question and undermine those who – apparently unproblematically – confuse patriotism and ethnic nationalism, a stance that can be seen as a way to temper the kind of cultural politics found in films like *Braveheart*. The bathetic opening of *Filth* with its bombastic voiceover showing off its Scottish pride ('It's great being Scottish' coming as an ironic antithesis to Renton's 'it's shite being Scottish' in *Trainspotting*), as Bruce comes out of Edinburgh castle, is put into perspective by its conclusion and the contrapuntal shots that immediately deflate such a nationalistic view with racist undertones. What is supposed to be a performative act of Scottishness is not associated with Burns Suppers but deep-fried Mars bars, and the 'uniquely successful race' is illustrated by a family of vacant-looking, greasy-haired, obese people wearing Saltire hoodies, drinking Buckfast and eating junk food in slow-motion to make them even more disgusting. These films sardonically denounce how sectarianism and racism underlie the class war dividing the nation, feed the canteen culture of Scottish policemen and are still rife in all strata of Scottish society. Football is a classic example. Most Irvine Welsh-inspired characters are Hibs supporters (as shown by the numerous scarves and posters seen in *Trainspotting*, *The Acid House*, *T2 Trainspotting*) while Bruce (*Filth*), who does not hide his anti-Catholicism, supports Hearts, and the Orangemen in *T2 Trainspotting* sing Rangers FC songs. The Japanese student who is the victim of a race crime (*Filth*) is defined as 'a kamikaze, sushi-eating, karaoke bastard' by policeman Bruce, a 'wog' by his Chief Inspector and as a 'gook' by the ned who killed him – representatives of Scottish middle, upper-middle and working/under-classes – as if to insist on the fact that this ideology can be found in supposedly rough and respectable sections of society alike, and does not simply result from multiple deprivation. *T2 Trainspotting* also offers a biting sequence mocking Scottish Orangemen who still look menacing despite their gullibility and supposed estrangement from modern, secular Scotland. As the camera pans over a pub called 'King William Arms' covered with Saltires, Union Jacks and banners depicting the Battle of the Boyne in which William III defeated the Jacobites while a member is singing 'Caledonia', Renton ironically explains: 'At least they have what we don't. A sense of identity.' He and Simon become the soul of the ongoing party thanks to their improvised hit generating loud cheers shot in increasingly distorted angles every time they repeat the chorus 'by the time it was over, there were no more Catholics left'. Renton keeps commenting: although 'sectarian songs have been banned, [these people] remain loyal to [...] a simpler, less tolerant time'. The two Catholic Scots have their revenge stealing all the credit cards of the club members whose pin number they easily guess – 1690 (the year when the Battle of the Boyne was fought).

Besides such satirising of bigoted attitudes, these films counterbalance racism and sectarianism with signs of a growing awareness of Scotland as a multicultural society. Older and more recent waves of immigration are noticeable with positive secondary characters that were absent from previous films, such as Bruce's ex-wife's Black partner (*Filth*). In *T2 Trainspotting*, Edinburgh's cosmopolitanism is perceptible in the presence of a Black security guard, a Chinese nurse and an Asian doctor whose accents testify to their Scottish roots, while the accent of the ladies who welcome tourists at the airport dressed in tartan micro-kilts with matching heels and sporting Nessie t-shirts reveals their eastern European origin. With these varieties of indigenous or identikit Scottishness, the film establishes Scotland as 'a post-imperial, devolved and multicultural nation'.[26] The soundtrack's magnum opus considered to be 'the heartbeat of the film' by its director[27] is a song, 'Only God Knows', performed with the Leith Congregational Choir and composed by the Edinburgh band Young Fathers, two of whose three members are of Liberian and Nigerian descent. The derided canteen culture of the Edinburgh police (*Filth*) could actually be interpreted as an invitation for Scotland as a whole to open up and move away from the Kailyard in literary/cinematic terms.

Irvine Welsh adaptations also play with the 'hard man' image that many men try to adopt and its consequences on their behaviour (alcoholism, machismo, misogyny, homophobia, violence). This stereotype, which appears in literature and films, is often associated with Glasgow and the Clyde Valley but is found in all of the Irvine Welsh-inspired films and used to undermine certain aspects of mythic Scottish masculinity. The stag may be used to signify renewed Scottish male potency (Lennox in *Filth*, Spud in *T2 Trainspotting*) and headbutting allegedly be part of tradition (*The Acid House*) but Begbie (*Trainspotting*, *T2 Trainspotting*), for all his comedic potential (literally chest-beating like an ape in an Argyle sweater), is addicted to violence. So is Bruce (*Filth*) who joined the police because he thinks of the force as the 'hardest firm', that is to say a legal form of hooliganism, and admits he cannot help bullying people, even his best friend Blade. He also suspects one of his colleagues' sexual orientation because he looks metrosexual. Interestingly, the colleague is called Inglis, the Middle Scots word for 'English', thereby reinforcing the cliché of Scotland as a male nation versus England as an effeminate one. Although most hard men are ridiculed in these films, notably through the grotesque or carnivalesque[28] nature of their scenes (Larry and Coco's father in *The Acid House*, Solo in *Ecstasy*) with their self-delusion, obsession with male genitalia and sexual performance if not sex addiction (Bruce 'the Stallion' Robertson in *Filth*, the Viagra-popping Begbie in *T2 Trainspotting*), their omnipresence might be perceived as a form of fascination.

Irvine Welsh has sometimes been criticised for his gender-biased stories focusing on men's perceptions while obliterating women.[29] The latter remain peripheral in the film adaptations and most of them might be insulted, objectified or assaulted (*Filth*, *T2 Trainspotting*) but enough is seen to understand that they better negotiate the changes occurring in Scottish society, being successful and independent (Gail and Diane in *T2 Trainspotting*). Amanda's (*Filth*) domineering position is symbolised by the duel she fights with Bruce on the stairs and, interestingly, Bruce's accent becomes more Scottish as he gets angry and acts like a hard man (see also Renton in *T2 Trainspotting*). Ambitious female colleagues are said to sleep their way to the top out of sheer misogyny, like Amanda 'who is strong in press relations', that is to say useless talk but their representation as dominatrices or witches symbolises male fear since most men remain stuck in a definition of masculinity that eventually brings them down (Begbie in *Trainspotting*, *T2 Trainspotting*, Bruce in *Filth*). The most thuggish men, like Dougie, express their homophobia with insults and blows but, even among higher classes, homophobia is such that Chief Inspector Toal cannot utter the word 'gay' or finish his sentence 'the idea of two men doing it to each other ...' without wincing (*Filth*). When Bruce provokes him by saying 'in some parts of the country the force even advertises in the gay press now', he retorts shouting and clutching his fists as the camera zooms on him: 'this isn't some parts of the country. This is Scotland, by Christ!' This moment is referred to as his 'Braveheart speech' by Irvine Welsh in the DVD commentary,[30] a way to ironically debunk the idea of Scotland as a male nation.

In fact, hard men may not be totally aware of their inner longings. Despite the prevailing homophobic tone in the film, some characters belong to homosocial circles where homoeroticism prevails. Homophobic insults abound in *Ecstasy* or *Filth* but the latter present clear signs of male bonding between Bruce, Lennox, Inglis, Toal and even Gorman for whom 'pussy is for faggots'. Veronica (*T2 Trainspotting*) senses the homoerotic nature of Renton and Simon's relationship from the start but as she expresses it in her native language, they cannot understand. Although ashamed of it, Begbie (*Trainspotting*) is seduced by a transvestite while Bruce (*Filth*) happens to be one, on his way to becoming fully gender-fluid. He is found in the women's toilets by Amanda, wears his wife's clothes and eventually his psyche seems to merge with that of his wife, which incidentally implies that 'manly' Scottish men like transvestites: he is very successful with punters and the leader of the gang of neds kisses him passionately, calling him 'sick, sexy, wee pansy'. Many comments and sex scenes reveal the homosexual (*Filth*) or gender inversion fantasies of Scottish hard men (*The Acid House*, *T2 Trainspotting*) and sometimes others. Blade's dancing with a gay couple (*Filth*) while he is high on ecstasy epitomises the return of the repressed. Some of these hard men eventually realise the suffering that is born out of their conception of being 'the man of the house and all that' (*Filth*), repressing their feelings for fear of looking too soft as exemplified by Bruce's final speech and recommendations (*Filth*) because that is the road to victimisation, illustrated by Johnny the 'soft touch' (*The Acid House*). Bruce's meltdown (*Filth*) partly results from his conflicting sexual tendencies and male insecurities.

This self-imposed male burden also takes its toll on Dougie who tries to kill himself as he loses both his wife and job, but Scottish masculinity seems to be changing. Signs accumulate to show the hard man is becoming obsolescent. Renton who was making fun of Begbie (*Trainspotting*) renews his feminist stance as he rants over the damages of social media on women in *T2 Trainspotting*: 'choose rape jokes, slut shaming, revenge porn, and an endless tide of depressing misogyny'. Besides his symbolic impotence, Begbie gradually realises, notably thanks to Spud's stories, that he was never loved but feared. Suddenly awed at his own monstrosity, he comes to terms with the fact that 'the world changes, eh? Even if we don't' and so gives his son his freedom as the latter looks forward to going to college rather than taking over his father's criminal activities. Franco Junior shows him another form of authority by resisting the temptation to settle arguments by resorting to violence. In a domestic scene that is shot like a Terence Davies film with a stilted frame of the family sitting in an old-fashioned living-room, Begbie finally opens up and admits that Franco Junior will be a better man than his alcoholic tramp grandfather and foolish father. The eye directions still diverge but hands are shaken and smiles exchanged before Begbie hugs his son. The deconstruction of the hard man's masculinity is apparently on its way.

(Re-)Shaping Scottish national identities: beyond the 'Scotch myths'

By interrogating the meaning of Scottishness in an often provocative way, notably through the debunking of 'Scotch myths', Irvine Welsh's adaptations may appear overly critical or shocking. But the vision of Scottish society presented in these films can be credited to the author's anarchistic streak, his endeavour to shake things up. Alcoholism, drug use, depravity and corruption are widespread among all social classes. The ultimate bastions of Scottish respectability and establishment are seen as greedy, hypocritical, mafia-type organisations, like the freemasons' lodge in *Filth*. Drug-dealing occurs just after the end of the assembly to the sound of 'God Save the Queen' defined as 'a moment of harmony' in a typically unionist-nationalist mindset.[31] *Trainspotting* and *Ecstasy* refer to well-known anti-drug campaigns ('choose life' and 'Scotland against Narcotics' that stands for the real 'Scotland against Drugs') better to deride the moralising attitudes of political leaders, always eager to stigmatise a section of the population they do not see as fit to embody the nation. 'These small groups of antisocial deviants are destroying the moral fibre of Scotland' one claims (*Ecstasy*) as a Saltire is clearly visible behind him as on all the posters of the campaign he promotes. The vision of drug-taking as an act of resistance against a certain sense of

Scottish respectability almost reaches a blasphemous level since churches are used for free parties (*Ecstasy*) and drugs are compared to God ('the acid shall inherit the Earth', 'LSD is the body of Christ' in *The Acid House* and *Ecstasy*). The level of provocation is such that some Scottish actors like John Sessions, who nonetheless played Toal in *Filth*, left the première of *The Acid House* saying that what they saw on screen was 'a disgrace to Scotland'.[32]

Although at first glance these films all seem to go along with Renton's logorrheic purple patch ('it's shite being Scottish!' in *Trainspotting*) and might explain why some producers were reluctant to finance them, Irvine Welsh-inspired films actually develop a subtler discourse which has more to do with a love-hate relationship, both undermining and celebrating Scottishness. These films provide an alternative to – while being on the verge of entering – the Scottish canon[33] or what Richard Butt has called the 'oligopoly' (Scott, Stevenson and Barrie), who 'account for all the adaptations of Scottish literature until 1922 […] and for the majority of adaptations of Scottish literature thereafter, totalling in excess of one hundred and fifty film releases'.[34] Irvine Welsh's work has, however, given birth to many different types of adaptations. Although he must still be far from the other three authors mentioned,[35] these films manage to show aspects of Scottishness without essentialising it, reminding the audience that identity is multiple and evolving or 'negotiable and situational',[36] that it takes all sorts to make up a nation, and that only a nation that can accept its past to better embrace the future can grow. The ultimate irony is that these films, which initially might be interpreted as voicing an anti-Scottish stance, are in fact deeply infused with Scottishness, just like their source material.[37] *Trainspotting* illustrates that with its reference to Sean Connery, another Scottish export, whose accent is imitated by Sick Boy who, for all his cynicism, is an obsessive fan of James Bond. The chase taking place between Begbie and Renton in the Old Town at night (*T2 Trainspotting*) evokes the Scottish gothic[38] whether architectural, literary or filmic.

The most telling example is that of *Filth* with its protagonist whose onomastics make him an allegory of the nation. Bruce Robertson, a policeman suffering from what increasingly looks like bouts of schizophrenia made worse by drug psychosis, is a perfect representative of Caledonian antisyzygy.[39] Symbolised by his long stare into the mirror, his fractured morality and psyche are also those of his country[40] and follow the likes of Stevenson's *Strange Case of Dr Jekyll and Mr Hyde* or Hogg's *The Private Memoirs and Confessions of a Justified Sinner*. His fear of everyone/everything, among which success, is related to his national identity by Irvine Welsh himself.[41] The film is pervaded with historical characters such as Bonnie Prince Charlie and Robert Burns, albeit with a non-politically correct twist since the first stands for cocaine and the second is reinterpreted as 'A wog's a wog for all that'. His hallucinations are just extrapolated visions of the personality of his colleagues and acquaintances. So, besides the onomastics of his name that potentially make him the subversive son of Robert the Bruce, the reason why he sees himself as a stallion in a herd of donkeys or sheep may have to do with the fact that he seems or pretends to be a descendant of the Clan Robertson. He tells his wimpish colleague Lennox that 'the Lennoxes [a Lowland clan] of this world will never oust the Robertsons [a Highland clan]' and he has a tattoo of their badge on his arm – as well as that of Hearts – with the motto 'Virtutis Gloria Merces' ('Glory is the reward of valour'). *T2 Trainspotting* also presents Renton as a sort of bipolar character, forever oscillating between the two extremes of his own personality embodied on the one hand by Simon (his cynical side), and on the other by Spud (his more humane and empathetic side).

Conclusion

Irvine Welsh-inspired films go against three cinematic 'Scotch myths': Tartanry, Kailyard and Clydesideism, by being anti-romantic, urban and focusing on the underbelly rather than on a 'noble' working class. The image given of Scottishness may not always be pleasing but the aim is to present it as 'authentically' as possible in the light of Irvine Welsh's own experience. Since he is often asked to supervise film production and to act as a location adviser, he requires some additional footage when he thinks the vision given of his hometown is too touristy.[42] Similarly, he strives for his heteroglossic use of language to be respected in his adaptations. Some parts of *Trainspotting* have been notoriously redubbed for American audiences[43] although their impenetrability was not planned. Irvine Welsh nonetheless felt that the film did not stress its Scottishness enough and thus wrote the screenplay for *The Acid House* himself, which was shot with a very small budget ('a wee daft film', in his own words[44]) and whose style was meant to be more faithful to the original material so that 'spoiled middle-class brats who want to shop around for their next culture fix will find it more impenetrable'.[45] *The Acid House* indeed presents thicker accents that are also emphasised by the HOH subtitles that keep the Scots spelling. Whether it is through characters' expression or cityscapes/landscapes, Scotland is never monolithic in these films, which recall the fact that nation does not obfuscate class and race, that identities should not be conflated even in the pursuit of national unity, and therefore that Scottishness remains multifaceted.

The position of Irvine Welsh's characters remains unclear as to Scottish identity and nationalism. Denouncing the damages of neoliberalism on both the livelihood and ethics of Scottish working-class men does not make one an independence supporter despite the numerous taunts at Unionists. Yet the films adapted from his books have undeniably contributed to avoidance of the Scottish Cringe[46] and cultural inferiorisation. They are statements of self-assertion, marking 'a new, and sometimes determinedly unsolemn, maturity',[47] developing a form of cultural nationalism that goes beyond football victories (though the latter do have potential political parallels[48]) and usual literary/cinematic clichés. In the end, the strength of Irvine Welsh's work is that these films can appeal to both local and international audiences with their multiple layers of reading/understanding. A theme like police brutality and terrible jail conditions can resonate in many countries but can also refer to a specific Scottish context as in *The Acid House* or *Filth*. Bruce's allusions are very reminiscent of jail films set in late 1970s Barlinnie such as *A Sense of Freedom* (John Mackenzie, 1981) and *Silent Scream* (David Hayman, 1990).

The ambivalent nostalgia and nostophobia at the heart of *T2 Trainspotting* can similarly have universal and very local implications. The scene in the pub when Renton 'the stranger' meets Simon again after twenty years away alludes both to a typical western saloon scene and the jealousy towards the 'Scottish expat done good'. Significantly, Renton and Simon can bond again once the former admits most of the perfect life he described is just lies, thus making him a suitable losing partner again and another embodiment of the Scottish Cringe. The films can also use foreign characters to present some lesser-known aspects of Scottish history to an international/ American audience (a Canadian girl in *Ecstasy*, a quizzical Bulgarian one in *T2 Trainspotting* to whom Renton explains the Battle of the Boyne in a sort of 'Scottish sectarianism for Dummies' crash-course). Their intertextuality has definitely put Scotland on the cinematic map establishing the Irvine Welsh brand as a self-referential cycle of films but also inscribing these films within a broader Scottish cultural history (through a reference to Bill Forsyth's *Gregory's Girl* in *Trainspotting*) and world cinematography (with citations of Murnau's *Nosferatu* in *T2 Trainspotting*, Scorsese's *Mean Streets* in *Trainspotting* and *Raging Bull* in *T2 Trainspotting*, Kubrick's *A Clockwork Orange* in *Trainspotting*, *T2 Trainspotting* and *Filth*, *The Shining* in *T2 Trainspotting*, Bryan Singer's *The Usual Suspects* in *Filth*). Irvine Welsh's adaptations thus appear like a major contribution to a new form of Scottish cultural nationalism, presenting a more diverse national identity in a transnational cinematic environment.

Corpus:
  Ecstasy, dir. by Rob Heydon (2012).
  Filth, dir. by Jon S. Baird (2013).
  The Acid House, dir. by Paul McGuigan (1999).
  Trainspotting, dir. by Danny Boyle (1996).
  T2 Trainspotting, dir. by Danny Boyle (2017).

Endnotes

1. Ian Brown, *Performing Scottishness, Enactment and National Identities* (London: Palgrave Macmillan, 2020), p. 223.
2. Duncan Petrie, *Screening Scotland* (London: BFI Publishing, 2000), p. 196.
3. Tim Edensor, *National Identity, Popular Culture and Everyday Life* (Oxford: Berg, 2002), pp. 145–51.
4. David Martin-Jones, *Scotland: Global Cinema. Genres, Modes and Identities* (Edinburgh: Edinburgh University Press, 2009), p. 64.
5. Jonathan Murray, *The New Scottish Cinema* (London: I. B. Tauris, 2015), p. 175.
6. Christopher Meir, *Scottish Cinema, Texts and Contexts* (Manchester: Manchester University Press, 2015), p. 68.
7. Colin McArthur, *Scotch Reels: Scotland in Cinema and Television* (London: British Film Institute, 1982). Related myths are further developed in Bob Nowlan and Zach Finch, *Directory of World Cinema: Scotland*, vol. 27 (Bristol: Intellect Books, 2015), pp. 91–92.
8. David Archibald, 'Why there's more to Scottish cinema than dour miserablism', *Financial Times*, 27 September 2013: www.ft.com/content/83076cac-251b-11e3-9b22-00144feab7de [accessed 29 May 2022].
9. Christopher Meir, 'Trainspotting', in Nowlan and Finch, pp. 256–59 (p. 256); Alice Ferrebe, 'Welsh and Tradition' in Berthold Schoene (ed.), *The Edinburgh Companion to Irvine Welsh* (Edinburgh: Edinburgh University Press, 2010), pp. 9–18 (pp. 14, 17); Robert Munro, 'Irvine Welsh and the Adaptation Industry: Filth, a case study', *International Journal of Scottish Theatre and Screen* 7.2 (2014), pp. 31–56 (p. 37): journals.qmu.ac.uk/index.php/IJOSTS [accessed 29 May 2022].
10. Duncan Petrie, 'Trainspotting, the Film', in Schoene, *The Edinburgh Companion to Irvine Welsh*, pp. 42–53 (p. 48).
11. Katherine Ashley, 'Welsh in Translation', in Schoene, *The Edinburgh Companion to Irvine Welsh*, pp. 113–25 (p. 115).
12. Rob Heydon, 'Commentary with director', *Irvine Welsh's Ecstasy* (Kaleidoscope Home Entertainment: KAL8190, 2012) [on DVD].
13. James McAvoy, 'Interview', *Filth* (Lionsgate Home Entertainment: LGD95076, 2013) [on DVD].
14. Meir, *Scottish Cinema, Texts and Contexts*, pp. 101–02.
15. Rob Heydon, 'Commentary' (15').
16. Peter Clandfield and Christian Lloyd, 'Welsh and Edinburgh', in Schoene (ed.), *The Edinburgh Companion to Irvine Welsh*, pp. 100–12 (p. 100); Meir, *Scottish Cinema, Texts and Contexts*, p. 67.
17. Aldona Reyes Mallet, 'Trainspotting 2: what have Renton and his pals been up to for the last 20 years?', (2017) www.visitscotland.com/blog/films/trainspotting-2/ [accessed 29 May 2022].
18. 'Trainspotting finally wins the backing of VisitScotland', *Scotsman*, 13 December 2016: www.scotsman.com/business/trainspotting-finally-wins-backing-visitscotland-609913 [accessed on 29 May 2022].
19. Meir, *Scottish Cinema, Texts and Contexts*, p. 31.
20. David McCrone, Angela Morris and Richard Kiely, *Scotland – the Brand, The Making of Scottish Heritage* (Edinburgh: Edinburgh University Press, 1995).

21 Petrie, *Screening Scotland*, pp. 8–9. See, for comparison, Colin McArthur, *Brigadoon, Braveheart and the Scots: Distortions of Scotland in Hollywood Cinema* (London: I. B. Tauris, 2013). For a comprehensive study of tartan, see Ian Brown, *From Tartan to Tartanry: Scottish Culture, History and Myth* (Edinburgh: Edinburgh University Press, 2010).
22 Petrie, *Screening Scotland*, p. 53.
23 Brown, *Performing Scottishness*, p. 214.
24 For an analysis of the concept in Scottish films, see Craig Cairns, 'Nostophobia', in Jonathan Murray, Fidelma Farley and Rod Stoneman (eds), *Scottish Cinema Now* (Newcastle: Cambridge Scholars Publishing, 2009), pp. 56–71.
25 Clandfield and Lloyd, pp. 102, 109.
26 Brown, *Performing Scottishness*, pp. 201–02.
27 Ninja Tune, 'Only God Knows by Young Fathers featuring Leith Congregational Choir', (2017) ninjatune.net/release/young-fathers-featuring-leith-congregational-choir/only-god-knows [accessed 29 May 2022].
28 David Borthwick, 'Welsh's Shorter Fiction' in Schoene (ed.), *The Edinburgh Companion to Irvine Welsh*, pp. 31–41 (p. 40); in the same book, see also Carole Jones, 'Welsh and Gender', pp. 54–64 (p. 55).
29 Jones, pp. 54–64.
30 Irvine Welsh and Jon S. Baird, 'Commentary', *Filth* (41').
31 Brown, *Performing Scottishness*, p. 84–86.
32 Irvine Welsh and Jon S. Baird, 'Commentary', *Filth* (3').
33 Meir, '*Trainspotting*', p. 258; Berthold Schoene, 'Introduction' in Schoene (ed.), *The Edinburgh Companion to Irvine Welsh*, pp. 1–8 (p. 3). In the same book, see Gavin Miller, 'Welsh and Identity Politics', pp. 89–99 (p. 89) and Ashley, p. 117.
34 Richard Butt, 'Literature and the Screen Media since 1908', in Ian Brown (ed.), *The Edinburgh History of Scottish Literature, volume 3: Modern Transformations – New Identities (from 1918)* (Edinburgh: Edinburgh University Press, 2007), p. 54.
35 Brown, *Performing Scottishness*, pp. 206–07, 230.
36 Ibid., p. 124.
37 Schoene, p. 3.
38 Duncan Petrie, 'Scottish Gothic and the Moving Image: A Tale of Two Traditions' in Carol Margaret Davison and Monica Germanà (eds), *Scottish Gothic: An Edinburgh Companion* (Edinburgh: Edinburgh University Press, 2017), pp. 181–94.
39 As defined by Petrie, *Contemporary Scottish Fictions*, pp. 117–18; Ferrebe, p. 17; Munro, p. 43.
40 The idea is borrowed from Ian Brown's study of John Byrne's television work (*Performing Scottishness*, p. 197).
41 Irvine Welsh, 'Interview', *Filth* (16').
42 Rob Heydon, 'Commentary', *Ecstasy* (23').
43 Petrie, '*Trainspotting*, the Film', p. 48; Ashley, p. 120.
44 Murray, p. 56; Petrie, '*Trainspotting*, the Film', p. 52.
45 Ferrebe, p. 11.
46 Karen Gardiner, 'Is it the end of the Scottish Cringe?', (2016): www.bbc.com/culture/article/20160114-is-it-the-end-of-the-scottish-cringe [accessed 29 May 2022].
47 Brown, *Performing Scottishness*, p. 231.
48 Petrie, '*Trainspotting*, the Film', pp. 49–50.

13. George Davie's *Democratic Intellect* in Context

ROBERT ANDERSON

George Davie's book *The Democratic Intellect: Scotland and her Universities in the Nineteenth Century*, published in 1961, was a pioneering if problematic work of university history, and a key influence on the development of cultural nationalism in Scotland in the 1960s and 70s. Davie has been described as 'one of that very small group of Scottish intellectuals who have shaped the way the nation thinks of itself'.[1] A book which is now sixty years old, on a somewhat esoteric subject – the teaching of philosophy in universities – and actually not very easy to read, is still in print (the latest edition was in 2019), and still capable of stimulating a creative response from scholars in several disciplines.[2] The phrase 'democratic intellect' has itself become a cliché of Scottish identity, though often without much connection with Davie's own use of the phrase. It is commonly employed to sum up the popular and usually unexamined view that Scotland is a more egalitarian and communitarian country than England. The aim of this paper is not to discuss Davie's relationship to other thinkers about Scottish culture and intellectual life, or the historical validity of Davie's account of university reform,[3] but to place Davie in the context of his time and reassess his book as a work of university history. Like all classics, it has changing meanings as times change.

Although it is usual to discuss Davie in a purely Scottish context, his book appeared in a period of intense British debate on university education. The Robbins committee was appointed in 1960 and reported in 1963, but university expansion was under way well before then, leading to fears, which today seem premature, of 'mass' higher education undermining cultural standards. It was in 1960 that the novelist Kingsley Amis pronounced that 'more will mean worse'. Often these critiques had a conservative or religious bias, as with Walter Moberly's *Crisis in the University* in 1949, or T. S. Eliot's *Notes Towards the Definition of Culture* in 1948, and the debate needs to be seen in a Cold War context, as part of a reassertion of liberal and humanistic values against 'materialism'.[4]

This was the age of the plate-glass or campus universities, re-examined in 2021 in the book on *Utopian Universities* edited by Miles Taylor and Jill Pellew.[5] The first, Sussex, opened in 1961. In 1962 the government introduced, in effect, free university education, combined with means-tested but generous maintenance grants, paving the way in the long run for the detachment of universities from their local roots.

The scientist and novelist C. P. Snow's celebrated lecture on the 'two cultures' was given in 1959, provoking a hostile response in 1962 from the literary critic F. R. Leavis. Much debate centred on the conflict between academic specialisation and general or liberal education. Science, technology and economic growth seemed to be government priorities. Eric Ashby's *Technology and the Academics* was a key text in 1958, and the historian J. H. Plumb edited a book called *Crisis in the Humanities* in 1964. Davie's restatement of the Scottish generalist tradition can be seen as a contribution to that debate. But he wrote for a Scottish readership, and the somewhat hermetic character of his book meant it did not have the wider influence that it might have.

There were several strands to Davie's account of Scottish university reform, which it may be useful to summarise. For most of the nineteenth century, there was a uniform Master of Arts degree for undergraduates, based on seven or eight compulsory subjects, including two philosophies, Logic and Moral Philosophy. This was replaced by a system of options after 1889, including the distinction between three-year Ordinary and four-year Honours degrees. Davie was critical of these changes and saw 'anglicisation' as the force behind them. Philosophy, from being a compulsory and central subject, and one whose spirit infused the teaching of other subjects, was reduced to being one speciality among others. Then for Davie there was the issue of what kind of philosophy was taught, as Scots turned their back on the distinctive 'common sense' school of the Enlightenment.

Davie's work linked the Enlightenment, the university question in the nineteenth century, and the problems of his own day. He argued that there is a perpetual tension between the demands of specialised expertise and the common interest. Common sense philosophy, as expounded by Thomas Reid in the eighteenth century, was able to bridge the gap between the university-educated elite and 'ordinary people'. This is an attractive idea, and Lindsay Paterson has stressed its relevance to the continuing tension between democracy and expert opinion, represented in modern society by the university-educated professions.[6] Politically, the issue seems newly urgent in the age of populism.

Davie took the idea of the 'democratic intellect' from the Conservative politician Walter Elliot, writing in the 1930s. Elliot saw this tradition as a product of the Reformation and of Calvinist theology, exemplified in the Scottish parish, where fiercely independent ordinary Scots continually challenged the authority of the minister, and were keen to enter into metaphysical and theological debate, reducing all issues to first principles.[7] As Davie put it, 'the minister's theological supervision of the congregation was checked and balanced by the congregation's common-sense scrutiny of the minister', providing the model for 'a sort of all-round spiritual participation by means of educational democracy'.[8] Davie spoke of 'the remarkable way in which the philosophic emphasis of the curriculum meshed in the democracy of the "open door" policy'.[9] Common-sense philosophy both ensured that the traditional elite remained responsive to social pressures and that the universities were open to poorer boys, the famous lads o' pairts, allowing a broader recruitment to the Scottish professions. This 'intricate balance of the national ideal of democracy *plus* intellectualism'[10] formed a cultural complex which was difficult to define simply, but which differed from the more basic concept of educational democracy current in the 1960s, which was about widening participation and removing the obstacles to equality of opportunity. Davie was concerned above all with the ethos of the university-trained elite, and was critical of the post-1945 'bureaucratic welfare state'.[11]

Davie's broader historical interpretation, clarified in later writings, could appeal to readers who had no special interest in philosophy or universities. He argued that after 1707 there was unity in politics between England and Scotland, but diversity in 'social ethics'. Scotland maintained a balance, in which the potentially theocratic inclinations of the Presbyterian church were countered by the rationalism of philosophy.[12] In the early nineteenth century, Davie argued, philosophy still provided a moral check on the utilitarianism of the industrial age. But the Scottish balance between the sacred and the secular was disrupted by the rise of evangelicalism, based on emotion rather than reason. The Disruption of 1843 was thus a cultural disaster, and religious sectarianism came to dominate contests for professorial chairs, which play a key role in Davie's story. It seems likely that Davie's hostility to sectarianism was influenced by the fifteen years he spent teaching in Belfast, though he does not talk about this (or give much other autobiographical information) in his writings. The bulk of *Democratic Intellect* was written before Davie moved to Edinburgh in 1960.

Particularly crucial professorial contests involved James Ferrier, whom Davie identified as the most creative philosopher of the mid-century, but who was twice rejected for chairs in Edinburgh (in 1852 and 1856), and had to remain banished to 'the obscurity of the tiny University of St Andrews'.[13] That put St Andrews in its place; but then a sub-theme of *Democratic Intellect* was that Edinburgh was the true 'metropolis of common sense', whose Old Quad had been 'the chief centre of light and philosophy in the whole English-speaking world'.[14] Ferrier's successful rivals (Patrick McDougall and Alexander Campbell Fraser) had both previously been professors in the Free Church's New College. For Davie, Ferrier's rejection marked the 'fatal crisis' of Scottish democracy, and the beginning of Scotland's 'intellectual fade-out' and 'slide into cultural provincialism', by which he meant the sectarian squabbles that paralysed Scottish intellectual vitality into the twentieth century, and prevented Scots from cooperating to defend their legacy.[15] For Davie, the 1850s were thus a historic turning point, which marked the end of continuity with the Enlightenment. But recent commentators sympathetic to him, notably Alexander Broadie and Cairns Craig, have not shared his pessimism, arguing that the Enlightenment was only part of a Scottish intellectual tradition that stretched both backwards into earlier centuries, and forwards into the twentieth. The common-sense tradition continued to inspire Scottish thought; and Davie himself seemed to change his mind later, finding worthy twentieth-century successors in his own mentor Norman Kemp Smith and the Scots-Australian philosopher John Anderson.[16]

Davie's hostility to sectarianism, and to religious 'fanaticism', was perhaps part of his appeal. He acknowledged the legacy of Calvinism in his interpretation of the Enlightenment and democratic intellectualism, and continued to argue that the distinctive blend of religion, law and education was Scotland's special contribution to civilisation. But by the 1950s and 1960s, the Church of Scotland and its ministers were widely regarded in intellectual circles as a repressive force, morally censorious and culturally philistine. Davie's work, it may be suggested, was attractive to the youthful intelligentsia created by post-war university expansion. Before the war, most Scottish graduates had gone into the professions, the civil service, or school teaching. But now there were new career fields in the media, politics, and college teaching which promoted a less conformist attitude. The Reformation had long been seen as the basis for Scotland's identity and its cultural difference from England, but Davie offered a version of Scottish identity which substituted a secular intellectualism for the well-worn themes of Calvinism and John Knox, and made no appeal, either, to Kailyard sentimentality. Davie became a cult figure for journals like *Cencrastus* and the *New Edinburgh Review*, to which he contributed himself.[17] Marxism was a significant influence at this time, but – perhaps surprisingly for a philosopher trained in the 1930s – Davie himself showed little Marxist influence, and hardly used social class as an explanatory factor. Nevertheless, he was a personal link between pre-war and post-war Scottish intelligentsias. Davie's view that Scots suffered a 'failure of intellectual nerve' in the nineteenth century,[18] turning their back on their heritage and accepting English or 'metropolitan' values, including Oxbridge notions of university education, struck a chord with many of his readers, who often applied the idea to their own age (while accepting without much question Davie's historical account).[19]

Though Davie read widely and deeply in nineteenth-century writing, he rarely cited secondary sources in his rather scanty footnotes, or referred to existing interpretations of the subject, or engaged in debate with critics. But his acknowledged inspirations were mostly from the early twentieth century. One was the critique of contemporary university reforms by the literary critic Herbert Grierson, Professor of English at Edinburgh when Davie was a student, and formerly at Aberdeen. As a student himself at Aberdeen in the 1880s, Grierson had experienced the old MA degree, and he lamented its abandonment as a uniform experience for students. These views were expressed in an essay of 1919, and repeated in 1937 in Grierson's inaugural address as rector of Edinburgh University, at which it is highly likely that Davie was present.[20] Another key influence was the classicist John Burnet, who published in 1917 a book on post-war university problems and the education of national elites, comparing Scotland and Prussia. Davie cited Burnet as the source for his conception of generalism.[21] At one level, this just meant that all subjects benefited from being studied in conjunction with others, but Davie also made a special claim for philosophy as introducing students to the epistemology or theory of knowledge which underlay all disciplines, including science. In the 1980s he warmly welcomed the interdisciplinary School of Epistemics set up at Edinburgh University. Davie's reading also included L. J. Saunders's *Scottish Democracy, 1815–1840* (1950), a pioneering but now rather forgotten work of socio-cultural history, and an article of 1927 by Kennedy Stewart which deplored the decline of university standards since they had become 'glorified technical colleges' for turning out teachers.[22] Davie followed Stewart in complaining that 'second-rate minds' were now getting to the university.[23] He was also influenced by the nationalist poet Hugh MacDiarmid, who campaigned for Scotland to draw on its own cultural traditions rather than accepting English models, and was already denouncing the anglicised universities. Davie met the poet as a student in the 1930s and became a close personal friend.[24]

An aspect of the contemporary context of Davie's book not discussed here is its influence on secondary education. It appeared at a time when the future of school leaving examinations was much debated, and he clearly had a real and long-lasting influence in ensuring that Scottish 'Highers' were less specialised than English 'A Levels', and over the common view that Scottish education had greater 'breadth', a concept which linked schools and universities. In 1961, Davie was responding more directly to current university developments. The number of Scottish students approximately doubled between 1938 and 1960, from 10,000 to 20,000; at Edinburgh the growth was from 3,826 to 7,373. There was already pressure on the Ordinary degree, especially as the graduate employment market became more diverse. In the early 1960s, about 67 per cent of women took the Ordinary MA, but only 35 per cent of men.[25] Since women had entered the universities in the 1890s, teaching had been the most common career choice, and it was possible to go on to training with an Ordinary degree. Thus, the growth of women students gave a boost to the Ordinary degree, but it later came to be seen as a 'woman's degree' – an aspect not considered by Davie.[26] However, changes in the system in the 1950s meant that women, like men, now needed an Honours degree or equivalent. Furthermore, the new student grant system limited grants to three or four years, and the traditional practice of taking an Ordinary MA before a degree in law or divinity died out.

Was anglicisation already a problem? The appointment of non-Scottish professors was nothing new, but before 1939 most lecturers and assistants were Scottish graduates. Now university expansion brought an influx of non-professorial staff, often from England, who might have no sense of Scottish universities being different from any others where they might find jobs.[27] Davie was also reacting against the analytical philosophy which was then dominant in British philosophy departments, and which certainly seemed lacking in social or ethical significance.[28]

F. R. Leavis has been mentioned as a significant post-war figure, and there are interesting parallels and contrasts with Davie. Both men put their own subject at the heart of a liberal university education. If Davie saw philosophy as the 'pivot' of arts degrees, Leavis, in his book of 1943, *Education and the University*, proposed English literature as the centre of a preliminary interdisciplinary curriculum common to all humanities students. Like Leavis, Davie was temperamentally a man of the Left, and both men attracted disciples of the same cast, despite their somewhat craggy personalities. Yet both were defenders of a traditional cultural ideal and looked back to a supposed organic society of harmonious social relations. For Leavis the enemy was 'technologico-benthamism'; for Davie it was what he called in his later work 'atomisation', and he saw the utilitarian philosophy of the early nineteenth century, despite its own roots in the Scottish Enlightenment, as hostile to the Scottish balance of reason and morality. Davie referred occasionally to Leavis and the 'two cultures' debate, but does not seem to have been acquainted with another key book of the period, Raymond Williams's *Culture and Society 1780–1950* (1958), which showed that England had its own tradition of moral critique of industrialism.[29]

Leavis had a real influence on the new universities of the 1960s, but did Davie? Lionel Robbins was an admirer of the Scottish generalist tradition, and a strong critic of the specialised English sixth form.[30] The clearest Scottish influence, via its founder the philosopher A. D. Lindsay, was on Keele, founded in 1949, with its four-year degree and general foundation year. Davie mentioned Lindsay along with the Scottish John Fulton, vice-chancellor of Sussex, as heirs of Grierson and Burnet.[31] He might have added another of Sussex's founding fathers, the Professor of English David Daiches, an Edinburgh graduate of the 1930s and thus a pupil of Grierson. The new universities of the 1960s could not afford to extend their curricula to four years, but all of them, as *Utopian Universities* makes clear, professed some sort of interdisciplinary ideal, often expressed in a broad first year. The Open University of the 1970s had a similar approach. Interdisciplinarity, however, usually meant trying to bridge the two cultures, by giving students a taste of both arts and science. That was not really Davie's vision, of a central unifying subject, although the relationship between science and philosophy was one of his themes. Later, the new English universities could not avoid the pressures of specialisation any more than the Scottish ones, and the common courses have fallen by the wayside. Besides, the new universities had two very un-Scottish features. First, they were campus universities, and in the early years often entirely residential. But Scottish students traditionally lived at home or in lodgings, and this was only beginning to change by the 1950s. Second, the new universities generally rejected lectures as the main mode of instruction, reacting against the older redbrick universities, and they emphasised tutorials and seminars. But Scotland was still wedded to the – often authoritarian – professorial model with firm departmental structures, and Davie's own account focused on professorial figures.

To turn to the academic context of Davie's work. He was writing long before historians and social scientists became interested in questions of national identity, national myths, and collective memory, but national identity was certainly one of Davie's themes. This has stimulated engagement with him by political scientists and sociologists. Sociology was itself a new subject in Scotland in the 1960s and was slow to focus on Scottish society.[32] But a Centre for Educational Sociology was founded at Edinburgh University, and some of the most useful critiques of Davie have come from sociologists, notably Andrew McPherson in the 1970s and 1980s, and Lindsay Paterson thereafter. Historians have been less enthusiastic. The leading historian of Scottish education, Donald Withrington, was an early and persistent critic.[33] It is also notable that Davie's work on the Scottish Enlightenment seems to have been largely ignored by historians of that movement, though this has become a flourishing branch of intellectual history.

It is fair to say that in 1961 Davie had very little to go on. The history of Scottish universities, as far as it existed, was of a traditional institutional kind. Projects like the eight-volume history of Oxford, the four-volume history of European Universities, or the Quincentenary series on the history of Aberdeen University were well in the future, and it was only in the 1970s that historians like Lawrence Stone and Fritz Ringer began to apply social history techniques to university history.[34] To answer the question of how far an educational system is democratic, or how far it promotes social mobility, it is necessary to look at quantifiable data like student enrolments, participation rates, or the social backgrounds of students. Sociologists were already looking at these questions, and the Robbins report itself was founded on social statistics. But this was an approach which had no interest for Davie. Apart from its deficiencies of historical method, Davie's book lacks a convincing comparative basis. Though it is structured around the theme of anglicisation, there is no serious examination of what was actually happening in England in the nineteenth century. To speak, when he is discussing the 1870s, of 'the ideal of extreme specialisation which was guiding academic policy in England' is unrecognisable as history.[35]

Davie associated specialisation with both Oxbridge and 'redbrick'. In the case of Oxbridge, Davie resorted to caricature. Oxford was noted for classics, Cambridge for mathematics: for Davie this meant learning 'all their Greek irregular verbs off by rote' and doing 'algebra with the inevitability of a calculating machine'. It was not difficult to see the superiority to this of 'the intellectual argumentative essay from first principles, which not merely formed the chief exercises in the philosophy classes but which was also developed into a mature and classic form by a whole series' of Scottish writers.[36] As for redbrick, this term was only popularised in the 1940s by Edgar Allison Peers, professor of Spanish at Liverpool, writing as 'Bruce Truscot'. The new civic universities of the nineteenth century generally awarded their degrees through London University, always associated by Davie with utilitarianism. But London degrees were not so different from the Scottish general degree, and included philosophy as an important element, as did the prestigious Oxford Greats degree. In London as in Scotland, greater specialisation came only in the 1890s; it would be possible to construct a comparative account showing how the rhythms of generalism and specialism worked out in parallel ways in England and Scotland. The two countries had different traditions of liberal education, but similar generalist aims underlay both.[37] Nor did Davie provide much international context. One narrative about universities already well established was that in the late nineteenth century the 'Humboldtian' model spread from Germany to other countries: it meant both that advancing knowledge was defined as the leading function of universities, and that students should share the spirit of research with professors. What Davie called specialisation was part of the general move towards the professionalisation of disciplines, their division into specialities, and their location in universities as the source of academic authority – where Scotland was arguably a pioneer, in medicine as well as philosophy. There was nothing specifically English about this; indeed, the older English universities were notoriously reluctant to follow the German model.

Within this general context, Davie's work invites comment on two relatively neglected aspects of university history: the pedagogy of higher education, and the relation between universities and schools. The growth of research specialisation posed problems for university teaching: how was the original work now required from academics to be reconciled with the task of giving a general or liberal education to undergraduates? Traditionally, Scottish philosophy professors had seen their role within the nation as 'not to push back the frontiers of knowledge [...] but to contribute to the education of the minds that would populate the professions', as 'social educators'.[38] Shaping the moral and civic conscience of their students was seen as a duty of professors, especially perhaps by those who were clergymen. The tension between scholarship and a pastoral or educational role was not confined to philosophy. Davie cited with approval the classicist John Stuart Blackie, writing in 1855:

> we demand a scholarship with a large human soul, and a pregnant social significance, which shall not seek with a feeble studiousness to avoid, but rather with a generous vigour to find contact with all the great intellectual and moral movements of the age.[39]

A hundred years later, academic ideals were narrower.

The classics provide a useful comparison in Christopher Stray's work on the history of classical teaching in England. In the early nineteenth century, schools and universities had the same ideal of liberal education. Oxbridge dons and public-school masters were part of the same world, and could move easily between the two careers. But when classical studies became professionalised, universities and schools drew apart. Stray calls this the move from culture to discipline. But there was a workable new pattern, as schools retained the task of basic (and admittedly often mind-deadening) linguistic teaching.[40] But philosophy was not taught in schools in Scotland, as we shall see, so university philosophers had to try to combine preparatory and specialised education. This was perhaps a special problem for philosophy, as a compulsory subject. Professors were faced with large classes of students who were not intending to take the subject further, who might be unenthusiastic or hostile, and who had not had any previous introduction at school. Davie explains very well how in the early nineteenth century professors met this problem by discussing general ethical, political, or economic problems in their classes, and by encouraging the 'intellectual argumentative essay' on such subjects. But when philosophy became more technical, this was less plausible. And even when departments expanded, the task of teaching in the Ordinary class limited the possibility for staff to give Honours teaching related to their research.

Davie also showed that in the early nineteenth century there was a Scottish form of pedagogy centred on the professor's class. He rediscovered George Jardine, Professor of Logic at Glasgow from 1787 to 1827, who published what was in effect a manual of university teaching in 1818. Part of the lecture hour should be used for catechetical questions and discussion of written assignments – which could range widely into general subjects – and this seems to have been common practice. Students were assessed by the professor within the class, and sometimes students themselves voted democratically on class prizes. But this was replaced, from around the 1840s, by written terminal examinations and the sorting of students into degree classes.[41] This was undoubtedly borrowed from England, specifically from Oxbridge. But arguably English and Scottish universities were responding to the same social pressures, for certification and professional qualifications, at much the same time, though in ways reflecting their own traditions.

Ordinary classes could be very large, and until the 1960s degree regulations meant that a philosophy course was a normal part of the experience of arts graduates, including those in Honours in other subjects. But Honours degrees in philosophy, though possible from the 1860s and expanded in the 1890s, were never a very popular choice. Davie himself took his first degree in Classics, then a second MA in Philosophy. When he graduated in Philosophy in 1938, he was one of only three at Edinburgh, compared with thirty in Modern Languages, thirteen in History, twelve in English, and so on, not to mention about sixty Honours science graduates. It was the same picture in the other universities, and earlier in the twentieth century.[42] Of the eighty-two Edinburgh Honours arts graduates in 1938, Philosophy accounted for 3.6 per cent, while English, Classics and Modern Languages together formed 57 per cent. Languages and literature were arguably as central to Scottish humanities culture as philosophy. The position of philosophy, and philosophy departments, depended unusually on the subject's role in the Ordinary degree, which helps explain why Davie was so concerned to defend it.

The main reason why there were so few philosophy Honours graduates was that the subject was not taught in Scottish schools, nor does anyone seem to have proposed this. Lindsay Paterson has suggested, interestingly, that in the twentieth century English literature in secondary schools replaced university philosophy as the basis of Scottish generalism.[43] But with no philosophy in schools, students had no opportunity to develop an early interest in the subject, and it could not be part of university entrance requirements. Most important, there was no demand for secondary teachers in the subject, then the main outlet for Honours arts graduates. Here there was a contrast with English literature, and with Leavis, who was able to disseminate his disciples through the sixth forms of England.

Scotland may also be contrasted with France, where philosophy was a school subject with high prestige, and where lycées and faculties were centrally administered as part of the same system, which was not the case in Scotland. Graduates in philosophy went on to teach in schools, and it was normal well into the twentieth century for leading university philosophers to start their careers there. In schools, philosophy was an essential element in the *baccalauréat*, and *Philosophie* was the name of the highest secondary form. The result was that educated French people were and still are familiar with philosophical problems and the ideas of the great philosophers in a way that is not the case in Britain. George Davie, who was very interested in the links between French and Scottish thought, drew a parallel between philosophy in the Scottish Ordinary degree and the *classe de philosophie*: In both countries, philosophy was being taught to adolescents.[44] But in Scotland, the age of starting university rose from fifteen or sixteen in the mid-century to seventeen or eighteen by the end. Logically, the elementary teaching of philosophy should have moved from the arts faculty back into the schools, as it did for other subjects. But this failed to happen. According to the Humboldtian model, general education should be completed in the secondary school, but in this respect Scotland remained pre-Humboldtian.

Moreover, in France the centralised system meant that curricula and professorial appointments were controlled by the state, which gave favoured individuals the ability to impose an official philosophy. This was famously the case with Victor Cousin in the early nineteenth century, whose 'eclectic' doctrines combined the influence of Thomas Reid and his Scottish successors like Dugald Stewart and William Hamilton with that of German idealism. According to Davie, Cousin supported the idea that the Scots could 'keep alive in the nineteenth century the compromise, initiated by the Union, of identifying politically with the English, but of maintaining a distinctive national identity before the world, in a cultural-spiritual sense'. There was undoubtedly a kinship between the social ethic of common sense, as interpreted by Davie, and Cousin's idea of a philosophy which would combat materialism and scepticism, and be reconcilable with religious belief, while remaining independent of ecclesiastical authority. In France, philosophical doctrines were to change later in the nineteenth century, but the principle of an official state-approved philosophy remained. Scotland, however, lacked a philosophical dictator to ensure the continuance of a national tradition.

Endnotes

1. Lindsay Paterson, quoted in Murdo Macdonald, 'George Davie 1912-2007: an Appreciation', *Scottish Affairs* 60 (2007), pp. 1-5 (p. 5).
2. George E. Davie, *The Democratic Intellect: Scotland and her Universities in the Nineteenth Century* (Edinburgh: Edinburgh University Press, 1961). The edition cited here is the second, of 1964; the third, of 2019, has the same text and pagination. The best guide is Lindsay Paterson, 'George Davie and the Democratic Intellect', in Gordon Graham (Ed.), *Scottish Philosophy in the Nineteenth and Twentieth Centuries* (Oxford: Oxford University Press, 2015), pp. 236-69.
3. See respectively Ben Jackson, *The Case for Scottish Independence: A History of Nationalist Political Thought in Modern Scotland* (Cambridge: Cambridge University Press, 2020), esp. ch. 2; R. D. Anderson, *Education and Opportunity in Victorian Scotland: Schools and Universities* (Oxford: Oxford University Press, 1983), esp. pp. 358-61.
4. Robert Anderson, *British Universities Past and Present* (London: Hambledon Continuum, 2006), esp. pp. 124-29.
5. Jill Pellew and Miles Taylor (eds), *Utopian Universities: A Global History of the New Campuses of the 1960s* (London: Bloomsbury, 2021).
6. Paterson, 'George Davie and the Democratic Intellect', pp. 251-52. Cf. G. E. Davie, *The Crisis of the Democratic Intellect: The Problem of Generalism and Specialisation in Twentieth-Century Scotland* (Edinburgh: Polygon, 1986), pp. 262-63. No attempt is made here to assess this later book.
7. W. Elliot, 'The Scottish Heritage in Politics', in Duke of Atholl and others, *A Scotsman's Heritage* (London: Alexander MacLehose, 1932), pp. 59, 62-63. Recent historians have tended rather to see the early modern parish as an instrument of social discipline.
8. George Davie, 'The Social Significance of the Scottish Philosophy of Common Sense', lecture of 1972 reprinted in G. Davie, *The Scottish Enlightenment and Other Essays* (Edinburgh: Polygon, 1991), p. 59. Cf. *Crisis of the Democratic Intellect*, pp. 262-63.
9. George Davie, 'The Importance of the Ordinary MA', *Edinburgh Review* 90 (1993), pp. 61-69 (p. 62).
10. *Democratic Intellect*, p. 209.
11. *Crisis of the Democratic Intellect*, pp. 9, 84, 166-67.
12. *Democratic Intellect*, pp. xi, xv.
13. 'Victor Cousin and the Scottish Philosophers', in George Davie, *A Passion for Ideas. Essays on the Scottish Enlightenment 2* (Edinburgh: Polygon, 1994), p. 72.
14. *Democratic Intellect*, pp. 255, 314.
15. *Democratic Intellect*, p. 298; 'The Discovery of Ferrier', in *Scottish Enlightenment and Other Essays*, p. 89-90; George Davie, *Ferrier and the Blackout of the Scottish Enlightenment* (Edinburgh: Edinburgh Review, 2003).
16. Both discussed (with Burnet and MacDiarmid) in *Crisis of the Democratic Intellect*.
17. Jackson, p. 37; Christopher Harvie, *Scotland and Nationalism: Scottish Society and Politics, 1707-1977* (London: George Allen and Unwin, 1977); Rory Scothorne, 'From the Outer Edge', *London Review of Books*, 6 December 2018.
18. *Democratic Intellect*, p. 337.
19. Notably Craig Beveridge and Ronald Turnbull, *The Eclipse of Scottish Culture: Inferiorism and the Intellectuals* (Edinburgh: Polygon, 1989), esp. ch. 6; Andrew L. Walker, *The*

Revival of the Democratic Intellect: Scotland's University Traditions and the Crisis in Modern Thought (Edinburgh: Polygon, 1994); Carol Craig, *The Scots' Crisis of Confidence*, 2nd edn (Glendaruel: Argyll Publishing, 2011).
20 H. J. C. Grierson, 'The Scottish Universities', in John Clarke (ed.), *Problems of National Education, by Twelve Scottish Educationists* (London: Macmillan, 1919), pp. 311–62; H. J. C. Grierson, 'The University and a Liberal Education', in *Essays and Addresses* (London: Chatto and Windus, 1940), pp. 193–97. See *Democratic Intellect*, pp. 99–102; Anderson, *Education and Opportunity*, pp. 282–83. Davie considered that my emphasis on nostalgia showed 'a complete trivialisation of twentieth-century Scottish cultural history': *Crisis of the Democratic Intellect*, p. 32.
21 John Burnet, *Higher Education and the War* (London: Macmillan, 1917), esp. ch. 7; *Crisis of the Democratic Intellect*, pp. 11–26.
22 Laurance J. Saunders, *Scottish Democracy, 1815–1840: the Social and Intellectual Background* (Edinburgh: Oliver and Boyd, 1950); Kennedy Stewart, 'The Problem of the Scottish Universities', *Nineteenth Century* 101 (1927), pp. 201–07.
23 *Crisis of the Democratic Intellect*, p. 9.
24 Alan Bold, *MacDiarmid: Christopher Murray Grieve, A Critical Biography*, paperback edn (London: Collins, 1990), pp. 51, 369, 395.
25 Andrew McPherson et al., *Eighteen-Plus: The Final Selection* (Bletchley: Open University Press, 1972), p. 17.
26 On gender and other 'blind spots' in Davie, see Jean Barr, 'Re-Framing the Democratic Intellect', *Scottish Affairs* 55 (2006), pp. 23–46.
27 Andrew McPherson, 'Selections and Survivals: a Sociology of the Ancient Scottish Universities', in Richard Brown (ed.), *Knowledge, Education, and Cultural Change: Papers in the Sociology of Education* (London: Tavistock, 1973), pp. 175–77.
28 Beveridge and Turnbull, pp. 63–70.
29 Another book not mentioned by Davie, but pertinent to his ideas on experts and elites, was Michael Young's *Rise of the Meritocracy* (1958).
30 Holger Nehring, 'Failed Utopia? The University of Stirling from the 1960s to the Early 1980s', in Pellew and Taylor, p. 191; L. Robbins, *The University in the Modern World* (London: Macmillan, 1966), pp. 64, 95.
31 *Crisis of the Democratic Intellect*, p. 40.
32 David McCrone, *Understanding Scotland: The Sociology of a Stateless Nation* (London: Routledge, 1992), pp. 4–8.
33 Donald J. Withrington, 'Raw, Pungent Spirit', *Universities Quarterly* 16 (1961–62), pp. 94–98.
34 Robert Anderson, 'Writing University History in Great Britain, from the 1960s to the Present', *CIAN. Revista de Historia de las Universidades* 20 (2017), pp. 17–40.
35 *Democratic Intellect*, p. 91.
36 Ibid., pp. 63, 83.
37 C. J. Wright, 'Academics and their Aims: English and Scottish Approaches to University Education', *History of Education* 8 (1979), pp. 91–97; Peter Slee, 'Scottish Higher Education – an Invented Tradition?', *Higher Education Quarterly* 41 (1987), pp. 194–97.
38 Gordon Graham, 'The Nineteenth-Century Aftermath', in Alexander Broadie (ed.), *Cambridge Companion to the Scottish Enlightenment* (Cambridge: Cambridge University Press, 2003), pp. 348–49.

39 J. S. Blackie, *On the Advancement of Learning in Scotland* (Edinburgh: Sutherland and Knox, 1855), p. 10; cited (slightly inaccurately) in *Democratic Intellect*, p. 239.
40 Christopher Stray, *Classics Transformed: Schools, Universities, and Society in England, 1830–1960* (Oxford: Clarendon, 1998).
41 Robert Anderson, 'Professors and Examinations: Ideas of the University in Nineteenth-Century Scotland', *History of Education* 46 (2017), pp. 21–38.
42 Robert Anderson, 'The Development of History Teaching in the Scottish Universities, 1894–1939', *Journal of Scottish Historical Studies* 32 (2012), pp. 50–73 (p. 57).
43 Lindsay Paterson, 'The Modernising of the Democratic Intellect: The Role of English in Scottish Secondary Education, 1900–1939', *Journal of Scottish Historical Studies* 24 (2005), pp. 45–79.
44 *Democratic Intellect*, p. 287. Also discussed in Burnet, pp. 168–71.

14. Writing Scottishness in Post-imperial, Post-devolution Theatre: a Conversation

PETER ARNOTT AND IAN BROWN

IB What does it mean to you to talk about 'Writing Scottishness: literature and the shaping of Scottish national identities'?

PA The answer's partly personal, partly cultural. From the latter perspective, the biggest event for my generation was the 1981 publication of *Lanark*. That offered a more expansive, modern, contemporary vision of Glaswegianness and Scottishness than I'd grown up with; versions of *The White Heather Club*; Andy Stewart and a tongue-in-cheek kitsch Scottishness nobody had to take too seriously, that was unrelated to our personal lives. What *Lanark* offered was quite different. I was nineteen in 1981. Before that I didn't know much.

IB For me the process was very similar, but slightly earlier, in the 1970s when playwrights began to draw on almost forgotten energy from the 1940s work of Glasgow Unity Theatre: Bill Bryden, Roddy McMillan, Hector MacMillan. Unromantic plays about Scottish history and contemporary society, using Scots language, pulled me in. My *Lanark* moment would be Stewart Conn's 1971 *The Burning*, about witchcraft trials under James VI. Your trigger was a novel; mine a play; but both rewriting what Scottish identities are.

PA Absolutely. Expanding what 'Scottish' might mean in literature, or rather literature as a means to express an expansion of personal possibilities. But I was, shamefully, unaware of Bryden's or McMillan's plays, or even John Byrne's *Slab Boys Trilogy*. I just didn't know. In my secondary schooling in the 1970s, the plays that made the biggest impression were those I acted in: *The Crucible* and *Death of a Salesman* – Arthur Miller, very important – or Robert Bolt's *A Man for All Seasons*. But Scottish plays, absolutely not. No idea there was such a thing. I went to Cambridge University where I met a Welsh poet, Jo Lloyd. She was completely horrified I knew nothing about Scottish literature. She knew far more than I did because she came from a culture with a sense of the interaction of its history and literature.

IB That fits with the long-term impact of Scottish Education Acts: we weren't taught Scottish literature. Though in my Highers year we once did Robert Burns at my school: 'A Cotter's Saturday Night', not typical of his work.

PA It contains Scottishness within a safe domesticated – and cringingly unambitious – culture.

IB Why does that background, shared not just by you and me, but by so many Scottish writers of the last forty years, see them strongly asserting Scottish identities in various forms – feminist, LGBTQIA+, BAME – but also in Scotland's languages? You write in Scots.

PA I write Scots, sometimes demotic, sometimes self-consciously, especially doing translations or versions. And sometimes, as a Scot, using standard English as a language that's available to me. My version of Brecht's *Herr Puntila and his Man Matti*, for example, used a literary Scots, consciously heir to MacDiarmid and Goodsir Smith in picking and choosing words of different origins. It's a utilitarian approach to the Scots language, a string to the bow, a tune you can sing. I'm perfectly happy singing in standard English, but sometimes an alternative seems right. *Puntila*, set in the Finnish countryside, was semi-stolen by a German playwright in exile from the Nazis. For him Puntila's Karelia was a kind of Never-Neverland, so I developed a Scottish Never-Neverland. I thought the story archetypally Scottish – a landlord who's decent when drunk, an absolute bastard when sober – and I thought that connected straight with a lot of archetypical Scottish culture, comic, rural, from the Kailyard through Compton Mackenzie to now. I felt two continuities I could bring to it: Scottish twentieth-century Renaissance language and Brechtian dramaturgy.

IB What you're doing there ties in with what Bill Findlay and Martin Bowman were doing with their Michel Tremblay translations. It's saying Scots language can handle international topics and themes.

PA I remember conversations about the international potential of being distinctively Scottish with Chris Hannan back in the 1980s. His first show adapted a Russian story, *Klimkov: The Life of a Tsarist Agent*, performed by 7:84. Then in 1985 – an *annus mirabilis* I like to think – he had *Elizabeth Gordon Quinn* at the Traverse, I had *White Rose* performed and Jo Clifford *Losing Venice*. All of us, including Jo whose origins are in the north of England, consciously extended what we thought a distinctly Scottish play could do. Chris's *Elizabeth Gordon Quinn* was like the Glasgow Unity plays but doing different things, revising kitchen-sink Glasgow drama. The original production caught something: it was almost like opera, so formal, so precise, a wonderful piece of writing. It was a Scots story and in Scots, but felt part of European theatre, absolutely self-consciously. My aim with *White Rose* was to dramatise a political story about a Russian woman fighter pilot, where the fourth wall wasn't there. It connected to Scottish variety theatre and Russian 1920s agit-prop, addressing the audience directly. I wanted to write a Scottish play that didn't have to be about Scotland but couldn't have come from anywhere else. I was very young then, twenty-three the week before we opened. I'd left Scotland at the beginning of 1980, with no intention of ever coming back. I went to London to the National Youth Theatre, then to Cambridge. I stayed in London after Cambridge but came home basically because I was broke. In the meantime, I'd met Tim Cribb, one of my key encounters, who used to teach at Glasgow University and was at Churchill College, Cambridge. He began talking to me about somebody called 'MacDiarmid'. I'd no idea who he was talking about. So, it was an Englishman who said 'Oh, for God's sake!' and threw a copy of the collected poems at me.

IB In 1977 I went to work for a time with the British Council in Istanbul and met a wonderful Turkish poet and scholar, Cevat Çapan, leading translator of many contemporary English-language writers including T. S. Eliot. He said, 'What do people think now of MacDiarmid?' And I'd no idea. Cevat is a leading literary scholar of international standing who cared about MacDiarmid's critical position and I, a Scot, knew nothing about the status of MacDiarmid and his work. Cevat's interest in his work made me think 'Hang on; we're missing something up here in Scotland'. That revelation made me realise it was parochial of Scots to think the work of their great writers was 'parochial'. And the other thing you've just discussed is the issue of language. By talking about your experience in 1985, you remind me that I'd been trying at university to write plays and they weren't working. One or two had amateur performances, but the first serious play I had produced I wrote for Hugo Gifford of Strathclyde Theatre Group. It was a version of *Antigone* in Scots. In 1969, given where my head was, it could only be in Scots. That was because I began exploring writing in Scots during university summer jobs working among miners, monolingual Scots-speakers with a wonderfully rich language. I'd then gone to work in London for two years but had to come back because my mother was ill for a time. Then, I was suddenly hearing the language in my ear again and I could write my version of *Antigone*. Since then, according to topic, roughly half my plays are in Scots and half in English. Both are indigenous to Scotland, but when the dialogue is in Scots there's certainly an additional sense that one's writing versions of Scottishness not just in content, but in linguistic form.

PA   The parallel for me is that in 1982–83 I was writing plays done as student shows, but the first play of mine presented as an adult work was *The Boxer Benny Lynch*. I hadn't read Bill Bryden's *Benny Lynch*. I'd seen the play in the 'Play for Today' series on the telly when I was a teenager. It was just after my discovery of MacDiarmid that in 1982 John Burrowes wrote a biography of Benny Lynch. I wrote my play in my last year at university in 1983. I'd a barely conscious sense that I could reach towards home. I remember my brother picking up the script and saying, 'This is *The Broons*, isn't it?' That's what Scots language was: for Sunday mornings, Burns Night and Scottish regiments. That may be difficult for current generations to understand, but it seemed almost completely unconscious. It didn't feel like anti-Scots prejudice because there was no realistic political project for Scotland until the 1970s and even then it didn't feel serious. Scottishness was an entertaining notion, but not necessarily a real one.

IB How, then, do you think the literary and theatrical processes you're talking about contribute to those that led to devolution?

PA First, perhaps coincidentally, in the 1970s – before the 1979 referendum – devolutionary cultural and political developments fed into theatre writing, poetry and the novel, which reciprocally recorded and reinforced rising social and politico-cultural interest in Scottish themes and, so, Scottish political identities in general. Second, specifically, theatre producers simply discovered that people would come and see new plays in a Scots voice.

IB Clive Perry, Lyceum Artistic Director from 1966, working with Bill Bryden who came in 1971, made a great critical and box-office success of producing Scots-language plays as did his successor in 1976, Stephen MacDonald. Stephen would say his box-office projections anticipated a new play in Scots would do at least ten per cent better than a new play in English. At the Lyceum, Edinburgh's so-called middle-class 'posh' theatre.

PA At the Traverse, too, Chris Parr, another Englishman, followed that path from 1975 to 1981. This programming of Scottish plays in Edinburgh theatre was led by Englishmen, as was my introduction to contemporary Scottish poetry. It's almost as if the English were more culturally confident to introduce Scottishness than Scots were. It's like that Douglas Dunn comment, 'I will know that devolution has had an effect if my Scottish students question me. If they're confident enough to think I might not know everything because I'm the dominie.'

IB We're talking about 1970s theatre developments that bear fruit in the 1980s when sales for playwrights, poets and novelists show people are not turned off by Scots-language work. Other versions of Scottishness in theatre flourished too. From the early 1970s into this century the Glasgow Citizens artistic triumvirate, led by Giles Havergal, a Scot, with Robert David MacDonald, another Scot, and Philip Prowse, explored a different strand of Scottish drama, a post-modern aesthetically daring European-focused English-language international repertoire. And interest in Gaelic developed too: Sorley MacLean was still around into the 1990s and the ghettoisation of Gaelic was being challenged. We all make the case that Gaelic, English and Scots are co-equal indigenous languages within Scottish literature and it's our absolute right as writers to use them. I don't think that was the attitude in the 1970s when there was much more institutionally of a hierarchy of language esteem.

PA Douglas Dunn's observation is part of the deep history of these attitudes. Scottishness was also contained in the semi-mythical and – as it turns out – fraudulent, yet incredibly important, Ossian poems of James Macpherson. James Macpherson is a great unsung genius of Scottish literature. I think he's great.

IB Ossian's on this book's front cover. Macpherson's accused of fraud, which is fair as far as it goes, but it's a certain kind of fraud: there's sincerity in it. He's trying to work with fragments of Gaelic poetry he understands and respect them by creating an epic from them.

PA Homer's the model but both French and the British imperial states assimilated classicism as a precursor of themselves! 'We are the continuation! "Civis Britannicus sum!"' But things were changing all round us. This is going to sound like a complete *non sequitur* – but I'm thinking of Scottish football fans. In the 1970s their idea was to rival English football-fan violence, culminating in 1977 when the Wembley pitch was torn up after Scotland beat England by all of 2–1. I was still at school, and everyone claimed to have a bit of Wembley in their garden. That chip-on-the-shoulder Scottishness attempted to rival a perceived Englishness and what Scottish football supporters did after the 1978 World Cup – well before theatre – was to reinvent themselves as entertainers. In those supporters' minds, the way to really piss off the English is for everyone to love us. After the Wembley riot, they created a genuinely post-modern self-parody with 'See-you-Jimmy' hats and kilts. That's a cultural vision of one version of Scottishness, having the self-confidence to make a popular cultural decision not to try to rival chauvinism but to invent a different kind of identity. I think that's a comic-book version of what the whole country has done since the

1970s. We've ceased being the world-beating nation's slightly pathetic younger brother, the subaltern, the sergeant, the capable sergeant-major who actually ran the regiment or the engineer who actually built the bridge, or the slavedriver. We had been all that, that had been how we saw ourselves – flattering ourselves as being 'useful but not in charge' – and now we'd decided to be different. It wasn't just us. It was what happened to the idea of Britain in the 1970s and 1980s. 'Britain' was reinvented, post-IMF 1976, Margaret Thatcher, the Falklands War. That reinvention of what 'Britishness' might mean left Scotland cold. I remember this vividly because I was commuting between Cambridge and Glasgow during the Falklands War and for the first time for me personally it felt like going to a foreign country.

IB So, what factors in your view, as a writer, have shaped the contemporary Scottish nation's identities?

PA I think the single biggest influence on modern Scottish consciousness is the break-up of Britain's Empire. The Suez crisis was a big traffic light on the way. That told the UK definitively that 'You don't run things anymore'. This may be simple self-dramatisation, but I see the decline of Britishness as dating back to 1916, to the Easter Rising and its aftermath and also to the battle of the Somme in the same year where so many Scots died. My grandfather was there on the first day. British cultural politics has been a reaction to the decline of an idea of Britishness, which was fostered by a now non-existent Empire, some of whose attitudes hang on, often poisonously. That steady process of what we've called since the 1970s 'managed decline' crystallised at Suez and the way the Americans stopped it – cease and desist – and the realisation that it was only as hosts to American nuclear weapons that we could pretend to be a 'Great Power'. Meantime, by 1960 we were begging to join the European Community. The idea of Britain had to be reinvented. It was just about possible to see devolution as part of that, and our cultural role in theatre-writing as part of devolution.

IB What we're saying here, as a generalisation, is writers shape identities, but also respond to changes already under way.

PA Absolutely, both. A classical dialectical process.

IB So, how far do you think devolution has had an impact on the Scottish world of letters? What cultural issues have emerged from devolution?

PA In purely pragmatic terms I remember talking to Hamish Glen, then director of Dundee Rep theatre, about this in his kitchen in Dundee in 1997. We thought, 'Well, if there's to be one time you can set up a Scottish National Theatre, the first years of devolution are it. At some point, we'll have a crash and we'll run out of money and then it will never happen. In the early years of devolution, we've a chance. If not now, when?' In other words, it was optimism tempered by experience even then. So, within the theatre – I don't know so much about publishing and other cultural endeavours – but within theatre and playwriting, the advent of the Playwrights Studio Scotland in 2004 – we were both part of that – and the National Theatre of Scotland in 2006 absolutely had to happen. They were a *sine qua non* whose moment was in the earlier days of devolution.

IB Accepting what you say, I'd look back forty years to a similar cultural surge, tied into the build-up to the 1979 devolution referendum. 1962 – Scottish Opera founded; 1969 – Scottish Ballet founded; 1977 – Scottish National Orchestra became 'Royal'. In terms of interaction of devolution and cultural events, let alone creative literature, we're clearly looking at waves, each going a stage further. For theatre, what's interesting about what you're saying is that when we set up the Scottish Society of Playwrights in 1973, part of that earlier wave, it was outside the Establishment, while those later things you're talking about – Playwrights Studio, the National Theatre of Scotland – are the Establishment.

PA Devolution's had a wide, but mutual, impact on culture. No National Theatre of Scotland without devolution, but it's part of a not entirely conscious, and therefore probably permanent, cultural transformation that almost nobody explicitly expressed when the Scottish Parliament was established and the Scottish Government was initially called the Scottish Executive. Then, the parliament appeared really only to have older Scottish Office functions, and the historical bits the Treaty of

Union handed on, with election of members added. The fact it's become much more than that is almost a cultural accident, it's a cultural event, really, deeply deplored by some of its very architects who thought that devolution would dish the Nats. It turns out Tam Dalyell was right all along: once you open that door and Scotland becomes a real place politically, a Scottish Parliament can no longer be a version of local government under Westminster. And now that Brexit has reinvented Britishness again – without any regard for the wishes of London let alone Scotland – who knows what happens next?

IB Would you say devolution has given Scots and Gaelic language culture more impetus?

PA It has, of course, institutionally speaking, in terms of language policies and Gaelic-medium schools. Creatively, too. I've worked with Donald S. Murray, the Gaelic novelist, whose new Gaelic play I dramaturged through an intermediate translation. Currently, I'm excited to be working, through Playwrights Studio Scotland, with Elspeth Turner who's written two epic historical plays about the Gaels in America, both set in Carolina, one in the present dealing with aspects of history and belonging that underlie the Black Lives Matters movement, the other set in the American War of Independence including slave-owning Gaels. Both plays are partly in English and partly in Gaelic. Both might be very important.

IB Gaelic's place is constantly developing. Just last Friday (10 June 2022) in a garden in Pollokshields I watched a promenade production of *Stùris*, a Gaelic version of *Antigone* by Rona Dhòmhnallach, supported by Playwrights Studio Scotland. Last year, the ASL 2021 annual volume was a Gaelic drama anthology, *Dràma na Gàidhlig: A Century of Gaelic Drama*. Before the twentieth century, socio-economic and non-urban structures in the Gàidhealtachd meant you didn't see playhouses. Once Gaelic-speakers moved to cities in a certain critical mass, you saw dramatic development: by 1900 people began writing Gaelic-language plays semi-professionally and professionally. Initially, they were rather didactic, but by the 1960s, let alone by the time you get to *Scotties* in

2018 which is included in the Gaelic drama anthology, they're serious drama, while contemporary playwrights like Catriona Lexy Campbell write amazingly.

PA Martin Travers is writing in a very vivid, realised Scots and he and Angela Darcy are setting up a Scots-language touring company based in Biggar. I think he's not nearly well enough known – he's writing a lot for young people but as a playwright for 'grown-ups', he's not nearly well enough known.

IB Would you say that Scots are now more at ease with themselves than forty years ago, or that contemporary politics has increased the sense of distinctiveness?

PA That question implies it's now possible for somebody to be self-consciously Scots and Scottish for a wider and more generous range of people. Let's take the example of Jimmy Somerville of the Communards, growing up gay in 1960s and 1970s working-class Glasgow, but having, in order to be himself, to get on the train south as soon as possible. The difference now – at least this is the hope – is that nobody has to feel that. It's now possible – maybe I'm wrong but in my optimistic moods I'd like to think – that for people of non-white ethnic backgrounds, or for people who are gay or trans, that Scotland and Scottishness can be part of who they are in a completely unself-conscious way.

IB We're not saying there's no prejudice, but we've had more women Makars than men and more gay than straight. The Scottish Society of Playwrights now has more women members than men. Leading writers like Jackie Kay and Hannah Lavery are embraced as part of a national identity. The other day women politicians of different parties married one another: Jenny Gilruth, an SNP government minister, and Kezia Dugdale, former Labour leader. Is that politics or wider culture?

PA It's dialectics again. It's not necessarily been a conscious project.

IB One of the things emerging from what you've been saying is that Scottishness has many constituent identities and its literature has been part of shaping and extending them. So, what d'you think would happen culturally if Scotland became a full-blown political entity?

PA That's a good question. It's really about cultural self-confidence, which was often weak when I was younger and probably even weaker when you were starting. But we do seem to have a kind of gradual self-assertion over recent generations. In some ways, everything depends on what you think 'independence' in the twenty-first-century European context actually might mean in terms of internal and external politics, but also for the general population. In institutional terms it should mean changing the 1948 Arts Council of Great Britain model with its specified art forms and dividing the amateur from the professional, from which we are gradually developing. Right now, I think we're living in a strange sort of paradox, that the possibility of radical change seems in the air but there's very little appetite, energy or bandwidth – to use the current phrase – among those with power and influence to think what that might mean for culture or cultural policy in Scotland.

IB We've got to imagine not just what 'full-blown political entity' would mean for us but for other countries and other cultures we interact with. I know you've done a lot of work overseas. I find often in my work overseas that people need an adjustment to recognise even what is the current nature of 'Scottishness'. In 2002, visiting a major Armenian university literature department, I was asked if there were any famous Scottish poets. I mentioned Robert Burns. They said, 'Robert Burns is Scottish?' They thought him a wonderful poet but within an imperialist English Literature framework: given their ages, they'd been educated within a Soviet-era view of him as a proletarian whose nationality was occluded within Soviet attitudes to nationalities. Scotland's becoming a full-blown political entity will inevitably change such frameworks. Indeed, they're changing now, post-devolution. Also, and however, in some senses internally Scotland for its own purposes has been a full-blown entity all along. Aspects of the Treaty of Union guaranteed that. It's just that for other people's purposes it's not always been seen that way.

PA I think that's very well put. Repeatedly, you find people thinking of Scotland as a region of England.

IB Europe-wide, there are examples of independent or quasi-independent nations that came to be seen as regions in other state entities and vice-versa. Think of, among many, Catalunya, Lombardy, Croatia, the Baltic States. Not to mention the bedevilled history of Poland or, indeed, Armenia. In many ways, how the Scandinavian kingdoms have linked and separated is closest to the Scottish/English experience.

PA Is there a way, I wonder, if you had the same conversation in Armenia about James Joyce, the question about being his being Irish would arise?

IB I'm sure there'd be no doubting his Irishness.

PA But when Joyce was writing *Ulysses*, he was a British subject, rather an unusual one, but nonetheless one.

IB But in the case of Joyce you see the impact of a century of Irish independence on the cultural sector. There, culture became a key element in nation-building. For example, in 1924, straight after Irish independence, Lady Gregory and W. B. Yeats, two of the Abbey Theatre's founders in 1904 as part of the British repertory theatre movement, offered the Abbey to the new Irish government as a gift to the Irish people. Despite initially refusing, in 1925 the Finance Minister Ernest Blythe offered an annual grant. The Abbey was the English-speaking world's first state-supported theatre. That support for the newly independent nation's cultural identity included Irish language promotion. Even now, such support continues, including tax exemptions for artists or the Aosdána, a group of artists receiving annual stipends, set up in 1981 by Charles Haughey, then Irish Prime Minister, as part of recognising national cultural identity.

PA Exactly. And Scotland already has a kind of market identity – at its most basic we're all familiar with it – from the shops on the Royal Mile. One feature about that market identity, I think, is that it's entirely compatible with Union status. I remember once being on radio with Nicola Sturgeon back in the 1990s before she attained her current standing. I ventured to suggest that modern Scotland's cultural identity was itself the creation of the Union. This did not go down well.

IB An interesting thing I've written about, is what I call the 'Rule Britannia Project'. Remember a Scot wrote 'Rule, Britannia'.

PA I didn't know that.

IB James Thomson. It concludes a 1740 opera, *The Masque of Alfred*, lyrics by Thomson, book by another Scot, David Malloch (who changed his surname to 'Mallet' to make it easier for English colleagues to say), music by Thomas Arne. Another Scot, John Arbuthnot, invented John Bull in 1712. David Hume sent his manuscripts away to have the 'Scotticisms' removed. For 'Rule Britannia Project' Scots, seeking a peaceful entity, Britain is a creation which culminates in their Scots version of 'Britain'. Meanwhile, for many in England, 'Scottishness' is just rather quaint.

PA My grandparents' vision of 'Britain' absolutely included Scotland and Scottish identity as a distinct and secure thing through which they were completely secure in their 'Britishness'. For anyone of our generation who's grown up with a post-colonial idea of Britain and the identity of Scotland, perceptions are different.

IB This book includes a chapter about the impact of Irvine Welsh's films. There's a quite different potential for a cultural identification of Scotland. I remember teaching in the O'Neill Theater Center's National Critics Institute – a summer school for mid-career newspaper and broadcast critics under the tutelage of senior mentors in the industry – in 1996 just after *Trainspotting* came out. The critics went to see the film at eleven a.m. in the late-July morning of a small Connecticut cinema, thinking they would see a cosy Scotland as in *Whisky Galore* or even *Brigadoon*. They came out absolutely gobsmacked, jaws literally dropped. This is a minor example; nonetheless, it's about the way the cultural changes and literary outcomes we talked about earlier affect the way the country's seen in other countries.

PA There are three strands here. One is how a new full-blown Scottish entity would be received abroad: George Orwell famously said that to the average Burmese, admittedly in the colonialist 1930s, the idea that Scotland is distinct from England was ridiculous. That'll change. Secondly, there's a post-devolutionary Scottish sense of self that's slowly having an international impact. Thirdly, there's the changing Anglo-British sense of self. Just now, you've people in Europe looking at the

UK, saying, 'My God! What's happening to you people?' Now there seems a deep lack of belief in Britain as a project. Empire that, as some kind of common enterprise, was holding Britain together, is long gone. We even tried the EU for a while in the role of external glue to hold Britain together. That's gone too. Maybe there's nothing left.

IB The Britain of the 'United Kingdom' isn't – and was never – a unitary nation. It's a union by treaty of two sovereign states who fudged a Treaty of Union to get through the Acts of Union in each country's parliament. In the last thirty to fifty years in England, as the Empire's gone, two things have happened. One is English nationalism has rather taken over from British nationalism, which in any case it always was to an extent. But also, with the post-Windrush generation, as Helen Tiffin and Gareth Griffiths nicely put it, the Empire has 'written back'. Suddenly, the concept of 'Britain' becomes much more problematic and that sometimes draws on underlying racism.

PA Often now, Brexit British-nationalism-as-English-nationalism is couched in terms of victimhood. In the whole debate about culpability of Empire, the Scots had felt for years they could blame the English for the Empire and congratulate themselves on not being its instigators. I'm again talking about my grandparents: they absolutely thought that the Scots did right in everything and the English were the imperialists. They could combine a sense of British nationalism with a sense of Scottish nationalism. This is absolute nonsense: recent historians have reminded us how mistaken such as view was. That's reflected in Elspeth Turner's play that I mentioned with slave-owning Gaels in the Carolinas. This conversation is happening in England too, but with a different inflection here.

IB If one asks if it's necessary for Scotland to be independent for it to reach cultural maturity, one can actually say it may be, but Scottish independence may certainly be necessary for England to reach cultural maturity.

PA I can't predict what shape I think English culture or Scottish culture will have in fifty years, but I'm absolutely certain people will have stopped talking about 'British' culture, meaning English culture. Shakespeare will finally belong to England!

Notes on Contributors

Peter Arnott FASLS(Hon)'s plays include *The Breathing House* (TMA Best New Play 2003), *Why Do You Stand There in the Rain?* (Fringe First 2012) and CATS Best New Scottish Play Award winners, *Monarch of the Glen* (2017) and *The Signalman* (2019). His novel *Moon Country* appeared in 2015. Formerly Writer-in-Residence at the Tron and Traverse theatres, National Library of Scotland and Edinburgh University, he is currently working for the Royal Lyceum and Vox Motus.

Robert Anderson FRSE is Professor Emeritus of History at Edinburgh University. He has written extensively on the history of education in Scotland, Britain, and Europe. His books include *Education and the Scottish People 1750–1918* (1995), *European Universities from the Enlightenment to 1914* (2004), and *British Universities Past and Present* (2006). He is joint editor of *The Edinburgh History of Education in Scotland* (2015).

Ian Brown FRSE FRHistS, Honorary Senior Research Fellow (Scottish Literature, Glasgow University) and Professor Emeritus (Drama, Kingston University, London), is widely published on theatre, literature, and cultural policy, editing a wide range of volumes. A playwright and poet, his most recent monograph is *Performing Scottishness: Enactment and National Identities* (2020).

Gerard Carruthers FRSE is Francis Hutcheson Professor of Scottish Literature at the University of Glasgow. He is General Editor of the Oxford University Press multi-volume edition of the Works of Robert Burns. Forthcoming is his co-edited *1820: Scottish Rebellion – Essays on a Nineteenth-Century Insurrection* (Birlinn, 2022) and he is currently editing the *Wiley-Blackwell Companion to Scottish Literature* (2023).

Bryony Coombs FSA Scot, Teaching Fellow (History of Art, Edinburgh University), works on Scottish Continental connections in the late-medieval and early modern periods. She is currently writing a monograph, *Visual Arts and the Auld Alliance: Scotland, France and National Identity c. 1420–1550* (Edinburgh University Press), as well as two chapters for *The Edinburgh History of the Book in Scotland*, vol. 1 (forthcoming).

Béatrice Duchateau, Teaching Fellow in British literature (University of Burgundy, Dijon), has published articles on Hugh MacDiarmid and the Scottish Renaissance Movement. Her most recent article is 'Hugh MacDiarmid: la poésie du "révolté métaphysique"' (*Études Anglaises*, July–September 2019).

Emma Dymock teaches in the Department of Celtic and Scottish Studies at Edinburgh University. Her research interests and publications focus on modern Gaelic poetry, particularly relating to politics and landscape symbolism, and the correspondence of Scottish Literary Renaissance figures. She has co-edited *Caoir Gheal Leumraich: Sorley MacLean Collected Poems* (2011) and edited *Naethin Dauntit: The Collected Poems of Douglas Young* (2016).

Clarisse Godard Desmarest FSA Scot FRHistS is senior lecturer in British Studies at the University of Picardie Jules Verne. Published widely on Scottish architecture and culture, she edited *The New Town of Edinburgh: An Architectural Celebration* (2019). Her current research, supported by an EU Marie Curie individual fellowship at Edinburgh University, focuses on questions of national and cultural identity in the architecture of William Burn (1789–1870).

Lesley Graham is senior lecturer in the University of Bordeaux's Department of Languages and Cultures and current president of the French Society for Scottish Studies. Her research centres on nineteenth-century Scottish literature, particularly travel writing and other non-fiction genres. Published widely on Robert Louis Stevenson, his entourage and afterlives, she is editor of the New Edinburgh Edition of Stevenson's Uncollected Essays 1880–94.

NOTES ON CONTRIBUTORS

Pamela King is Professor Emerita of Medieval Studies in Glasgow University. Her research interests range across late medieval literatures and culture. Her books include *The York Cycle and the Worship of the City* (2006) and *Medieval Literature 1300–1500* (2011). Her selected essays were edited by Alexandra Johnston as *Reading Texts for Performance and Performances as Texts* (2020).

Anne-Lise Marin-Lamellet, a senior lecturer in English (Université Jean Monnet, Saint-Étienne, France), works on contemporary British studies and cinema, mainly on issues of class, race, gender and nation as well as their relation to space (especially urban areas) and genres. Her latest edited volume is *La Ville industrielle à l'écran: objet cinématographique à identifier* (2022).

Emily L. Pickard is an independent researcher focusing on gender, class, and maternity in Willa Muir's published and unpublished writings. Her most recent publication is 'Re-Evaluating Willa Muir's "Mrs Muttoe and the Top Storey" in Light of COVID-19 Labour Disparities' (*Scottish Literary Review* 14.1, 2022).

Pauline Pilote is senior lecturer in English and American literature at the Université Bretagne-Sud in Lorient, France. A member of HCTI (Héritages et Constructions dans le Texte et l'Image), she works on nineteenth-century transatlantic literature. Her *Wizards of the West: Walter Scott et le roman historique américain* (2022) deals with American historical fiction and the reception of Walter Scott in nineteenth-century America.

Kristel van Soeren is an independent scholar of early modern music history, specialising in Jacobite songs, political protest, and identities in the British Isles. Her research focuses on the role of contrafacta in the dissemination of cultural resistance in Scotland and England. She is currently working on a 'songs as archives' theory in the context of early modern song cultures.

Index

Aberbach, David, 87–88
Achaius, 57
Act of Union *see* Union, Act of
Adair, James, 123
   History of the American Indians, 123
Aeneas, 108
Agandecca, 105
Albion, 51, 107
Alexander, George, 3
Alexander VI (Pope), 51
Alexander the Great, 112
Alfred the Great, 10
Allen, Kevin (dir.), 214
   Twin Town, 214
Alloway, 7–8
Alston, David, 16
American Revolution, 134
Amis, Kingsley, 232
Anderson, Benedict, xiii–xiv, 117
Anderson, Elizabeth, 199
Anderson, John, 236
Anderson, R. R., 9
Anderson, Robert, xi
Andrew, Christopher, 162
Apollo (sun god), 90–91
Arbroath, 12
Arbuthnot, Alexander, 22
Arbuthnot, John, 261
Archibald, David, 215
Armenia, 260
Arne, Thomas, 261
Arnott, Peter, xi–xii
   The Boxer Benny Lynch, 252
   White Rose, 251
Ashby, Eric, 233
   Technology and the Academics, 233
Aston, Anthony, 4
Athens, 7, 168
Aubry-Lecomte, Jean-Baptiste, 102
Auden, W. H., 162
Augusta, Isabella (Lady Gregory), 260
Augustus, 112
Australia, 9
Austria, 102, 105
'Awa Whigs Awa', 88

Bacon, Francis, 10
Baird, Jon S. (dir.), 215, 229
   Filth, 215, 217–26, 228–29
Bàn, Donnachadh, 181
Bannatyne, Richard, 31
Baldwin, Stanley, 168
Bannockburn, Battle of, 133, 165
Bara, Joseph, 103
Barbour, John, vii, 20, 65, 132
   The Brus, 65, 132
Barnard, John, 10
Barra, 148
Barrie, J. M., 75, 78, 226
   Farewell Miss Julie Logan, 78
Barrow, Geoffrey, 12
Barzun, Jacques, 109
Bateman, Meg, 177, 192
Baxter, Charles, 141–42
Beauharnais, Joséphine de, 98, 112, 114
Bell, Gavin, x, 138, 141–42, 151
Bell, Ian, 140, 148, 151
Bellenden, John, 44–45, 59
   The History and Cronikils of Scotland, 45
Beveridge, Craig, xi
The Bible, 12, 24, 28, 74
Bidauld, Jean Joseph Xavier, 100
Blackie, John Stuart, 242
Blair, Hugh, ix, 4
'Blind' Hary, vii, 20, 214
   The Wallace, vii, 214
Blythe, Ernest, 260
Boece, Hector, 44–45, 59–60
   Historia Gentis Scotorum, 44
Boffey, Julia, 28
Bohemia, xiii
Bold, Alan, 166
Bolt, Robert, 249
   A Man for All Seasons, 249
Bonaparte, Napoleon, ix, 98–100, 106–07, 111–18
Book of the Dean of Lismore, 2
Bothwell, Richard, 47
Boulainvilliers, Henri de, 109
Bowd, Gavin, 171
Bower, Walter, 45, 47, 59
   Scotichronicon, 45, 47, 57, 61 (fn. 9)

INDEX

Bowman, Martin, 250
Boyle, Danny (dir.), 215, 229
   Trainspotting, 214–19, 221–27, 229, 261
   T2 Trainspotting, 215, 217–24, 226–29
Boyne, Battle of the, 221–22, 229
Brand, Jack, 159
Brecht, Bertolt, 250
   Herr Puntila and his Man Matti, 250
Brer, Simon, 57
Brewster, Patrick, 71
Brexit, vi, 257, 262
Britain, ix, xiii, 10, 12, 45, 68, 72, 81, 106, 116, 121, 131, 157, 161, 204, 244, 255, 259, 261–62
British Isles, ix, 46, 66, 68, 87, 116–17, 161
British Union of Fascists, 162
Britishness, ix, 1, 7, 10–11, 13, 72, 75, 118, 131–35, 183, 255, 257, 261–62
Brittany, 111
Broadie, Alexander, x, 235
Broch, Hermann, 198
Brooman-White, Richard, 164, 169
Brown, George Douglas, 75
   The House with the Green Shutters, 75
Brown, George Mackay, 80–81
Brown, Ian, vi, xi, 66, 167
   Antigone, 252
Brown, Mary Ellen, 86
Brown, Oliver, 164
   Hitlerism in the Highlands, 164
Brussels, 47, 58
Bryden, Bill, 249, 252–53
   Benny Lynch, 252
Buchan, John, 78, 138, 147, 158
   Witch Wood, 78
Buchanan, George, 31–33
   The Buke of the Howlat, 30
   Chamaeleon, 31–32
   De Jure Regni apud Scotos, 33
Budapest, 210
Burguière, André, 114
Burke, William, 72
Burnet, John, 237, 239
Burns, Robert, ix, 6–10, 67–70, 76–77, 82 (fn. 9), 86, 91, 227, 250, 259
   'Address of Beezlebub', 68
   'The Braes o' Killiecrankie', 67
   'The Cotter's Saturday Night', 250
   'The Highland Laddie', 91
   'Holy Willie's Prayer', 77
   'Tam o' Shanter', 7

Burrowes, John, 252
Butt, Richard, 226
Byrne, John, 80, 249
   'Slab Boys' trilogy, 80, 249

Caesar, Julius, 115
Caffarelli-Dufalga, Louis-Marie-Joseph, 102–04
Caird, James, 178
Caledonia, 106, 116
   see also Scotland
Campbell, Catriona Lexy, 258
Campbell, John (1st Earl of Breadalbane), 68
Campbell, Thomas, 124
   Gertrude of Wyoming, 124
Camus, Albert, 187
   The Myth of Sisyphus, 187
Canada, xii, 6, 9
Çapan, Cevat, 251–52
Calvinism, 26, 67, 73–78, 82 (fn. 16), 144, 198–99, 207–09, 234, 236
Capitalism, 75, 207, 214
Carlyle, Thomas, x
Carmichael, Alexander, 184, 192
   Carmina Gadelica, 184, 192
Carruthers, Gerard, viii, 19 (fn. 41)
Catalunya, xiii, 259
Catholicism, 65–73, 75, 78–81, 82 (fn. 9, 16), 221–22
Catullus, 34
Celticism, 13–14, 72–73, 105–07, 111–18, 149, 160–61, 176, 179–80, 194
Cesarotti, 115
Championnet, Jean-Étienne, 103
Charlemagne (Holy Roman Emperor), 57, 113, 116
Charles I, 67
Charles VIII (King of France), 48
Chastenay, Victorine, 112
   Mémoires, 112
Chauveau, Gilbert, 48–49, 59, 62 (fn. 21)
China, v, xii
Choate, Rufus, 122
Choice Collection of Serious and Comic Scots Poems, 67
Chorùna, Dòmhnall Ruadh, 189
Chowdbury, Sajid, 28
Christianson, Aileen, 200, 202, 204
The Chronicle of Fredegar, 107
Church of England, 66
Church of Scotland, viii, 66, 73, 75, 198–99, 208–09, 236

INDEX

Churchill, Winston, 172
Clancy, Thomas Owen, 1
Clark, Steve, 139
Classics, ix, 8, 12, 33–34, 44, 90–91, 105–06, 116, 128, 237, 240–43, 254
Claverhouse, John Graham of see Graham, John
Clifford, Jo, 251
  Losing Venice, 251
Clifford, Margaret, 30
Colinton, 143, 145
Colvin, Sidney, 140
Communism, 157, 162–63, 165, 167, 169, 171–72, 179
Conn, Stewart, 249
  The Burning, 249
Connery, Sean, 226
Connolly, James, 179–80
Constantinople, 132
Conway, Moncure D., 121
Coombs, Bryony, vii
Cooper, James Fenimore, ix, 126–32, 134–35, 137 (fn. 18)
  The Last of the Mohicans, 126–27, 129
  Leatherstocking Tales, 126–27
  The Prairie, 126
  The Red Rover, 126
  The Spy, 134
  The Wept of Wish-ton-Wish, 127
Cormack, John, 78
Cotton, Richard, 30
Cousin, Victor, 245
Covenanters, 66–68, 74
Craig, Cairns, x, 14, 76, 235
Craig, David, 76–77
Crawford, Barbara E., 1
Crawford, Robert, 4
Cribb, Tim, 251
Croatia, 260
Crockett, S. R., 149
Cromwell, Oliver, 12
Cruickshank, Helen, 205, 211
Cuke, Thom, 49
Culloden, Battle of, 13, 84, 176
Cummings, Mansfield, 168
Cunningham, Alison, 140
Cunninghame Graham, Robert Bontine, 160
Cuthullin, 104–05

D'Auria, Matthew, 110
Daiches, David, 150, 239

Dalyell, Tam, 257
Dampierre, Auguste Marie Henri Picot de, 103
Dante Alighieri, 7
Darcy, Angela, 258
David, Jacques-Louis, 99–100
Davie, George, xi, 178, 232–45
  The Democratic Intellect, xi, 232, 235
Davies, Hunter, 138, 140, 148, 152
Davies, Terence, 225
Day-Lewis, Cecil, 162
Denmark, 49
Delitiae Poetarum Scotorum, 30
Desaix, Louis, 102, 104–05
Devine, Tom, 16, 158
Dhòmhnallach, Rona, 257
  Stùris, 257
Di Mambro, Ann Marie, 80
  Tally's Blood, 80
Diaspora, 10, 151
Disruption of 1843, 75, 235
Domat, Bremond, 45–47, 49–52, 54–55, 57–60
Donaldson, Arthur, 163–64, 166
Donaldson, William, 92
Douglas, Gavin, 20, 69
Drake, Francis, 10
Dràma na Gàidhlig: A Century of Gaelic Drama, 257
Duchateau, Béatrice, x
Dugdale, Kezia, 258
Dugommier, Jacques François, 103
Dumfries, 7–8
Dunbar, William, 20–21
Dundas, Henry (1st Viscount Melville), 16
Dundee, 49, 256
Dunn, Douglas, 253–54
Dunnigan, Sarah, 28, 167
Dunouy, Alexandre-Hyacinthe, 100
Duphot, Mathurin-Léonard, 103
Dupin, Étienne, 110
Dymock, Emma, x

Edinburgh, 4, 8–13, 16, 32, 47, 49, 65–66, 72–73, 78, 80, 140, 142–43, 145–48, 151–52, 158, 160, 164, 166, 178–80, 186, 191–92, 214–15, 219–22, 235, 237, 239–40, 243, 253
Edward III, 54
Edward VIII (Duke of Windsor), 168
Edward the Black Prince, 10
Egypt, 112, 115
Eliot, T. S., 76, 232, 251
  Notes Towards the Definition of Culture, 232

INDEX

Elizabeth I, 10
Elizabeth II, 15
Elliot, Walter, 234
Elphinstone, Margaret, 207, 209
England, vii–viii, 9–10, 12, 31, 36, 49, 68, 74, 76, 86, 125, 131, 133, 161, 207, 210, 211, 223, 232, 234, 236, 238–44, 251, 254, 259, 261–62
Englishness, 1, 10–11, 254
Enlightenment, viii–xi, xiii, 1, 5, 8, 68–69, 123–24, 130, 233–36, 238, 240
Erraid, 147, 151
Evangelism, 184, 235
Ewing, Winnie, xi

Fascism, 78, 157, 162, 171, 174 (fn. 41)
Fergus I, 44, 51
Ferguson, Adam, 123
 An Essay on the History of the Civil Society, 123
Fergusson, Robert, ix, 8
Ferrier, James, 235
Feuchtwanger, Lion, 198
Findlay, Bill, 250
Findlay, Jessie, 140, 154 (fn. 8), 155 (fn. 41)
Finlay, Richard, 158, 163
Flodden, Battle of, 41
Floyd, George, 16
Fontaine, Pierre, 99
Forsyth, Bill (dir.), 215–16, 229
 Gregory's Girl, 216, 229
France, vii, ix, xii, 45–46, 54–55, 57–60, 99, 104–07, 109–11, 113–14, 116, 211, 244–45
Francis I (King of France), 108
Francis II (Holy Roman Emperor), 105
Fraser, Alexander Campbell, 235
Frederick II (Holy Roman Emperor), 51
Free Church of Scotland, 75, 235
Frith, Simon, 95
Fukuyama, Francis, v
Fullarton, Billy, 79
Fulton, John, 239

Gàidhealtachd, x, 73, 177, 181, 186, 192, 257
Galt, John, 70, 78
 Annals of the Parish, 70
Gaul, 107–10, 113
Gaythelos, 54
Geddes, Alexander, 69–70
 'Epistle to the President', 69
Gellner, Ernest, xiii–xiv, 117
George II, 93
George IV, 12–14, 214

Gérard, François, 100–02, 119 (fn. 5)
Germany, xii, 104, 164, 211, 241
Gibson, Mel (dir.), 214
 Braveheart, vii, 214, 221, 224
Gide, Andre, 77
Gifford, Douglas, 167
Gifford, Hugo, 252
Gilmour the Scot, 57
Gilruth, Jenny, 258
Girodet-Trioson, Anne-Louis, ix, 100, 102–03, 105–07, 111, 114, 116–18, 119 (fn. 5)
Glasgow, vii, 9–10, 45, 47, 72–73, 78–79, 147–48, 151–52, 168, 171, 179, 186–89, 207, 222, 243, 249, 251, 253, 255, 258
Glen, Duncan, 149
Glen, Hamish, 256
'Glorious Revolution' (1688–89), 66, 68
Godard Desmarest, Clarisse, ix
Gold, John, 10
Gold, Margaret, 10
Goodsir Smith, Sydney, 250
Graham, James, 67
Graham, John, of Claverhouse (1st Viscount Dundee), 66–67
Graham, Lesley, x
Grassic Gibbon, Lewis, 207
Gray, Alasdair, 79
 Lanark, 79, 249
Gray, Rev. John, 79
 Park, 79
Greece, 8, 34, 57, 157
Gregory of Tours, 107
 Decime Libri Historiarum, 107
Gresham, Thomas, 10
Grierson, Herbert, 237, 239
Grieve, Christopher Murray, 73, 157, 160, 165, 171, 173 (fn. 20)
 see also Hugh MacDiarmid
Griffiths, Gareth, 262
Gringore, Pierre, 46
 Abus du monde, 46
'Gude and Godlie Ballatis', 65
Guiomar, Jean-Yves, 111
Guthrie, Charles John (Lord Guthrie), 140, 146

Haddington, 21, 34
Hagemann, Susanne, 201
Hamilton, xi
Hamilton, Clayton, x, 138, 140–42, 144–47, 149, 154 (fn. 8)
Hamilton, Thomas, 8, 18 (fn. 24)

270

INDEX

Hamilton, William, 245
Hampden, John, 10
Hannan, Chris, 251
   Elizabeth Gordon Quinn, 251
   Klimkov: The Life of a Tsarist Agent, 251
Hare, William, 72
Harker, O. A., 171
Harris, 178
Harvie, Christopher, 158, 161
Harvie, Jen, 8, 11–12
Haughey, Charles, 260
Havergal, Giles, 253
Hay, George Campbell, 169
Hayman, David (dir.), 228
   Silent Scream, 228
Hebrides, 178–79, 191
Henley, W. E., 138
Henryson, Robert, 20
Hepburn, James (Earl of Bothwell), 31
Hercules (demi-god), 90
Heydon, Rob (dir.), 215, 217, 229
   Ecstasy, 215, 219–21, 223–26, 229
Hibernia, 57, 63 (fn. 39)
   see also Ireland
'Highland Laddie', 85, 87, 91–94
Highlands, ix, xi, 3–4, 13–15, 116, 127–28, 130, 143, 147, 152, 176, 186–87, 93–94, 101, 116, 191, 199, 207–09, 214, 218
Hitler, Adolf, 163
Hoche, Lazare, 103
Hogg, James, 66, 69, 77, 86, 227
   The Brownie of Bodsbeck, 66
   Private Memoirs and Confessions of a Justified Sinner, 77, 227
Hogg, Ulrike, 2
Homer, 112, 116, 254
Hotman, François, 108–10
   Franco-Gallia, 108, 110
Hubbard, Tom, 149
Hume, Alexander, 30
   'Of the Day Estivall', 30
Hume, David, ix, 4–5, 16, 68–69, 261
   History of England, 68
Hungary, xiii, 209–10
Hunter, John Dunn, 126
Huppert, George, 108
Hutton, James, 8

Immigration, vi, 70, 73, 222
India, xii, 6
Industrial Revolution, 74, 80, 235, 239

Innocent IV (Pope), 51
International Companion to Nineteenth-Century Scottish Literature, x
International Companion to Scottish Literature of the Long Eighteenth Century, x
Ireland, xii, 71–72, 80, 86, 116, 118, 179–83, 260
   see also Hibernia
Irish, 70–74, 78, 80, 149, 157, 179–83, 260
Isabey, Jean-Baptiste, 99
Italy, xii, 7, 30, 45, 57, 59, 105, 108, 112–13, 115

Jackson, Ben, 159
Jacobites, 15, 67–69, 78, 84–95, 116, 125, 129, 161, 185, 221
James III, 46, 87, 90
James IV, 2, 46, 49
James V, 45–46, 59, 69
James VI (and I), 3, 22, 29, 31, 33, 69, 249
James VII (and II), 67–68
Jardine, George, 243
Jenkins, Robert, 77
   The Cone Gatherers, 77
Johanneau, Éloi, 115–16
John of Fordun, 45, 54, 59, 61
Johnson, Samuel, ix
Johnston, Alastair (Lord Dunpark), 140
Jones, Inigo, 10
Jonson, Ben, 30, 33
   'To Penshurst', 30
Joubert, Barthélemy Catherine, 103
Joyce, James, 260
   Ulysses, 260

Kafka, Franz, 198
'Kailyard', 75, 218–19, 222, 227, 236, 250
Kay, Jackie, 258
Keirstead, Christopher, 138–39, 150, 152
Kennedy, Walter, 2
Kent, William, 10
Kerins, Andrew, 72
Kerrigan, Justin (dir.), 214
   Human Traffic, 214
Kesson, Jessie, 79
   Another Time, Another Place, 79
Keswick Jencks, Maggie, 9
Killiecrankie, Battle of, 67
Kilmaine, Charles Edward Jennings de, 103
King, Pamela, vii
The Kingis Quair, 28
Kingussie, 146
Kléber, Jean-Baptiste, 102, 104

INDEX

Kojève, Alexandre, v
Kolkata, 6
Knox, John, 21, 31, 65, 69, 74, 236
   Book of Discipline, 31
Kubrick, Stanley (dir.), 229
   A Clockwork Orange, 229
   The Shining, 229

Labour Party, xi, 164, 258
La Tour d'Auvergne, Malo de, 103, 111, 113, 115–16
Lanyer, Amelia, 30, 33
   'Description of Cooke-ham', 30
Lauder, Alexander, 29, 34
Lavery, Hannah, 258
Le Bris, Michel, 138, 142, 148, 150
Lays, François, 112
Le Sueur, Jean-François, 115
   'Ossian ou les Bardes', 115
Leask, Nigel, 6
Leavenworth, Maria Lindgren, 139
Leavis, F. R., 233, 238–39, 244
Leith, 78, 148, 219–20, 222
Lemercier, Nepomucène, 112
Lewis, 178, 184, 188–89
Lewis, Wyndham, 200
   Apes of God, 200
Levitine, George, 102, 105–06
Liber Pluscardensis, 45, 47, 51, 55, 57–58, 61 (fns 9 and 14)
   MS Advocates' Library (Edinburgh), 47
   MS Bibliothèque Royale (Brussels), 47
   MS Cavers, 47
   MS Marchmont (Glasgow), 45, 47, 49–51, 54, 58
   MS Bodleian (Oxford), 47, 62 (fn. 14)
   MS Bibliothèque Sainte-Geneviève (Paris), 47, 51
Lindsay, A. D., 239
Linlithgow, 65
Lloyd, Jo, 249
Loach, Ken, 215–16
   The Angels' Share, 216
Locke, John, 10
Lockhart, John Gibson, 13
Lombardy, 260
London, 10, 151, 161, 164–66, 169, 219, 241, 251–52, 257
Lorma, 105
Lorne, Tommy, 15
Lorimer, William, 41
Louis XIV (King of France), 109

Lowlands, 2–3, 13–15, 123, 176, 179, 187–88, 207–08
Lucan, 34
Lyall, Scott, x, 157
Lynch, Benny, 252
Lyndsay, Sir David, 65
   An Satyre of the Thrie Estatis, 65–66

Mac Colla, Fionn, 73–75
   The Albannach, 73
   And the Cock Crew, 73
Macartney, Wilfred, 162
MacCormick, John, 165
MacDiarmid, Hugh, x, 73–74, 157, 159–62, 164–67, 169–72, 178, 200–01, 203–05, 237, 250–52
   A Drunk Man Looks at the Thistle, 170, 203
   Greek Memories, 157
   see also Grieve, Christopher Murray
MacDonald, A. A., 30, 42 (fn. 4)
MacDonald, Robert David, 253
MacDonald, Stephen, 253
Macdonell, Alasdair Ranaldson, 13–14
Macedonia, 107
MacFadyen, John, 182
MacFarlane, Murdo, 184–86
MacFie, Kathleen (Lady Dunpark), 140
MacGillivray, Alan, 167
MacGregor, Martin, 2
Machiavelli, Niccolo, 31
   Il Principe, 31
MacIntyre, Donald, 187
MacKechnie, Alasdair, 152
Mackendrick, Alexander (dir.), 216
   Whisky Galore!, 216, 261
Mackenzie, Compton, x, 157, 159–62, 165–72, 250, 266
   The Golden Treasury, 171
   Greek Memories, 168
   The Monarch of the Glen, 168
   The North Wind of Love, 167
   'Quo Vadis', 160
   Whisky Galore, 167
   The Windsor Tapestry, 168
Mackenzie, John (dir.), 228
   A Sense of Freedom, 228
MacLean, Dougie, 182
   'Caledonia', 182
Maclean, John, 165, 179–80
MacLean, Sorley, 169, 177–82, 191, 254
MacMillan, Hector, 249

INDEX

MacNeacail, Aonghas, 177, 181
MacNeill, Florence, 164, 170
Macpherson, James, ix, 104–05, 112, 116, 254
 'Ossian', ix, 4, 72, 100–02, 104–06, 112–16, 254
 Temora, 112
MacPherson, Mary (Màiri Mhòr nan Òran), 177, 181
Mair, John, 169
Maitland, James, 21, 29, 35
Maitland, John, 22–23, 27, 29, 33–34, 37
Maitland, John (nephew of Marie), 41
Maitland, Helen, 34
Maitland, Isabel, 34
Maitland, Margaret, 34
Maitland, Marie, 22–23, 26–29, 31, 33–34, 37, 41
Maitland, Richard, 21–23, 27–29, 33, 36–37
Maitland, Thomas, 30, 32–34, 37
Maitland, William, 29, 31–33, 37
Maitland Quarto, vii, 20–21, 27, 29–30, 32, 41
Malloch, David, 261
 The Masque of Alfred, 261
Malmaison, 98–100, 112
Marbot, Marcellin, 103
Marceau, François Severin, 103
Marengo, Battle of, 100, 102, 105
Marin-Lamellet, Anne-Lise, xi
Martin, Dean, 219
Martin, Joanna, 22, 30
Marvell, Andrew, 30, 33
 'Upon Appleton House', 30
Mary of Guise, 31, 41
Mary, Queen of Scots, 9, 31–32, 41, 68–69
Mary II, 67
Matos, Jacinta, 145
McAvoy, James, 217
McDougall, Patrick, 235
McDougall, Peter, 79
 Just Another Saturday, 79
McDowell, Paula, 88–89
McGinn, Clark, 6
McGuigan, Paul (dir.), 215, 229
 Acid House, 219, 221–24, 226–29
McIntyre, Robert, 158
McMillan, Roddy, 249
McNeil, Kenneth, 13–14
McNeill, Florence Marian, 200
McPherson, Andrew, 240
Melville, Andrew, 69, 74
Melville, Elizabeth, 20
Menace of the Irish Race to our Scots Nationality, 73, 78

Mhaighstir Alasdair, Alasdair Mac, 177
MI5 *see* Secret Services
Milan, 113
Millar, John, 123
 Origin of the Distinction of Ranks in Society, 123
Miller, Arthur, 249
 The Crucible, 249
 Death of a Salesman, 249
Milton, Colin, 13
Milton, John, 10
Minneapolis, 16
Mitchell, James, 159
Mitchell, John, 71–72
 'A Braid Glow'r at the Clergy', 71
Moberly, Walter, 232
 Crisis in the University, 232
Moderate Party, 67, 75
Modernism, xiii, 73, 139, 194, 200–01, 204–05
Montesquieu, 124
Montgomerie, Alexander, 22, 69
Montgomery, Mary, 177, 181, 183–85
Montjoie, 47–49, 51, 54–55, 58
Montrose, 67, 198, 200
Morata, Olympia Fulvia, 26
Morgan, Edwin, 79, 149
 'King Billy', 79
Morigia, Camillo, 7
Morris, Michael, 16
Morrison, Murdo, 189
Morton, Graeme, 7
Mosley, Oswald, 162
Motherwell, 158
Motherwell, William, 70
Muir, Edwin, 73–76, 80, 178, 198–201, 211
 'Scotland 1941', 74
 Scott and Scotland, 74, 204
 Scottish Journey, 74
 Variations on a Time Theme, 202
Muir, Willa, x, 166, 178, 197–211
 Belonging, 198, 201
 'Clock-a-doodle-doo', 197, 199–202, 206, 211
 Imagined Corners, 199–200, 202
 Mrs Grundy in Scotland, 197, 199–202, 205–08, 211
 Mrs Ritchie, 199
 Women: An Inquiry, 201
 'Women in Scotland', 197, 199, 201, 205–07, 211
Muirhead, R. E., 160
Mull, 146–48, 151–52, 178–79
Mullan, Peter, 215

INDEX

Murnau, F. W. (dir.), 229
Nosferatu, 229
Murray, Donald S., 257

Nairn, Tom, xi
Napoleon *see* Bonaparte, Napoleon
National Party of Scotland, 73, 160–61, 163, 169
　see also Scottish National Party
Nationalism, v–vi, ix, xiii–xiv, 7, 10, 69, 72, 76,
　106, 117–18, 119 (fn. 20), 121, 135, 157–60,
　162–72, 177, 181, 183, 188, 194, 200–01, 204,
　209–10, 214, 220–21, 225, 228–29, 232, 262
Native Americans, 123–30, 134
Netherlands, 30
New York, 9, 46
New Zealand, xii
Newlyn, Evelyn, 22, 26
Newton, Isaac, 10
Nimmo, Ian, x, 138, 146–48, 151–52
Niven, Barbara, 200
North Berwick, 146
Northern Ireland *see* Ulster
Norway, 164
NPS *see* National Party of Scotland

O'Connell, Daniel, 71
O'Hagan, Andrew, 80
Oban, 147, 190
Ogilvie, John, 167
Orange Order, 70, 72, 79–80, 221
Origines gauloises, 111–13
Orwell, George, 261
Ossian *see* Macpherson, James
Ovid, 34
Owen, Wilfred, 146
Oxford, 47, 240–41

Pacific Islands, 149
Palmer McCulloch, Margery, 197
Paris, vii, 47, 48, 58, 98, 126
Parnassus, 34, 106
Parr, Chris, 253
Paterson, Lindsay, 234, 240, 244
Peden, Alexander, 74
Peers, Edgar Allison, 241
Pellew, Jill, 233
Percier, Charles, 99–100
Perfect, Peter, 164–65
Perry, Clive, 253
Perth, 125, 129, 131

Perthshire, 2
Philips, Katherine, 27
Phillips, Williams, 163
Pickard, Emily, x
Pilote, Pauline, ix
Pinkie, Battle of, 21
Pitcairne, Archibald, 66, 70
　The Assembly, or Scotch Reformation, 66
Phoebus, 90–91
Phrygia, 107
Pius VII (Pope), 100
Plato, 112
Plockton, 191
Plumb, J. H., 233
　Crisis in the Humanities, 233
Pollitt, Harry, 162
Pope, Alexander, 10
Popular Party, 67
Pound, Ezra, 202, 204
Presbyterianism, 66–69, 71–73, 78, 216, 235
Prestonpans, Battle of, 129
Priam, 107
Protestantism, 3, 30, 33, 65–66, 69, 72, 75, 77–81,
　82 (fn. 25), 108, 184
Prowse, Philip, 253
Prussia, 237
Putin, Vladimir, v

Quinlan, Kevin, 166

Raleigh, Walter, 10
Ramsay, Lynne, 215
Ramsay Snr, Allan, ix, 4–5
Ravenna, 7
Rankin, Nicholas, x, 138, 140–42, 144–45, 147,
　149, 151
Reid, Thomas, 234, 245
Renaissance, twentieth-century Scottish, x, 73, 75,
　158–59, 167–72, 176–78, 197, 199–207, 250
Retallack, R., 164
Reuil, 98
Riach, Alan, 159, 172
Riccio, David, 31
Ringer, Fritz, 240
Robbins, Lionel, 239–40
Robert I, 65, 74, 132, 227
Robert III, 130
Robertson, Fiona, 132
Robertson, James, 77
　The Fanatic, 77

INDEX

Robertson, William, 69
Rodger, Johnnie, 7
Romanticism, ix, xi, xiii, 67, 69, 101, 121–22, 124, 126, 128, 130, 135, 186
Rome, 57, 106, 108, 115
Ros, Uilleam (William Ross), 181
Roscrana, 101
Rousseau, Jean-Jacques, 124

Sallust, 12
  War of Cataline, 12
Samoa, 148–50
Sappho, 26
Sassi, Carla, 16
Saunders, J. L., 237
  Scottish Democracy, 1815–1840, 237
Scipio, 115
Scorcese, Martin (dir.), 229
  Mean Streets, 229
  Raging Bull, 229
Scota, 54
Scotland, v–ix, xi–xiv, 1–3, 5–10, 12–16, 21, 27, 29, 31–33, 36–37, 41, 45–60, 65–66, 68–70, 72–81, 86, 91, 104, 106, 116, 118, 121, 125–26, 129–35, 138, 140, 142–43, 147–53, 158–60, 163, 168–72, 176, 178–83, 185, 187–88, 190–92, 194, 197–202, 204–07, 209–11, 214–19, 221–26, 228–29, 232, 234–37, 239–42, 244–45, 250–52, 254–62
  see also Caledonia
Scott, F. G., 200–01
Scott, Thomas, 122
Scott, Sir Walter, ix, 9, 13–14, 66, 77, 121–26, 128–35
  Anne of Geierstein, 132
  Castle Dangerous, 125, 131–34
  The Chronicles of the Canongate, 125
  Count Robert of Paris, 132
  The Fair Maid of Perth, 125–26, 129, 131–33
  Ivanhoe, 123
  The Lady of the Lake, 122
  A Legend of the Wars of Montrose, 123
  Life of Napoleon, 126
  The Pirate, 123
  Rob Roy, 14, 122–23, 125–27
  The Tale of Old Mortality, 66
  Tales of My Landlord, 132
  'The Two Drovers', 123
  Waverley, 126, 129, 131
  Waverley Novels, 121–22, 124–25, 130–32, 135
'Scottish Cringe', 2, 229, 231 (fn. 46)

Scottish National Party, vi, xi, 3, 158–59, 160–61, 163–64, 170, 258
  see also National Party of Scotland
Scottish PEN, 210–11
Secret Services, 157, 161–72, 174 (fn. 41)
Selbach, 57
Semple, James, 31
  Bird in the Cage, 31
Sessions, John, 226
Shakespeare, William, 9–10
Shelford, T. M., 165
Shetland, 164, 172
Sicily, 34
Sieyès, Abbé de, 110–11
Singer, Bryan (dir.), 229
  The Usual Suspects, 229
Singer, Jefferson A., 143
Skelton, John, 31, 35, 42 (fn. 16)
Skene, William F., 61 (fns 9, 14, 15)
Skinner, Rev. John, 68
Skye, 178, 181, 192
Slessor, Mary, 9
Soeren, Kristel van, viii
Somerville, Jimmy, 258
Somme, Battle of the, 255
South Uist, 192
Soviet Union, v, 167
Smith, Adam, 68, 123
Smith, Anthony D., xiii–xiv, 117, 181
Smith, James, 163
Smith, Iain Crichton, 177, 187, 189–90
  'A Poet in Scotland', 190
Smith, Norman Kemp, 236
Snow, C. P., 233
SNP *see* Scottish National Party
Spain, xii, 57
Spark, Muriel, 77, 80–81
  The Prime of Miss Jean Brodie, 77, 81
Spence, Lewis, 163
Spence, Alan, 79
  'Its Colours They are Fine', 79
Spender, Stephen, 162
Spiller, Michael, 43 (fn. 19)
Starno, 104–05
St Andrews, 201
Stevenson, David A., 148
Stevenson, Margaret, 140
Stevenson, Robert Louis, x, 138–53, 226–27
  A Child's Garden of Verses, 144
  Edinburgh: Picturesque Notes, 138

275

INDEX

Stevenson, Robert Louis (*cont.*)
   'Ille Terrarum', 145
   Jekyll and Hyde, 227
   Kidnapped, 138, 146–48, 152
   'The Lantern Bearers', 146
   'The Manse', 144
   'Memoirs of an Islet', 147
   The Merry Men, 147
   'An Old Scotch Gardener', 145
   'Pastoral', 145
   Silverado Squatters, 148
   St Ives, 145–46
   'To Any Reader', 144–45
   Weir of Hermiston, 150
Stevenson, Thomas, 140
Stewart, Andy, 249
Stewart, David, 13
Stewart, Dugald, 245
Stewart, James (1st Earl of Moray), 31–32
Stewart, Kennedy, 237
Stirling, Kirsten, 203, 206–07
Stirling Bridge, Battle of, 9
Stone of Destiny, 165–67, 170
Stone, Lawrence, 240
Stokes, Martin, 84
Stuart, Charles Edward ('Bonnie Prince Charlie'), 91, 227
Stuart, Henry (Lord Darnley), 32
Stuart, James Francis Edward ('the Old Pretender'), 91
Stuart, John (Duke of Albany), 46–47, 49, 51, 54–55, 58–59, 63 (fn. 30)
Sturgeon, Nicola, 260
Stratford, 10
Stray, Christopher, 242
Switzerland, 132

Tacitus, 109
   Germania, 109
Tallaght, 183
Taunay, Nicolas-Antoine, 100
Taylor, Miles, 233
Taylor, Thomas, 74
Temple, Richard (Viscount Cobham), 10
Terry, Daniel, 13
Thatcher, Margaret, xi, 255
Thibault, Jean-Thomas, 100
Thomson, Derick, 177, 187–88
Thomson, James, 77, 261
   The Seasons, 77
Tieghem, Daniel Van, 112

Tiffin, Helen, 262
Travers, Martin, 258
Treaty of Union *see* Union, Treaty of
Tremblay, Michel, 250
Trevlyn, Valda, 200–01, 205
Troy, 107–08
Trump, Donald, v
Turkey, 10
Turnbull, Ronald, xi
Turner, Elsepth, 257, 262
Turner, J. M. W., 13
Tytler, William, 68–69
   An Inquiry Historical and Critical, 68

Ukraine, v, 118
Ulster, 70, 72, 163, 180
Union of the Crowns (1603), viii, 131, 133, 161
Union, Act of (1707), 4, 262
Union, Treaty of (1706), 1, 4, 259, 262
Unionism, ix, 2, 7, 225, 228
United Kingdom, vi, 4, 10, 106, 118, 121, 123, 135, 262
USA, v, xii, 6, 9, 122, 124

Victoria, Queen, 199, 207
Villebresme, Macé de, 46
   Epistres du Turc, 46
Virgil, 34, 108, 112
Voltaire, 112
Vulto, Renée, 90

Wagner, Richard, 9
Wallace, William, 8–9, 74, 126, 132–33
Waverley Novels *see* Scott, Sir Walter
Watt, James, 9
Weber, Max, 75
   The Protestant Ethic, 75
Welsh, Irvine, xi, 73, 80, 214–18, 220–29, 261
   Ecstasy, 216
   Trainspotting, 80, 216, 220–21
Whatley, Christopher, 6–7, 11
'Wherry Whigs Awa', 85, 87–91, 94
Whitney, Geoffrey, 30
   A Choice of Emblemes, 30
Whyte, Christopher, 192–94
Whyte, James, 201
   The Modern Scot, 201–02
Wilde, Oscar, 79
   The Picture of Dorian Gray, 79
William III, 10, 67, 221
Williams, Raymond, 239
   Culture and Society, 239

Wilson, Alexander, 71
'Hollander, or Light Weight', 71
Winsloe, Christa, 198
Winzet, Ninian, 65, 69
Withrington, Donald, 240
Wodrow, Robert, 66, 68
  Sufferings of the Church of Scotland, 66

Wood, Wendy, 165–66, 170
Woolf, Virginia, 201
  A Room of One's Own, 201

Yeats, W. B., 72, 260
Young, Douglas, 164–65, 169, 178–79
Young, Ronnie, 6

www.ingramcontent.com/pod-product-compliance
Lightning Source LLC
Chambersburg PA
CBHW052104230426
43671CB00011B/1922